China and Autocracy

China and Autocracy

*Political Influence and the Limits
of Global Democracy*

Edited By
Miao-ling Lin Hasenkamp

I.B. TAURIS

LONDON • NEW YORK • OXFORD • NEW DELHI • SYDNEY

I.B. TAURIS
Bloomsbury Publishing Plc
50 Bedford Square, London, WC1B 3DP, UK
1385 Broadway, New York, NY 10018, USA

BLOOMSBURY, I.B. TAURIS and the I.B. Tauris logo are trademarks of
Bloomsbury Publishing Plc

First published in Great Britain 2020

Cover design by Charlotte James
Cover map by Free Vector Maps, http://freevectormaps.com

A catalogue record for this book is available from the British Library.

A catalogue record for this book is available from the Library of Congress.

ISBN: HB: 978-1-7883-1264-6
ePDF: 978-1-7883-1838-9
eBook: 978-1-7883-1839-6

Typeset by Deanta Global Publishing Services, Chennai, India
Printed and bound in Great Britain

To find out more about our authors and books visit www.bloomsbury.com and
sign up for our newsletters.

Contents

About the authors

Rupakjyoti Borah works at the Institute of South Asian Studies (ISAS) at the National University of Singapore (NUS). Before joining the ISAS, NUS, he was Research Fellow at the Japan Forum for Strategic Studies (JFSS), Tokyo. He has also worked as Assistant Professor of International Relations at Pandit Deendayal Petroleum University (PDPU), India. He received his PhD from the School of International Studies (SIS), Jawaharlal Nehru University (JNU), India. He has published in the *Journal of Asian Politics and History*, the *Journal of East Asian Studies, Straits Times, Japan Times, Jerusalem Post, Jakarta Post, Nikkei Asian Review* among others. He has also been Visiting Fellow at the Japan Institute of International Affairs (JIIA), Tokyo, the University of Cambridge (U.K) and the Australian National University (ANU). His recent book is *The Elephant and the Samurai: Why Japan Can Trust India?* He has also contributed chapters in edited books and has been interviewed on BBC World, NHK World, Channel News Asia, Bloomberg, Australian Broadcasting and many Indian television channels. He is presently working on his second book which will look at the relations between India, Japan and ASEAN.

Alexander Brand is Professor of Political Science and International Relations at the Rhine-Waal Applied University Kleve (Germany). He obtained his PhD in political science from the Technische Universität, Dresden. His main fields of research are theories of international relations/foreign policy, US foreign policy, global politics of development, and sport and international politics. Recent publications include 'Die Europäisierung des Fußballs: Von der Umsetzung politischer Vorgaben zur Gestaltung europäischer Realitäten', in Jürgen Mittag et al. (eds.): *Auf dem Weg zur europäischen Sportpolitik?*, Baden-Baden: Nomos 2018 (with Arne Niemann); 'Progressive Politik als Markenzeichen der Administration Obama? Dynamiken US-amerikanischer Entwicklungspolitik eingangs des 21. Jahrhunderts', in Michael Dreyer et al. (eds.): *Always on the Defensive? Progressive Bewegung und Progressive Politik in den USA in der Ära Obama*, Trier: WVT, 2015; 'Farewell to Leadership? Ideas of Hegemony and Counter-Hegemony in the Americas', *International Area Studies Review* 17 (4) 2014 (with Wolfgang Muno).

Earl Conteh-Morgan is Professor of International Studies in the School of Interdisciplinary Global Studies (SIGS) at the University of South Florida. A former Senior Research Fellow at the Norwegian Nobel Institute, Oslo, he is the author of, among other books, *Democratization in Africa: The Theory and Dynamics of Political Transitions* (Praeger, 1997); *Collective Political Violence – An Introduction to the Theories and Cases of Violent Conflicts* (Routledge, 2004); he has co-authored *Sierra Leone at the End of the Twentieth Century: History, Politics, and Society* (Peter Lang,

1999); and he has co-edited *Peacekeeping in Africa: ECOMOG in Liberia* (St. Martin's, 1998). His most recent book is *The Sino-African Partnership-A Geopolitical Economy Approach*. Dr Conteh-Morgan has published on topics such as human security, conflict and peace-building, state failure, the impact of globalization on state cohesion, and Sino-American rivalry in Africa, among others, in refereed journals such as the *Journal of Global Security and Intelligence Studies, Air and Space Power Journal, Armed Forces & Society, The Journal of Conflict Studies, Peace and Conflict Studies, The International Journal of Peace Studies, Journal of Social Philosophy, Journal of Military and Political Sociology* and *Insight Turkey*. Dr Conteh-Morgan is currently working on a book-length manuscript on Sino-American rivalry in Africa.

Ceren Ergenc is Assistant Professor in the Department of International Relations and Chair of Asian Studies Program at Middle East Technical University, Ankara, Turkey. She is also affiliated with Xi'an Jiaotong-Liverpool University. She earned her PhD in political science with a particular focus on area studies from Boston University. Her research interests include state–society relations in contemporary China and East Asia, urban politics, political participation, as well as comparative methodologies and debates on global history. Following are her publications: (1) *A Political Analysis of Middle Class-Based Social Movements: India and Turkey Compared in Past Connections, Contemporary Debates: India and Turkey*, Routledge (2018); (2) 'Rethinking the "International": Theoretical and Methodological Debates' (ed), Heretik Press (in Turkish) (2017); (3) 'Can Two Ends of Asia Meet? An Overview of Contemporary Turkey-China Relations', East Asia (2015); (4) 'Political Efficacy through Deliberative Participation in Urban China: A Case Study on Public Hearings', *Journal of Chinese Political Science*, 19(2): 191–213 (2014).

Miao-ling Lin Hasenkamp has served as staff at the UNESCO-Chair of human rights education and Chair of comparative political systems in the Department of Social Sciences, Otto-von-Guericke University (OVGU), Magdeburg, Germany. She earned her PhD in political science, sociology and economics from the Westfälisch-Wilhelms-University (WWU), Münster, Germany. Her research and teaching interests include China and democracy; international human rights (politics and instruments); gender justice; transitional justice in East Asia; public policy analysis (particularly the nexus between migration, security, development and refugee labour integration); and political corruption. Her recent editor work and publications include the following: (1) 'Renegotiating the City: Surveillance and Refugee Integration in German Urban Communities', Special Issue 'Contentious Politics of Migration', edited by Hans Schattle, Kelsey Norman and Willem Maas, *Globalization (2020, forthcoming)*; (2) *International Human Rights Politics: A Handbook*. Barbara Budrich UTB (2020) (in German); (3) Editor *Human Rights, Development and Governance in International Politics – Conflict or Convergence of Policy Goals?* Münster: Lit-Verlag (2017) (in German and in English). She also has given a number of speeches and comments concerning human rights violations, migration and refugee integration issues, international criminal justice, and North–South development cooperation in different fora including in her website www.ihrr.net.

Wolfgang Muno is Professor and Chair of Comparative Politics, University Rostock. He has a PhD in political science from the University Mainz, Germany. His main fields of research are problems of development and underdevelopment and democracy in Latin America. Additionally, he works on Latin America in international relations and regional integration. Recent publications: 'Europa spielerisch erlernen. Didaktische Überlegungen und Praxisbeispiele zu EU-Simulationen', Wiesbaden 2018, Springer, Editor with Arne Niemann and Petra Guasti; 'Populism in Argentina', in Daniel Stockemer (Ed.), *Populism around the World*, Wiesbaden: Springer 2018; 'Winter is coming? Game of Thrones and Realist Thinking', in Ulrich Hamenstädt (Ed.), *The Interplay Between Political Theory and Movies: Bridging Two Worlds*, Wiesbaden: Springer 2018.

Susan McEwen-Fial is Lecturer at the University of Mainz (Germany). She earned her PhD in international relations and sociology from Boston University and an MSc in international relations from the London School of Economics. Her main fields of research are US–China relations, Chinese economy and China–EU relations. Recent publications: 'Navigating Stormy Waters: The Triangular Relationship between the United States, Vietnam and China and the South China Sea Disputes', in Enrico Fels, Truong-Minh Vu (Eds.), *Power Politics in Asia's Contested Waters. Territorial Disputes in the South China Sea*, Springer 2016 (with Alexander Brand); 'Das Ringen um Vietnam. Machtpolitische Rivalitäten zwischen China und den USA, strategische Optionen Vietnams und Dynamiken der regionalen (De-)Stabilisierung', in: Sebastian Harnisch, Mischa Hansel and Nadine Godehardt (eds.), *Stabilität und Krisen: Sicherheitspolitische Dynamiken in Asien*, Baden-Baden: Nomos 2018 (with Alexander Brand).

Dirk Nabers is Professor of International Political Sociology at the University of Kiel, Germany. Previously, he has been Senior Research Fellow at the GIGA German Institute of Global and Area Studies in Hamburg. At GIGA, he was the head of the Research Programme on Power, Norms and Governance in International Relations and Academic Director of the Hamburg International Graduate School 'Regional Power Shifts and Global Order'. His main research interests include Poststructuralism in International Relations, Security Policy, Comparative Regionalism and the study of Regional Powers. His recent publications include articles in journals such as *Politics, Review of International Studies* and the *Journal of International Political Theory*. He is the author of *A Poststructuralist Discourse Theory of Global Politics*, New York: Palgrave.

Robert G. Patman is Professor of International Relations in the Department of Politics at the University of Otago. He served as an editor for *International Studies Perspectives* (2010–14) and Head of Department of Politics (2013–16). Robert is the author or editor of twelve books. Recent publications include *Strategic Shortfall: The 'Somalia Syndrome' and the March to 9/11* (Praeger, 2010) and three co-edited books titled *China and the International System: Becoming a World Power* (Routledge, 2013); *Science Diplomacy: New Day or False Dawn?* (World Scientific Publishers, 2015); and *New Zealand and the World: Past, Present and Future* (World Scientific Publishers, 2018). Robert is currently writing a volume called *Rethinking the Global Impact of 9/11* (Palgrave Macmillan,

2019). He is Fulbright Senior Scholar, Honorary Professor of the New Zealand Defence Command and Staff College, and provides regular contributions to the national and international media on global issues and events.

Yean-Sen Teng is Professor of Law at the School of Law, Soochow University in Taipei, Taiwan. He served as the director of Chung Fo-Chung Center for the Study of Human Rights and of the Master Program for Human Rights at Soochow University (2008–10) as well as of Yuen-Li Liang International Law Centre at the School of Law (2006–14). His research and teaching fields include international law, human rights and the rule of law and human rights education. Some of his important publications and papers are as follows: (1) *International Human Rights Law: Theory and Practice* (in Chinese) Angle Publishing (2017); (2) 'Who is Afraid of Human Rights? A Taiwanese Perspective', In Rainer Arnold (ed.), *The Universalism of Human Rights*, Springer (2013); (3) 'A Protean-Face of Human Rights in Taiwan', International Law Association, Asia-Pacific Regional Conference, Taipei (2011); (4) 'Human Rights: a Concept or an Idea, Human Rights Meet Legislation – Cross Cultural and Legal Perspectives', Roundtable, University of Magdeburg, Germany (2010). Being member and adviser of important human rights bodies (e.g. Human Rights Advisory Committee and the Human Rights Working Group at the Executive Yuan), Professor Teng has been involved in diverse consultancy and teaching work for the government in Taiwan since Taiwan ratified international human rights treaties in 2009.

Liang Qiao received a PhD in political science from Louisiana State University, Baton Rouge in 2012. He is Assistant Professor of political science at Renmin University of China, Beijing. He is also a specialized political analyst and advanced researcher at CGTN. His research interests include Chinese government and politics, political elites in China, political communication and China's global image. Among his many studies, his book *Political Mobility of Chinese Regional Leaders* was published by Routledge in 2017.

Acknowledgements

This book is the result of panel organizations and discussions during the annual conventions of the International Studies Association (ISA) in 2011 and 2014, respectively. It would not have been possible without precious contributions from a group of distinguished scholars in the fields of area studies, international relations (IR), international law and comparative politics. The idea of this book sprang from the editor's research on rights and institutional issues in China and from her public speech and lecture activities at the Helmut-Schmidt-Universität/Universität der Bundeswehr Hamburg in Hamburg, Otto-von-Guericke-University (OVGU) in Magdeburg and at the adult education centre (*Volkshochschule*) in Münster in Germany from 2007 onwards. In 2007, China's economic miracle had impressed European audiences and professionals. Many followed the conventional wisdom that continuing economic development might well pave the way for political reforms, thereby launching an incremental democratization in China, as the emerging middle class would demand the introduction of democratic institutions and rights agendas to secure their property rights and the newly obtained space of civil liberties. Despite the 2008–09 financial crisis, the democratic world led by the United States and the European Union (EU) was convinced that democracy was the best form of regulating human affairs, particularly in an era of globalization with multiple challenges. China should be encouraged to become part of the democratic community through enhanced dialogue and engagement.

Today, more than ten years later, the global environment has completely changed. We are witnessing a soaring competition between authoritarian and democratic states – a reality which was hardly thinkable shortly after the demise of the Cold War in the 1990s. One perceives a rising authoritarian influence in countless cultural and investment activities and educational programs and the development of media enterprises and information initiatives with global reach. China's authoritarianism has become a symbol of soft power which allures neighbours and partners to imitate. Meanwhile, some describe such rising authoritarian influence as 'sharp power' which, unlike 'soft power' that involves gaining hearts and minds, centres on manipulation and distraction while pursuing autocracy's interests *internationally*. On the part of the democratic world, sceptical voices questioning the ability of democracy to tackle multiple challenges and to address public discontent grow. The malaise of democracy has reached a tipping point, with democratic regression reflected in the spread of authoritarian populism and neo-nationalism. Heretical anti-democratic ideas presented by academics and philosophers are gaining ground and warnings of the imminent collapse of global democracy are heard daily.

In reflecting upon such a sea change and attempting to explore possible links between China's rising influence and democracy's recession, the contributors of this volume adopt a combined macro–micro view and address different aspects of China's authoritarianism and their implications for democracy at the domestic, regional and international levels. They not only cover several novel issues but also some familiar issues are viewed through a fresh prism (the special relationships between economic development, corruption, and anti-corruption from an economic neo-institutionalist and social trust perspective, the Chinese human rights discourse between universalization and localization, China and India, and China in Africa and its consequences for democracy promotion). My deep thanks first go to Maximilian Meyer and Karl-Peter Fritzsche for their comments on the limited diffusion power of democracy as a global norm. Thanks are also owed to Tomasz Hoskins from the IB Tauris publisher and anonymous reviewers as well as to the helping hands of Andreas Gottfried Hasenkamp. Finally, the content in this volume represents the opinions of the contributors, and they are also responsible for any mistakes contained therein.

Miao-ling Lin Hasenkamp

China's authoritarianism goes global?
Domestic and international dimensions

Miao-ling Lin Hasenkamp

China becoming the world's second largest economic power without undergoing fundamental political reform and without there being the prospect of such reform challenges the basic tenet of democratic theory, which suggests a positive correlation between economic development and democratization (for details about the economic theory of democracy see Chapter 2). With its successful economic performance, China represents a 'resilient autocracy' (Nathan and James 2003, see Chapter 4), which has set up an alternative development model demonstrating the strengths and potentials of authoritarianism in the international system. As a multipolar world takes its form following the decline of the United States as a superpower in shaping norms and agenda in world politics, one observes new group dynamics with concurring values and conflicting interests. On the one hand, China, Brazil, India, Russia, South Africa and Turkey have become the leading voices in those emerging and competitive economies in the developing world. A power diffusion of authoritarianism appears to take the stage, beginning with China's authoritarian capitalism and increasing technological progress, followed by the power grabs of autocrats in Brazil, Cambodia, Cuba, India, Paraguay, the Philippines, Russia, Turkey, Venezuela and Vietnam.

On the other hand, the camp of liberal democracy once led by the United States and the European Union has come under unprecedented pressure in three respects. First, both old and young democracies are in danger of backsliding while confronting challenges from *within*, ranging from rising inequality resulting from the economic and financial crises, identity politics, falling trust, to the rise of populism and nationalism. For instance, the 'America First' nationalist course of the United States under President Donald Trump has impaired the traditional Atlantic cooperation framework. Within the EU (notably Hungary and Poland), the populist victory has begun to threaten the functioning of democratic institutions with the erosion of civil liberties and frustrations towards and declining trust in those established and non-elected institutions (e.g. international and supranational organizations such as the European Union (EU), the United Nations (UN), International Monetary Fund (IMF) and the World Bank (WB)). Indeed, the spread of 'populist *Zeitgeist*' (Mudde 2004) haunting many countries can be considered as an expression of new cultural cleavages between cosmopolitanists who have profited from economic and cultural deterritorialization and communitarianists and economic have-nots, who often see themselves left behind in periods of uncertainty and instability (Norris 2017; Ingelhardt and Norris 2016: 3; Merkel 2016; O'Brian 2015; Betz 1993). For some authors, the rise of populism is a direct result of the inherent agonistic tensions with self-disruptive forces between (neo)liberal and democratic principles, which is in itself highly ambivalent being a corrective and threat for democracy (Kaltwasser 2012; Mouffe 2018: 16; Sandel 2018), as found in the increased voter turnout and the gradual end of people's parties.[1] The death of democracy seems to be probable which may not result from military coups or violent seizures of power. Instead, it may be the consequences of a subversion process in which democratic systems have been plagued and hollowed out by a widening gap between the electorate and their representatives and its inability and inefficiency to tackle many looming threats (Runciman 2018; Mounk 2018; Levitsky and Ziblatt 2018). Secondly, many democracies also face pressures from *without* reflected in disruptive elections, rightist populists' successful tactics in mobilizing the discontented electorate against mainstream parties and their transnational connection to illiberal regimes (notably Russia). Furthermore, although the West has considerably contributed to international development, due to the increasing active investment activities of new donors (i.e. China and India) and the declining size of Western Official Development Assistance (ODA), both the United States and the EU have failed to support sustainable development models in much of the developing world (Keijzer 2012; EU 2018).[2] These three conditions have become part of the West's gradual decline which makes the threat and promise of 'the Chinese model' increasingly relevant.

Doubtlessly, the success and efficiency of the Chinese communist regime to modernize China and to tackle a variety of political, economic and social crises at national and local levels deserve appraisal. Under President Xi Jinping, China has launched its 2013 *Belt and Road Initiative (BRI)* designed to expand China's global influence through the building of a trade and infrastructure network connecting Asia with Africa and Europe (the realization of 'globalization 2.0', see Acharya 2015; Xinhua 2017).[3] The comprehensive governance reforms at home have strengthened the one-man leadership surrounding President Xi, thereby enhancing the power and legitimacy of the CCP's authoritarian rule. Meanwhile, despite China's efforts to augment its global influence and to dance with those mainstream discourses (democracy, human rights and the rule of law), the giant country has encountered many paradoxes, conflicts, discrepancies and anxieties. Critics are concerned with Xi's one-man rule in violating the CCP's ruling principles with a collective elite rule introduced by Deng Xiaoping since the reform era onward. The risks of suffocating the dynamics of economic development and civic engagements, alienating citizenry and nurturing courtier culture are real (Fan 2018; Nick Besley, cited in Campbell 2018). The questions this edited book aims to address are: Is China changing the world and has become the leading role model of development that counterbalances the spread of liberalism and democracy? What are the specific characters of China's autocracy found in its state–society relationships, reform politics including rule of law, party recruitment and disciplinary anti-corruption measures and articulation of the human rights discourse? How has the world perceived China's ambition to become a great nation with its Chinese Dream? Are there causal relationships and links between China's rise, authoritarian diffusion, the persistence of hybrid regimes and the democratic recession?

Aims and structure

Unlike most current China studies which focus either on China's domestic state–society relationships in the reform process or China's foreign relations (Bader 2015; Bell 2015), this book provides a holistic perspective and analyses China's authoritarian rule reflected in domestic developments and its effects upon international relations. It has a unique format in combining scholarship from comparative political systems, IR and geopolitics, area studies, international law and human rights expertise for the elicitation of some disillusioning facts surrounding China's political, social, economic and human resource developments at home (institutional reforms, CCP's recruitment's policy, the state–society relationship, anti-corruption campaign and localization of human rights discourse) and its engagements and influences abroad (foreign policy change of the United States, China's relations to India and engagement activities in Latin America and Africa).

As such, the book pursues two aims. First, it aims to decipher the China puzzle and to detect if and to what extent authoritarianism as a global or regional phenomenon is challenging liberal democracy. If so, how does it work and what are its implications for international relations? The authors detect the strengths and limitations of China's autocracy against the backdrop of Xi's move towards dictatorship and the faltering influence of liberal democracy following the rise of populists and autocrats in domestic and international affairs. Treated issues include the prospect of democracy in China under one-man leadership, representation politics and the changing state–society relations, political mobility within the CCP, the relationship between economic reforms, corruption, and anti-corruption campaigns and its transnational implications, the domestication of the human rights discourse, and China's expanding influence abroad as perceived by the United States, India, Latin America and Africa involving the questions of the 'adversary' dynamic in the US foreign policy, the nexus building of authoritarianism in Latin America and democracy promotion in Africa. Secondly, through the adoption of inter- and intra-disciplinary approaches (international relations, comparative political systems, international political economy, institutional choice, new economic sociology, political geography, international law and human rights, and regional studies), the book explores and tests the combination of different approaches in explaining the diffusion and limitations of authoritarianism against the backdrop of the erosion of global democracy.

The book is divided into two major parts. Part 1 covers the domestic dimensions of China's authoritarianism in terms of its political, institutional, governance reforms and human rights discourse development (Chapters 1–6). Part 2 explores how important allies and regional powers perceive and react to China's growing assertiveness and influence in shaping international affairs (Chapters 8–11). Chapter 2 adopts neo-institutional and constructivist approaches and analyses if democracy still has a chance amidst institutional and governance reforms under Xi's rule. While a strategy of incremental institutional tactics has been helpful in addressing urgent social inequality issues, the tendency towards a one-man leadership has created an increasingly repressive environment, thereby making the birth and development of a pluralist and power-sharing system impossible. Nonetheless, the author reminds us of the logic of China's long history and upholds the relevance and potential of crisis situations in pushing for progressive institutional change. Chapter 3 takes a micro perspective by studying how the CCP shapes public opinion and inspirations through the control of the careers and work of its provincial propaganda leaders. Chapter 4 provides a further sophisticated picture and highlights the changing state–society relationship reflected in the project of 'administrative democracy' during the Hu Jintao era and the principle of 'ruling the country with law' under President Xi. Increasingly, the CCP faces challenges posed by citizens' demands for participation through the introduction of new representation tools (rural administrative reforms; collective but uncoordinated legal action such as public hearings). Albeit its authoritarian nature, the mutually defining character between public participation and political representation might pave the way for further structural changes driven by the dynamic of the changing meanings of the rule of law. Nonetheless, the extent to which the changing state–society relationship could influence CCP's anti-corruption campaigns remains unclear. Chapter 5 analyses the special relationship between economic performance, corruption, and anti-corruption campaign and its transnational implications. It illuminates the paradox of Xi's comprehensive anti-corruption campaign and the ambiguous nature of public attitudes towards corruption. On the one hand, the introduction of new institutionalized disciplinary mechanisms has helped address public discontent and enhance the CCP's legitimacy to rule. Beijing also has adopted a gradual approach in accommodating international pressure to combat corruption with transnational links. On the other hand, Xi's anti-corruption efforts have served as a powerful instrument in eliminating his enemies and centralizing his rule. Due to the lack of an institutionalized check-and-balance system, the level of corruption turns out to be a matter of subjective tolerance and acceptance, as long as it follows social norms and codes of conduct found in many informal institutional mechanisms and its costs do not threaten the profit-sharing of economic development and the CCP's rule. In a similar manner, Chapter 6 demonstrates how the launching of China's National Human Rights Action Plans (2009–10; 2010–15) has marked progressive localization efforts with the emphasis of collective and economic rights (e.g. the right to development), thereby signifying the incorporation of and connection with international human rights law as part of China's constitutional rights. At the same time, such localization efforts with cultural arguments could easily become a powerful political instrument in justifying the suppression of those who criticize the CCP's rule.

As a transition chapter connecting the domestic and international dimensions of China's rising political influence, Chapter 7 pays attention to the BRI and Chinese Dream (their meaning, purpose and implications), which represents the main domestic and international dimension of Chinese aspirations. As to the possibilities and limitations of the diffusion power of China's autocracy abroad, Chapter 8 highlights the 'adversary' dynamic in US foreign policy discourses towards China in the twenty-first century. With the focus on two issue areas (i.e. the currency question and nuclear proliferation), this chapter recurs to the notion of 'antagonism' and examines how the US construction of China as a 'significant Other' has shaped the US foreign policy discourses since 2000 onward. The changing dynamic of antagonist construction can be considered as a result of discursive dislocation. It has served a ubiquitous foreign policy goal, namely, to stabilize the US identity in the economic and security realms. This goal has constantly been in change: Whereas the Bush administration took the role of defending freedom and liberty, the US foreign policy entered a period of long-term decline of the US leadership in the democratic world and welcomed China to be a strong and prosperous member in the international community under the Obama administration. The Trump administration has projected a vision of a strong and smart America, supported by an adversary construction of China as the future superpower. In a similar manner, Chapter 9 echoes an evolving dynamic of India's self-identification process vis-à-vis China between traditional mistrust, on the one hand, and readiness for cooperation, on the other. Despite areas of divergences (e.g. concurrence for energy resources in Africa, unclarified territorial status within India, mutual threat perceptions), the status of leading emerging economies has provided facilitating moments for rapprochement and cooperation between China and India, particularly in the areas of trade and climate politics (e.g. the 2018 informal Wuhan summit). Albeit the United States' recent efforts to expand its alliance system by including the Indo-Pacific, the Indian Ocean and South Asian regions (Mishra 2016), a strengthened political will to talk about divergences and to overcome mistrust may constitute a breakthrough in the Sino-Indian relations. This is based on the mutual recognition that peace between China and India is crucially important for Asia as the central stage of global politics in the twenty-first century.

Chapters 10 and 11 go further to ask if China's foreign policy helps stabilize other authoritarian regimes in Latin America and Africa and if China's engagements abroad have threatened Western programmes of democracy promotion. Supported by a technique of structured focused comparisons, Chapter 10 tests the hypothesis of an 'authoritarian nexus' following China increasing its influence in Latin America and compares China's engagements in Cuba and Venezuela (being authoritarian regimes) with China's relations with Costa Rica and Chile (being democratic countries). The results are compelling and confirm the lack of evidence for direct influence from authoritarian external actors, as found in the studies of other regions (i.e. in Central Asia, see Ziegler 2016: 549; the weaknesses of Russia to promote autocracy in the 'near abroad' see Way 2015 and 2016). China's strengthened engagements in the region obviously have a cross-regime feature, marking *no* preferences towards authoritarian regimes. One observes 'the absence of the emergence of an authoritarian nexus through soft power instruments (that is producing cultural affinity as a means for stabilizing any special relationship' in Latin America (Muno et al. in this volume). At the same time, in addressing the question if China's close ties with African states have undermined democracy promotion and their observance of human rights, Chapter 11 shows the consequences of strengthened ties between China and the ruling elites in Africa, notably in Zimbabwe and Sudan: China has become an indispensable cooperation partner for African states, particularly for African autocrats and dictators. Its presence has proven to be detrimental for Africa's fight for economic independence, democracy and human rights in diverse post-colonial contexts. For many Africans, China has a very mixed reputation. On the one hand, China has been highly appreciated for its solidarity with Africa during Africa's fight against colonialism and oppression as well as its investment activities in varied sectors, thereby helping improve the infrastructure of many African countries. On the other hand, China's neglect of labour standards and non-interference policy have directly or indirectly influenced the behaviour of African ruling elites and become a source of conflict between the incumbent regime and the opposition parties. For many African leaders, cooperating with China provides an alternative choice not to abide by Western requirements of conditionality. As such, they even have found a justification to suffocate the burgeoning of a civil society, particularly in the areas of the environment, labour and working conditions. In this sense, China's growing influence in Africa has more negative than positive consequences in terms of democracy and human rights promotion.

In conclusion, this volume highlights the features, developments, implications and limits of China's autocracy in shaping domestic and international affairs. Chapter 12 particularly detects the link between China's rise, the diffusion of authoritarianism, the democratic recession in old and young democracies, and the future of democracy. Confronting an assertive China with a projection of becoming a superpower, major leading powers and regional political elites have adapted to new circumstances, specifically in terms of geostrategic and economic interest and alliance building (e.g. the development of the antagonistic reasoning of the US foreign policy). At the same time, the outreach of China's influence in the examined regions to build up an authoritarian nexus is far from secured. The diffusion of China's soft and sharp power backed by a toolkit has not seldom been countered with scepticism, critiques, resentment and vigilance (Hoover Institution 2018; Conteh-Morgan in this volume). Several reasons might account for the limits of the diffusion of authoritarianism. They include the inconsistency of autocracy's policy agenda in promoting authoritarianism, the lack of an encompassing normative framework, autocracy's narrow pursuit of its own interests, and the lack of credibility and transparency in promoting international norms.

In this respect, China's autocracy proves to pose less a challenge for democracy than other challenges and deficiency democracy faces today. The challenges and deficiencies are multifaceted, ranging from the crisis of representative politics including the emergence of a new form of domination found in power fragmentation in different elite groups (Gauchet 2016), social fragmentation and the rise of authoritarian populism, vulnerability to manipulation and lying, and the lack of efficient regulative mechanisms to protect data privacy, to uncertainty and insecurity engendered by social and technological change and the accompanying disruption.[4] The future of democracy hence will depend on how it can reinvent itself through reform and innovation efforts that inspire imaginary communities of meaning being able to reconnect the state and the society and to tackle those varied challenges for ensuring autonomy, social cohesion and welfare.

Notes

1 Braun (2019).
2 In its 2018 *Communication*, the European Commission regretted the consequences of delays in fulfilling the EU's obligations and commitment towards partners at the beginning of the budget period 2014–20. It promised to increase its external action budget to €123 billion for the next long-term budget period 2021–27 to support partner countries' economic and political transformations towards sustainable development, stability, consolidation of democracy and eradication of poverty. See the European Commission (2018).
3 Xinhua (2017).
4 Emcke (2018: 5), Bouée (2018: 20).

Bibliography

Acharya, Amitav, *The End of American World Order* (Uttar Pradesh, India: Oxford UP, 2015).

Bader, Julia, 'China: Autocratic Patron? An Empirical Investigation of China as a Factor in Autocratic Survival', *International Studies Quarterly*, 59 (1) (2015), pp. 23–33.

Bell, Daniel, *The China Model: Political Meritocracy and the Limits of Democracy* (Princeton, New Jersey: Princeton UP, 2015).

Betz, Hans-George, 'The New Politics of Resentment: Radical Right-Wing Populist Parties in Western Europe', *Comparative Politics*, 25 (4) (1993), pp. 413–27.

Bouée, Charles-Edouard, 'Populisten überlisten', *Süddeutsche Zeitung (SZ)*, 13 November (2018).

Braun, Stefan, 'Die Gewissheiten sind dahin' (The Certainties Have Gone), *SZ*, 1 September (2019). Available at https://www.sueddeutsche.de/politik/wahlen-sachsen-brandenburg-analyse-1.4583725 (accessed 1 September 2019).

Campbell, Charlie, 'China's Lurch Toward One-Man Rule Under Xi Jinping Should Worry Us All', *Time*, 26 February (2018). Available at https://www.yahoo.com/news/china-lurch-toward-one-man-081755124.html (accessed 24 September 2018).

Emcke, Carolin, 'Manipulation. Wie verlässlich ist die demokratische Willensbildung der Bürger in Zeiten der Desinformation und Diskurs-Sabotage' (Manipulation: How Reliable Is the Democratic Process of Voters' Will in the Age of Fake News and Discursive Sabotage), *SZ*, 29/30 September (2018).

Fan, Jiayang, 'Xi Jinping and the Perils of One-Person Rule in China', *The New Yorker*, 1 March (2018). Available at https://www.newyorker.com/news/daily-comment/xi-jinping-and-the-perils-of-one-person-rule-in-china (accessed 28 July 2018).

Gauchet, Marcel, *Comprendre le malheur français* (Paris: Stock, 2016).

Hoover Institution, *Chinese Influence & American Interests. Promoting Constructive Vigilance*. Report of the Working Group on Chinese Influence Activities in the United States, Co-chairs Larry Diamond and Orville Schell (Stanford, CA, 2018).

Inglehart, Ronald and Pippa Norris, *Trump, Brexit, and the Rise of Populism; Economic Have-Nots and Cultural Backlash*. Faculty Research Working Papers, Harvard Kennedy School, RWP16-026 (2016).

Kaltwasser, Cristóbal R. 'The Ambivalence of Populism: Threat and Corrective for Democracy', *Democratization*, 19 (2) (2012), pp. 184–208.

Keijzer, Niels, *The Future of Development Cooperation: From Aid to Policy Coherence for Development*. European Centre for Development and Policy Management (ECDPM) (2012).

Levitsky, Steven and Daniel Ziblatt, *How Democracies Die* (New York: Penguin Random House LLC, 2018).

Merkel, Wolfgang, *Kosmopolitanismus, Kommunitarianismus und die Demokratie*, WZB Mitteilungen, Heft 154 (2016), pp. 11–14.

Mishra, Vivek, 'US Power and Influence in the Asia-Pacific Region: The Decline of "Alliance Mutuality"', *Strategic Analysis*, 40 (3) (2016), pp. 159–72.

Mouffe, Chantal, *For a Left Populism* (London: Verso, 2018).

Mounk, Yascha, *The People vs. Democracy: Why Our Freedom Is in Danger and How to Save It* (Cambridge, MA: Harvard UP, 2018).

Mudde, Cas, 'The Populist Zeitgeist', *Government and Opposition* 39(4) (2004), pp. 541–63.

Norris, Pippa, 'Is Western Democracy Backsliding? Diagnosing the Risks', available at *SSRN Electronic Journal*, DOI: 10.2139/ssrn.2933655 (2017), pp. 1–24.

O'Brian, Thomas, 'Populism, Protest and Democracy in the 21st entury', *Contemporary Social Sciences*, 10 (4) (2015), pp. 337–48.

Runciman, David, *How Democracy Ends* (London: Profile Books, 2018).

Sandel, Michael, 'Populism, Liberalism and Democracy', *Philosophy and Social Criticism*, 44 (4) (2018), pp. 353–9.

The European Commission, 'EU budget: Making the EU Fit as a Strong Global Actor', 18 June (2018). Available at https://ec.europa.eu/europeaid/news-and-events/eu-budget-making-eu-fit-its-role-strong-global-actor_en (accessed 2 September 2019).

Way, Lucan A. 'The Limits of Autocracy Promotion: The Case of Russia in the "Near Abroad"', *European Journal of Political Research* (2015). Available at https://doi.org/10.1111/1475-6765.12092 (accessed 15 August 2018).

Way, Lucan A., 'Weaknesses of Autocracy Promotion', *Journal of Democracy*, 27 (1) (2016), pp. 64–75.

Xinhua, 'Spotlight: Belt and Road Initiative Strives to Reflect "Globalization 2.0"', editor: Huaxia, 26.03, (2017). Available at http://www.xinhuanet.com/english/2017-03/26/c_136158971.htm.

Ziegler, Charles E., 'Great Powers, Civil Society and Authoritarian Diffusion in Central Asia', *Central Asian Survey*, 35 (4) (2016), pp. 549–69.

Part 1

Domestic dimensions

2

The prospect of democracy in China

One-man leadership and institutional change

Miao-ling Lin Hasenkamp

Introduction

Being the second largest economic power of the world, China's centralized market system has set up a development model of authoritarianism without fundamental political reform. Some authors call such a model a Chinese brand of 'authoritarian mercantilism' (Meyerson 2010; Petersmann 2011), whose well-tailored mercantilist policies (including massive subsidies, forced technology transfer, pilfering of intellectual property and denial of access to Chinese markets) have fostered the basis of the political legitimacy of the CCP's rule. Drawing lessons from Mao's brutal dictatorship, the reformist leader Deng Xiaoping had installed, in the aftermath of the Tiananmen event, a collective leadership guided by the principles of top leader's term limit (one generation, two terms and ten years – Yi Dai, Lian Zen, Shi Nien), the nomination of successors in a cross-generational manner and leaders' age limit (no older than sixty-seven years). Indeed, the clarification of the successor question constructed the basis for political stability and economic prosperity of the communist regime for the next twenty-five years. Despite its double-edge repressive and reform measures, the CCP has been able to weather a series of social and economic crises and launched several reform efforts at the local and elite levels since the 1980s. For instance, regular village committee elections strengthened local governance and the 2007 internal party mobilization for suggesting Hu's successor demonstrated the CCP's attempt to introduce some democratic elements in its recruitment policy. As such, the CCP's elite rule has increasingly gained recognition and is regarded as a stabilizing force against a backdrop of uncertainty, crises and turbulence (Shi 1999; Schubert 2006). Towards the end of 1990s, in view of virulent corruption, mounting social inequality and unrest, the CCP even allowed competing voices to suggest different reform models ranging from a strong leadership under the CCP, a system of consultation guided by the rule of law, to incremental democracy.

Yet, the change from the collective elite rule towards one-man leadership under President Xi Jinping in 2017/2018 has silenced those arguments for pluralism and civil society. Here arise questions regarding the real face of institutional change in China: How far can existing theories explain the patterns and development of institutional change during the reform era? What are the factors that have pushed for the institutional transformation towards a one-man rule? Why has Xi decided to break the norm of collective rule set up by Deng? Does democracy still have a chance? This chapter uses neo-institutional and constructivist approaches to analysing institutional change under Xi's rule and the prospect of democracy in China.

To date, a variety of economic, political and comparative studies on China highlight China's modernization paths and its rise as a great power (Shin and Cho 2010; Liu 2010; Ding 2009; Shi 2008; Chu et al. 2008; Huang 2008; Peerenboom 2007; Zheng 2004; Whiting 2001; Fewsmith 2001; Shirk 1993). One group of studies explains China's development path through the prism of mainstream development thinking. Zheng (2004) explores how China's leaders have embraced global capitalism and market-oriented modernization. With successful reform measures and tactic investment strategies, China has not only survived globalization. It has also reinvented itself through outside influence by establishing a capitalist system with Chinese characteristics (Zheng 2004; Scott 2002). Another group of studies adopts rational choice institutional and historical approaches to explain institutional change and the flexibility of China's leadership to carry out market reforms and to tackle social crises without fundamental political reform (Shirk 1993; Whiting 2001). Susan Shirk (1993) demonstrates that Chinese communist political institutions are more flexible and less centralized than their Soviet counterparts. An analysis of detailed histories of economic reform policy decisions suggests how the political logic of Chinese communist institutions justified its focus on economic growth and shaped those decisions (Chow 2004: 129ff). Backed by the Chinese people's desire to abandon the planning system, the CCP resumed its modernization efforts (in the fields of agriculture, industry, science and technology, and defence), announced by Premier Zhou Enlai in December 1964, which were interrupted by the Cultural Revolution. Furthermore, in challenging mainstream views of China as an anachronistic and authoritarian regime, several comprehensive empirical studies have shed light on China's performance in human rights issues and grassroots movements either from a comparative perspective in the context of the developing world (Peerenboom 2007) or from a bottom-up micro perspective (Ahlers and Schubert 2012). Peerenboom (2007) shows China's efforts in improving its legal system and detects non-liberal variants of the concept of the rule of law in different Asian countries while pursuing a similar developmental path. In particular, in the midst of various economic and social crises, Chinese moderate elites have looked to the Western mainstream democracy and the rule of law theories and presented several models that might serve as a road map for the next stage of institutional change. It turned out to be that, knowing the political correctness of the primacy of the party over the law, suggestions have been largely limited to uphold Chinese cultural and political integrity and to launch its own style of political reform. Hu Angang, a vocal apologist for the government, for instance, made 'collective rule the centerpiece of his book on the superiority of the Chinese political system'.[1]

Though observers share the opinion that China's collective leadership has become institutionalized which played an important role in stabilizing political and economic developments, Xi's move towards dictatorship has surprised the world. Some critiques warn that such a regression may signal the beginning of the end of China's successful authoritarian rule. Others attempt to shed light on Xi's motivation and the long-term effects of such a move.[2] The existing literature and analyses have provided insights into the nature, development and features of the CCP's rule. However, a solid theory-based explanation of the CCP's change from collective rule to a strongman leadership appears to be overdue. This chapter attempts to address this deficit and uses new institutional (choice) and constructivist approaches to trace this change. It examines the basic tenets of the functioning of the China model of institutional reforms as well as the reasons for its move towards one-man rule. It aims to provide a synthesized approach to explaining some aspects of China's current political developments and to assessing the prospects and limitations of a systemic change in China. It is argued that the drastic move towards a one-man rule reveals the continuing anxiety and paranoia in China's ruling circles that have haunted the CCP since the collapse of the Soviet Union. It constitutes not only a necessary survival strategy for the CCP to restore its authority and legitimacy through strengthening law enforcement and adopting assertive diplomacy. Xi's total control of all levels of power proves to be tactically necessary in order to keep his enemies at bay. Ironically, Xi's move may destabilize the CCP's rule caused by an enhanced likelihood of calamitous mistakes that trigger the emergence of crisis situations.

To follow my arguments, the first section elaborates an institutional choice and constructivist framework and presents four variants of the theories of institutional change. The second section examines the three basic tenets of the Chinese model without ignoring negative social, political and ecological consequences as a significant malaise, situational and structural, behind China's economic successes. It then presents six models of political developments suggested by Chinese intellectuals and explains their applicability in light of evidence found in several reform efforts at national and local levels. The third section detects the (dys)functioning of collective rule and traces the driving factors responsible for the change towards Xi-ism. In recalling the preconditions of democratization found in theoretical explanations and historical experience, the final section summarizes the chapter's findings and draws a dim prospect of democratic reform under Xi's rule.

Tracing China's development model: New institutional and constructivist approaches as a theoretical framework

Through mutual engagement and accommodation, the combination of new institutional and constructivist (legitimacy-based and trust governance) approaches is supposed to explain China's institutional change. A mid-way synthetization of institutional and ideational approaches, according to Robert Lieberman (2002), shall facilitate the development of more convincing accounts of political change. It will ensure not just better self-critical understanding about the interactions of ideas, norms, agents and structure in the time span of a given historical setting but also a genuine cross-fertilization and collaboration within the ambit of work on the China model.

To be sure, both rational choice institutionalism (RCI) and historical institutionalism (HI) as forerunners of new institutionalism have revitalized the hard-core institutionalist tradition. The rational choice (RC) perspective can be defined as the analysis of the choices made by rational actors under conditions of interdependence. It is the study of strategic action of rational actors, using tools such as game theory (Immergut 1998: 12). In their efforts to build general theory through the micro–macro link, institutional choice models allow the analysis of social behaviour that is constrained by social institutions. For instance, in her analysis of the management of common pool resources (CPRs), Elinore Ostrom (1990) shows not only how varied institutional structures affect rational decision-making but also how rational decisions affect the institutional structures themselves. She argues that when individuals make choices, they affect not only the current operational situation (i.e. the adoption of their current behaviour). Their decisions also affect the operational rules (institutions) that govern future operational situations. In other words, by imputing ex ante preferences to individuals without worrying much about their larger sources, RC institutional theory emphasizes the role played by regulative, normative and cultural-cognitive processes in shaping social behaviour and social structure (Scott 2002). At the same time, as RC is motored by rational actor considered as 'an atom unconnected to the social structure in which he or she is embedded' (Shepsle 1989: 134–5), this approach has been criticized as having ignored the sources of preferences and beliefs as results of socially constructed ideas and rules (Katznelson and Weingast 2007: 5). In comparison, with its focus on historical context, HI argues that preferences are shaped primarily by macro-level dynamics. As argued by Kathleen Thelen (2002: 93–4), a good deal of historical–institutional scholarship shows that the impact of institutions is often heavily mediated by features of the overarching political or historical context. For instance, a strong professional bureaucracy in the context of a one-party state plays a very different role and has a very different impact on politics compared with a strong professional bureaucracy in the context of a democracy. Moreover, HI's focus on temporality and sequencing has helped establish the validity of particular causal claims and provided a more holistic and differentiating picture of the order in which various games get played in comparison with the order of moves in a particular, more or less well defined, game found in the RC tradition (Thelen 2002: 98).

Despite their distinct features and different emphasis, the common interest of RCI and HI in exploring institutions and preferences has opened some overlapping possibilities for the strengthening of their explanatory power. As suggested by Katznelson and Weingast (2007: 2), as institutions often generate sufficiently strong incentives for actors, we can derive a form of preference based on the compelling logic of institutions embedded in particular historical situations. As such, the overlapping dimension of RCI and HI enhances our understanding of how a given institutional milieu both constrains and shapes the repertoire of available preferences.

In view of RCI's and HI's respectively distinct features and their common focus on institutions and preferences, institutional change can be approached as follows. According to Bruce Gilley (2008: 259), institutional change can be defined as 'changes to the governing structure of a state'. The use of this term leaves open the evolutionary endpoint of such changes and the possibility that the magnitude of such changes may be as great within certain regime types as across them. Within the RCI, while economic institutionalism explains changes to institutions in light of the demands of economic interests at the micro and macro levels (Frey 1976; North 1990; Acemoglu and Robinson 2005), sociopolitical institutionalism focuses more on social or political power than on economic interests (see, for example, Bueno de Mesquita 2003). HI focuses on historical process of institution (its genesis, reproduction and change) and explains the impact of prior events, where exogenous technological change or endogenous facets of the institutions themselves trump conscious social control (Thelen and Steinmo 1992; Mahoney 2001; Thelen 2002: 98–9). Furthermore, in taking a more nuanced and historically informed focus on institutions, RCI examines how players mutually anticipate the actions of others and select strategies that respond to those decided by others. An exploration of the dynamics of adaptation and accommodation strategy choices may also help explain institutional change. For instance, in his study of emerging economies, Zhichang Zhu (2018: 371) finds that an actor-centred, process-oriented and uncertainty-sensitive reorientation backed by the notions and theory of 'uncertainty', 'adaptive efficiency' and 'entrepreneurship' may well enrich the methodological toolkit of RCI while explaining institutional change. For Katznelson and Weingast (2007: 8 and 10), these induced preferences concerned with instruments at times can be observed with sufficient regularity that they can be legitimately imputed as ends towards an individual's fundamental goals or underlying preferences. Meanwhile, despite their explanatory strengths, institutional choice approaches suffer from the absence of any subjective normative coherence to institutional change. They have been also criticized as being limited to reductionism, reliance on exogenous factors and excessive emphasis on order and structure (Lieberman 2002). For instance, Michael Collier (1999) notes the failure of Ostrom's CPRs analysis (1990) to clarify specific causal mechanisms that link institutional structures to actual decision-making processes.

Constructivism with its varied ideational perspectives may well provide these causal linkages. According to Nicholas Onuf (1997: 7), a principal constructivist tenet is that people (agents) and society (structure) co-constitute each other in a continuous process. Rules as general prescriptive statements are always implicated in this process, which make people active participants (as agents) in society. As such, rules form agent's relations into the institutionalized arrangements, or institutions that give society a recognizable pattern or structure. Any change in a society's rules redefines agents, institutions and their relation to each other. It follows that any such change also changes the rules, including those rules agents use to effectuate or inhibit changes in societies. Therefore, a main goal of constructivism is to provide both theoretical and empirical explanations for the constitutive processes of the emergence, maintenance and change to social institutions. Theoretical explanations focus on the analysis of the interaction of rules, agents and structures. Constructivists examine how these interactions constitute or cause individual behaviour by providing agents with direction and incentives for action, and how these interactions influence changes to institutions (rules) (Adler 1997: 329). In challenging the tendency of institutional theories to take the interests and goals of political actors as given, constructivist ideational accounts of politics consider actors' understanding of their own interests is apt to evolve as the ideological setting of politics changes. Hence, a focus on ideas suggests the possibility that human agency can defy the constraints of political and social structures and create new political possibilities (Smith 1992).

In accommodating both the institutionalist and constructivist perspectives, we introduce a further approach to explain institutional change, namely, the legitimacy-based and trust governance approach, which accords its central explanatory power to the role of popular preferences based on the common good demands of a political community (Roland 2004). According to Bruce Gilley (2008: 259ff), legitimacy is the degree to which citizens treat the state as rightfully holding and exercising political power. It puts forth the critical importance of ideas, norms or values, which are viewed as part of the common good aims of a political community. Once established, legitimacy furthers the emergence and maintenance of trust between citizens and government, which is a rational compact based on a fair exchange of information and the public's ability to evaluate government performance. As argued by Valerie Braithwaite and Margaret Levi (1998), a strong government can itself be a source of trust, which can be found in the evidence how public commitment increases through establishing clear goals and accountability procedures within government agencies facilitates greater public commitment. However, despite its effective economic performance, a strong government with repressive measures violating civil and political rights cannot fully guarantee the maintenance of citizens' trust, not to mention the maintenance of political legitimacy in a longer term.

Derived from David Easton's (1965) model of political systems, the legitimacy-based approach conceptualizes institutions as being at the centre of an endogenous system of performance (outputs), legitimacy and feedback. Institutions then are the infrastructure for generating the performance, on which legitimacy is based. Maintaining legitimacy means managing institutions to generate valued performance and enhance trust among citizens. When that performance fails, pressures grow for more radical institutional change. In this sense, the legitimacy-based trust governance approach is explicit in modelling institutions endogenously, where they are both a consequence and a cause of legitimacy (Gilley 2008: 259–60). In particular, from a historical and empirical viewpoint, it is unlikely that any one perspective mentioned above (economic, sociopolitical, historical and legitimacy-based/trust governance) alone is ever sufficient in explaining institutional change. As noted by Gilley (2008: 262), the South African case shows that the fall of apartheid was not only a direct result of the *de*legitimation of the regime, but also an indirect result of how that *de*legitimation generated structural conditions that magnified the impact of illegitimacy (the rise of a reform faction within the National Party, or the application of economic sanctions, that is international pressure). In other words, we can describe the relationship between the structural and legitimacy-based theories of institutional change in terms of four variants (Gilley 2008: 261ff). Legitimacy and structural factors may be causally autonomous in their effects on institutional change (Variants 1 and 2). Or they may be causally interdependent (Variants 3 and 4). In the latter case, either one could be the critical cause. The structural factors can be further deductively ordered into domestic and international circumstances and factors. As emphasized by Gilley (2008: 261), both structural (Variants 2 and 4) and legitimacy-based (Variants 1 and 3) theories

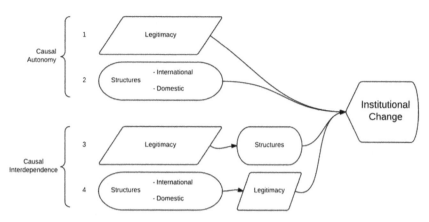

Figure 2.1 Four variants of the theories of institutional change (Gilley 2008: 261, with an addition of a sub-category of structures).

of institutional change can be justified deductively. From the structural perspective, the demands of legitimacy may run into a situation of inertia without the means with which to act (Variant 4). Skocpol's study (1979) of state weakness and international pressures in explaining revolutions shows that legitimacy may be driven by those structural factors themselves (Variant 4). In many cases, changes in power relations play a critical role in creating the openings in which new scripts can become more central (Thelen 2003: 217). Similarly, Gilley (2008: 261) continues, the argument for the legitimacy-based theory of institutional change can likewise be made deductively, either in the autonomous or interdependent way. Legitimacy might have autonomous effects (Variant 1). It may also lurk in the fabric of economic, sociopolitical or historical accounts of institutional change (Variant 3). Figure 2.1 illuminates these four variants of the theories of institutional change.

Which approach to institutional change – legitimacy-based or structural – can best explain the pattern of post-1989 institutional change in China? What can the case of China tell us about the theory of institutional change? The following sections first describe and explain major features of institutional change in the China model. It then highlights the driving forces that have pushed for the change from collective rule towards a strong leadership under President Xi in the post-reformist era.

Exploring a Chinese model of institutional change

The China model and its basic tenets

The past two decades have seen a proliferation of academic terms in describing and explaining China's development paths with new combination of concepts state authoritarianism, neo-authoritarianism, Leninist corporatism, commercial Leninism, single party capitalism, developmental state, Confucian capitalism, Confucian Leninism, plural authoritarianism, soft authoritarianism, etc. Despite their seemingly contrasting combination of political ideological and economic terms (which appeared unthinkable forty years ago) and a lack of consensus about what the China model really is, these terms, as observed by Ding Shuai-Liang (2009: 41), have demonstrated at least two essential aspects of China's modernization paths: a political one involving its nature, characteristics and structures of power; and an economic one involving its rules, characteristics and institutions. In this sense, we assume that Variant 4 of the theories of institutional change may turn out to be the proper one to explain China's modernization and the ensuing institutional change. Namely, legitimacy may be driven and enhanced by those structural factors themselves. The ensuing institutional reforms remain under the control of the overarching power of the CCP, what some analysts have called 'institutional tactics for democracy' (Shi 1999) or 'contained institutional change' (Gilley 2008).

Regardless of the initial doubts about the sustainability of such a model, the post-1989 period has at least witnessed a China model in the making, whose relatively stable structures can be discerned in three iron angles: the Leninist one-party rule and its overarching power structures; social control with Chinese characteristics that regulates the relationship between state and society; and a state-controlled market economy.

First, despite its much improved international reputation as a global player and a wide range of reform efforts (including some democratization steps within the CCP, legal reforms, local democratic elections, etc.), the core power structures of the communist regime remain a political monopoly, guided by Leninism and ruled by the CCP (Ding 2009: 44ff). Following the Leninist doctrine, a one-party state consists of a hierarchical disciplinary order in regulating party and state affairs, led either by a strong leader (during the Mao and Deng era and since 2012 led by Xi) or by a group (between the mid-1990s and 2012 led by Jiang Zemin and Hu Jintao). Since the end of the 1970s, while some elements of Leninism have been largely diluted or modified (i.e. with the introduction of the economic opening policy and several elements of capitalism), China's political development has demonstrated a high degree of continuity of the one-party rule through the CCP's successful crisis management and the implementation of adaptation strategies (e.g. the introduction of property laws and financial and political measures against inflation). Meanwhile, the 19th party congress in October 2017 that 'called for the strengthening of the party's leadership role in almost every aspect of public life'[3] and the ensuing modification of the Constitution in removing the term limits of presidency in March 2018 has destroyed some earlier reform efforts to separate powers between the party and the state and to further partial intra-party democracy once listed as a priority by late leaders Deng, Jiang and Hu (details about Xi's move back to the past in imitating Mao's totalitarian rule will be discussed later in the chapter).

The second iron angle of the China model is what Ding (2009: 47–54) has called 'a social control system with Chinese characteristics'. There are six components of this social control system that includes traditional control mechanisms and the new Social Credit System (SCS) planned for launch in 2020. The first one involves a state bureaucratic control system, which has survived, been rebuilt and enhanced following domestic political turbulence, social unrest, international isolation and changes in the international system during the past decades. The second component of this social control system is the establishment and cooperation of the CCP and its Youth Corps. The third one involves the organization of specific control units found in every working unit (in cities and rural areas, in private and public sectors), which has been endowed with the power and mission to monitor its employees and employers. A further control mechanism deals with a comprehensive social control network which can be found in the form of 'residents committees', 'residents units', 'township control units (*chen guan duei*)', etc. Although the establishment and definition of the tasks of '*chen guan duei*' cannot be found in any officially written legal documents (including the *Constitution* of People's Republic of China (PRC) after the amendment on 14 March 2004 and relevant legislation documents), *chen guan duei* have become the forerunner of the Chinese social control system. Both the third and fourth control units have emerged and evolved against the backdrop of a Leninist–Stalinist control system with Mao's blueprint. Whereas these control units with a strong Maoist tradition suffered from disorganization and functional weaknesses during the 1950s and 1960s, since the 1970s, they have successfully adapted to new circumstances (increasing interactions between China and the external world, new economic lifestyle, rapid social changes, etc.) and become revitalized and supported by modernization efforts. For instance, the power of *chen guan duei* has been refined and expanded particularly with the task to monitor migration flows from the rural areas to big cities within China.

Besides the physical control, China has extended its control system into the wireless world. With the help of information technology, internet police have been charged to undertake non-physical control and to filter messages communicated among laptops and smart phones. In a 2018 propaganda conference, Xi urged 'unity of thinking' and insisted that the internet must be 'clean and righteous', devoid of content that 'upsets the CCP's preferences'.[4] These remarks reflect an intensified censorship policy under Xi since 2017 that pursues the goals to improve state-sponsored propaganda and to suppress 'political criticism, Western culture and anything that could lead Chinese people questioning the wisdom of their leadership'.[5] Finally, in a 2014 policy document published by the State Council, the Chinese government has planned to launch a SCS that will enable the state to monitor and evaluate its citizens' daily activities. It involves what Botsman (2017) calls a marriage 'between communist oversight and capitalist can-do' while pursuing the aim to establish a nationwide trust system and to build a culture of 'sincerity' in every sphere of public and private affairs (e.g. government affairs, social and commercial sincerity and the construction of judicial credibility). As noted by Botsman (2017), the Chinese government adopts a 'watch-and-learn approach' and has given a licence to eight private companies to come up with systems and algorithms for social credit scores. For instance, the Ant Financial Services Group (AFSG), an affiliate company of Alibaba, has introduced Sesame Credit, with which people will be rated based on five categories (i.e. credit history, fulfilment capacity, personal characteristics, behaviour and preference, and interpersonal relationships). With these rating categories, the system not only scrutinizes behaviour but also shapes it in nudging citizens away from purchases and behaviours the government dislikes in order to make their score go up.[6] Moreover, while posting critical voices and links mentioning Tiananmen Square has always been dangerous in China, it now could directly worsen a citizen's rating. A further kicker of this 'Big Brother' system is that citizens' score will be indirectly influenced by the posting (negative or positive) of their online friends (Botsman 2017). Contrasting opinions have emerged towards this newest social control scheme. On the one hand, some welcome such regulation efforts that uphold the moral standards designed to reduce risks in digital economy, can prevent irrational behaviour and violence, and result in more effective oversight and accountability.[7] Other observers see the SCS as being like 'Amazon's consumer tracking with an Orwellian political twist' and compare it to 'Yelp reviews with the nanny state watching over your shoulder'.[8] Increasingly, such a SCS began to shape the mind-set of the Chinese population in a bizarre digitalized world, whose effects bring an illusion of security and can already be observed in normal cultural and business exchanges between the Chinese young generation and their European counterpart. A Chinese intern in Hamburg expressed her insecure feelings due to the lack of surveillance and face recognition systems in the public sphere in Europe.[9]

Whereas the first and second iron angles of the China model have created an environment of political and social stability, the third iron angle – a state-controlled market economy – has provided fresh air, blood and dynamics for an effective functioning of the whole system (Ding 2009: 58). As such, the development process of the China model is constituted by close interactions among these three iron angles. To be sure, a state-controlled market economy has been a common phenomenon in most East Asian economic development (Japan, Taiwan, South Korea, Singapore, Hong Kong and Vietnam), in which the government has explicitly and implicitly controlled those strategic key sectors including bank, finance, energy, communication, defence and education affairs (Wade 1990; Aoki et al. 1996; Kojima 2000). China has been following the 'flying geese' (FG) development model of Taiwan and Singapore. In the midst of industrialization process since 1978, the CCP not only has a strong grip in those key sectors (developed as a form of party capitalism) while elaborating strategies for attracting huge volumes of foreign direct investments (FDI), establishing alliances (such as joint ventures) and following a clear division of labour (found in the Sino-Japanese economic relations, see Kwan 2002; UNCTAD 2013). The CCP has also been strongly involved in corporate governance ranging from the recruitment and employment of managers to the control of shares, etc. Meanwhile, as observed by Ding (2009: 60–1), China has created a variation of the East Asian economic development model: the scope and degree of market intervention controlled and manipulated by the communist officials in those sectors such as real estate, finance, stock and energy sectors in the post-1990s can no longer be compared with the development experience found in Taiwan and Singapore. For foreign investors in China, the definition of market gaps and demands are often *less* important than the fostering of contacts with the mayors and CCP's officials. In this light, the China model provides a compelling example of an economic miracle and the likely durability of one-party rule in the developing world. The state-controlled economic reforms have improved the living standard of millions of people, thereby pushing the emergence of a middle class with strong purchasing power the global market can no longer ignore. At the same time, increasing social inequality, the slowdown of domestic economic growth resulted from recent trade barriers set by China's key partners (notably the United States and the EU)

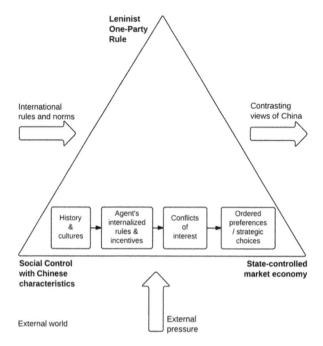

Figure 2.2 *The China model with its iron triangles – an institutional-constructivist framework.*

and the transformation towards a totalitarian rule under President Xi have cast shadows upon the further development of this model.

Viewed from an institutional–constructivist perspective, Figure 2.2 illustrates how the China model works.

To be sure, China's post-Deng era has seen two phases of political and institutional change. The first phase has been characterized by the continuation of China's productive exchanges with the West which have helped China change itself and contributed to China's domestic prosperity and its rise to global economic power (Gewirtz 2017). Under former presidents Jiang and Hu, China remained open to Western ideas and kept a *low* profile in international affairs set by Deng. Signs of political and social pluralism began to emerge and have been tolerated by the CCP. For instance, reform-minded thinkers and conservative hardliners within the CCP have debated over the direction of political reforms; social movements, local non-governmental organizations (NGOs), philanthropic associations and blogs fighting against social inequalities and environmental pollution have emerged. Nevertheless, the Chinese government has been less eager to publicize its engagement with Western-style innovations and maintains that China's economic miracle was the achievement of CCP alone.[10] It has presented its own development discourses in emphasizing the collective right to develop and uphold traditional values and norms such as 'harmony' and 'trust' found in the Confucian teaching. In particular, it has propagated nationalism and patriotism in countering Western pressure and protesting against Japan's revisionist efforts towards its past aggressor role during the Second World War (Hasenkamp 2018).

The second phase of change began with President Xi's gradual move towards one-man rule since November 2012. Backed by the slogan 'China Dream', a fundamental change is taking place (for more details about the China Dream, see Chapter 7). Measures are introduced to reorganize the top leadership, suffocating liberal thinking within the CCP and in society, monitoring NGOs' activities and strengthening internet censorship. The policy change can also be found in China's aggressive diplomacy coming from Xi's 'own aspirations, beliefs and strategic requirements'.[11] This diplomacy is designed to vault China to world greatness through even bigger spending in military and space projects as well as the launching of overseas infrastructure programmes (i.e. the One Belt and One Road Initiative (BRI)). Meanwhile, though Western media has declared Xi as the most powerful leader on the world stage, Xi's move towards dictatorship and increasingly aggressive diplomacy have prompted concerns and mistrust worldwide.[12]

Both phases witness how China's history and culture have shaped actors' incentives and rules, the scope of conflict of interests among different factions and the outcome of elites' ordered preferences. Gerrit Gong (2001) particularly upholds the role of history by offering value to *what* individuals and countries remember and *what* they forget. The spread of social media and public opinion has further nationalized individual feelings under the banner of nationalism and patriotism. At the same time, as noted by Callahan (2004: 200), instead of nurturing greater democracy or freedom, such popular politics might add 'another dimension to the broad forms of governance that rely on culture and history for political and economic projects'. The way Chinese history and culture provide values and incentives can be described in a set of complex and incompatible pictures with the following characteristics: a China-centric identification of greatness and superiority, nationalization of victimhood and suppression of the dark past through forgetting and a volatile potential of destruction and violence.

First, the Chinese mind has been and remains convinced of its rightful place as a Middle Kingdom with an enduring allure of its rich old civilization. The Chinese history with its past twenty-four dynasties has shown how it has survived foreign occupation, subordination, civil wars and internal division while absorbing different foreign cultures and cultivating barbarian peoples. After more than a century of 'national humiliation' (Callahan 2004; Kingston 2013) and backwardness, the restoration of its greatness constitutes a compelling legitimate basis for contemporary Chinese leaders. Secondly, China's collective psyche has been beleaguered by those unprecedented turbulent events of the past century (i.e. loss of territories, Japan's aggression and atrocities, civil war, political turmoil and violence during the Mao era (notably the Great Leap Forward and the Cultural Revolution between 1966 and 1976)). These events have defined China's mind-set which is characterized of a psyche of victimhood with a persistent humiliation narrative as well as conscious forgetting and silencing towards its dark past.[13] The enormous sufferings of the Chinese people at the hands of Western and Japanese imperialists and Mao's dictatorship are unique. However, the painful remembering began belatedly and selectively almost three decades ago, very often for political expedient reasons (Kingston 2013; Hasenkamp 2018). Despite the hosting of the 2008 Beijing Olympics being celebrated as an end to China's humiliation, deliberate acts of humiliation continue to be used as the bedrock of the founding of modern China and serve as a rally call for nationalism and an easy political cause for elaborating grand strategy (Callahan 2004; Kingston 2013; Wu 2015). Thirdly, China's historical experience has revealed a high degree of volatility of self-destruction and violence which has provided a facilitating bedrock for revolution and systemic change. Their root causes often lie in economic scarcity, severe social tensions, class antagonisms, blind dedication to deified leaders and the political cause, and conflicts between the state and the mass/society. Several studies reveal for instance why the Cultural Revolution can be described as 'a social revolution at all levels of society' and how social tensions and the Red Guard factionalism have led to *uncontrolled* violence, destruction and barbarism (Lee 1978; Chan et al. 1980). Albeit its strong economic performance and growing political influence, China remains vulnerable to the danger of domestic instability due to the high volatility of social conflicts and the unsettled dark past, as its future depends on how the narrative of history and culture might be framed, selected and manipulated for political purpose.

Coupled with the historical ghost of victimhood and a specific set of cultural traits (i.e. national pride and destruction), the exposures of structural and ecological malaise and the mounting social unrest as consequences of rapid economic development have further challenged the legitimacy of the CCP's rule. A brief look at the dark sides behind China's economic successes reveals inherent structural drawbacks of the China model.

Structural and ecological malaise and suggestions for reforms

From a macroeconomic and sociopolitical perspective, China's development model bore consequences reflecting the shadow of China's economic miracle in four areas: the continuing exploitation of marginalized rural areas and socially marginalized groups, structural corruption, ecological destruction and the lack of transparency and rationality in the sphere of public policy.

First, following Huang's analysis of two Chinas (2008), there exist an entrepreneurial rural China and a state-controlled urban China. In the 1980s, rural China gained the upper hand, and the result was rapid as well as broad-based growth. However, in the 1990s, urban China triumphed: the Chinese state reversed many of its productive rural experiments with long-lasting damage to the economy and society. It follows that a weak financial sector, income disparity, rising illiteracy, slowdowns of productivity and reduced personal income growth turn out to be the product of a capitalism with Chinese characteristics. While GDP grew quickly in the past three decades, the marginalized rural areas, regions and social groups (peasants, workers and particularly migrant workers and women) remain exploited and excluded from the accumulation and distribution of economic wealth. China's poor political governance and its bureaucratic centralized system are responsible for the increasing social disparity between the rich and the poor.

Secondly, though the conventional wisdom holds that corruption is damaging for maintaining social trust, empirical studies reveal its crucial role in serving as an incentive for officials and stimulating China's economic reforms and growth (Bergsten et al. 2008; Wang and You 2012). However, its omnipresence at every level of government and the loss of control on the part of the CCP deeply involved in collective profit-sharing in both business and state affairs have constituted structural barriers for China's further economic development. The ensuing negative political and social effects have particularly threatened the CCP's political legitimacy. Despite the state government's efforts in carrying out a series of anti-corruption campaigns and trials (in 1982, 1986, 1989, 1993 and since 2013 under Xi's leadership), their deterrence effects remain largely limited (for more details about the CCP's anti-corruption campaigns and its relationship to economic development, see Chapter 5). As long as there exist no *independent* anti-corruption institutionalized channels in regulating social and public affairs, the scope and degree of corruption and the filtration of corruption in every aspect of social life will continue (Quade 2007; Ding 2009: 134). Thirdly, behind the GDP growth, China's inhabitants (particularly those socially marginalized groups) have been suffering ecological deteriorations in various forms (water, air, land pollutions and food poison) as negative or (un)intended consequences of economic development. The corresponding violations of social and economic rights (including the rights of producers and consumers in the global chains of capitalism) have not only prompted a surge of social protests, but also the emergence of environmental activism (e.g. following the poison protests in 2011, see Kelly 2006).[14] Finally, in the sphere of public policy (ranging from the issues of public health, education, religion and cultural affairs to population control, etc.), as Chinese intellectuals have been continually prevented from engaging in discussions in an open, rational and creative manner, many problems remain unaddressed and intentionally covered, which have often led to outbreaks of tragic crises. Ding (2009: 135–6) calls the obstruction of an active role of intellectuals in the public arena and the consequent lack of transparency and rationality in the articulation and implementation of public policy as 'an institutionalized bêtise'.

In view of the poor political governance and existing institutionalized bêtise, various discourses surrounding possible political reforms emerged within the CCP circle towards the end of the 1990s. Moderate and conservative CCP intellectuals have proposed the following six models.[15]

The first model emphasizes that it is necessary for China to become a strong, authoritarian state to restore its national greatness and to concur against the United States. Wang Huning, the CCP's famous strategist under the presidents Jian, Hu and Xi, has proposed the idea of 'neo-authoritarianism' and argued already in the late 1980s that a nation as big and poor as China 'needed a firm hand to push through modernization before it could consider becoming a democracy'.[16] Wang doubts the adequacy of US-style democracy for China and suggests an *enlightened* autocracy that would be 'highly effective in distributing social resources' in order to 'promote rapid economic growth' through the centralization of party rule and tight control of society.[17] The second model involves a political system which should be guided by the principle of the rule of law with consultation. Supporters of this model like Pan Wei view that political reforms are necessary for the fight against corruption, misuse of power and increasing social disparity. The goal is to revitalize the political legitimacy of the CCP. Such a consultative political system based on the rule of law consists of several institutional reforms: the establishment of an independent state bureaucratic system; an independent judicial system; independent anti-corruption institutions as well as a social consultation system; and the legal protection of the freedoms of opinion and associations. In this system, the CCP should play a leading role to manage the timing and phases of the transition from a non-democracy towards institutional change.

The third model is – what Kang Xiaoguang calls – a cooperation state with a combination of authoritarianism, liberal market economy, corporatism and a welfare state. Kang argues that such a power-sharing system between the state, the market and society should be based on the principles of autonomy, cooperation, checks and balances, and participation. To be sure, to adapt to the globalized age, Chinese leaders have encouraged individual firms to build an entrepreneurial class at different levels (Zheng 2004). A unique, country-specific formula for cautious deregulation, state ownership and selective government intervention in the economy has been the case for Chinese economic development. Two examples help illustrate the emergence and growth of Chinese entrepreneurship backed by state-supported adaptation and regulation strategies. They also show how economic growth successfully follows from an *adept* tailoring of economic policies and institutions to their local contexts rather than from an application of universal economic principles (Huang 2008). First, the success of Lenovo as a product of Hong Kong institutions becomes a story of rule of law and market-based finance.[18] As noted by Huang (2008), that corporate success in China requires a combination of Chinese management and foreign legal status is 'probably the cleanest illustration of the massive distortions in China's business environment'. In other words, China's success has *less* to do with creating efficient institutions and more to do with permitting access to efficient institutions *outside* of China (Huang 2008). In view of China's corporate success stories, Western researchers have begun to argue that microeconomic and macroeconomic successes do *not* depend on adoption of Western-style financial and legal institutions. Instead, *informal* finance is nearly as good as market-based financial institutions in channelling capital to the private sector (Allen, Qian and Qian 2005, cited in Huang 2008). Another example deals with the growth of township and village enterprises (TVEs) in rural China during the reform period, which has been praised as the emergence of 'local state corporatism' growing out of the statist tradition (Oi 1992, cited in Whiting 2001: 11). However, as Susan Whiting (2001: 12) reminds us, local state officials in China do intervene actively in local economies, and they do so in highly politicized ways. As a result, publicly owned TVEs, while experiencing dramatic growth, share many of the same pathologies of state-owned enterprises (SOEs) throughout the developing world.

The fourth model, as suggested by Wang Shaoguang und Hu Angang, is based on the theory of democratic institutional building which pursues the goal of 'good governance' in fostering the government's capacities in eight areas: the capacity of safeguarding state security and public order (coerce capacity); the capacity of mobilizing and dispatching social resources (collect capacity); the capacity of fostering and consolidating national identity (legitimacy capacity); the capacity of maintaining economic and social orders (regulatory capacity); the capacity of retaining the control, supervision and coordination within state institutions (leadership capacity); redistribution capacity; the capacity of bringing the demand of citizens participation into the channel of official institutions (administrative capacity); the capacity of coordinating different interests and formalizing public policies (integration capacity). The evidence has shown that at least the CCP has proved to be successful in demonstrating their legitimacy capacity and leadership capacity in the past two decades. Gilley (2008: 263) mentions that, in most cross-national comparative studies of legitimacy, or the closely related concepts of political trust or support, China's party state has been ranked with high legitimacy. Following a series of institutional reforms including bureaucratic downsizing, party institutionalization, major central-provincial and corporate tax reforms, bureaucratic centralization, semi-competitive elections in self-managing villages, enhanced legal institutions, the rise of the regulatory state and the discussions of an independent anti-corruption institution (2007), a stray of hope that China would begin to move towards more democratic institutional reforms emerged. However, as long as the CCP's constitutional monopoly of political power remains, such institutional reform can be described as 'contained institutional change' (Gilley 2008: 264). In combining with the role legitimacy may play for the launching of institutional change, Gilley (2008: 264) observes that the party's programme of institutional change has successfully responded to public preferences at the macroscopic level. As such, the post-Mao state's emphasis on bureaucratic efficiency and state strengthening is consistent with the post-Mao public's emphasis on what Inglehart and Welzel (2005) call 'modernization' values, which are empirically strong in contemporary China: economic development and national defence. In other words, we can argue that CCP's trust governance has functioned well. Its significant but contained institutional change so far has enhanced the political legitimacy of the CCP, which might have obstructed the fundamental steps for democratization. In particular, at the local and microscopic level, various studies show how the party has responded to social demands for more efficient rule. For instance, in their cross-province study of the organization and administration of population control policies, Y. Huang and Yang (2002: 30) find that the shift to more professionalized and non-coercive institutions was driven by public demands. Concerned about the legitimacy problem, there was a perceived political need to shift the contentious issue from the political arena to an administrative 'neutral' zone.

Furthermore, Yu Keping proposed a fifth model based on the theory of incremental democracy, which regards democratization as a gradual process through the introduction of an *electoral democracy*. It upholds the importance of fostering a socialist market economy, of putting the CCP also *under* the rule of law, and of emphasizing grassroots democracy. Despite the contrasting views of the impacts of semi-competitive village elections,[19] some elements of electoral democracy have been introduced since the end of 1980s. Even though the CCP still organizes such elections, which contrasts with the principle of democracy, according to Shi (1999: 386ff), elections in rural China did create uncertainty for village rulers. Such uncertainty is the driving force of political and institutional change. Evidence has shown that candidates in many places have even begun to purchase votes, testimony to the ability of the elections to put an entrenched power at risk. In Shandong Province, turnover in the 1995 elections reached 30 per cent. It indicated that voters ousted between 9,900 and 19,800 incumbent CCP officials from office. At the same time, in countering Shi's argument (1999) that views such local village elections as an institutional tactic for the CCP to maintain its power, Chen Jie and Yang Zhong (2002) re-examine voters' subjective motivations and get a more differentiating picture. They find that people with stronger democratic orientation and a keener sense of internal efficacy are less likely to vote in those semi-competitive elections. In comparison, people who are identified with the regime and have affective attachments to the CCP are likely to vote in the elections. Here we detect the emergence of more or less pluralist voices within Chinese village voters, which may pave the way for further incremental democratization.

The final model suggested by Wang Guixiu is a rigorous one that should follow the imperative of the rule of law supported by democratic principles in order to effectively address the existing political, social and ecological malaise of the old system. Instead of the CCP's power monopoly, further decentralization backed by citizens' participation should be introduced. However, China's current political development might have from the very beginning countered such a suggestion, as it would not only pose a fateful challenge to the one-party state rule but also implicate social and political instability and insecurity following a systemic change without or with a democratic CCP, which is unthinkable in current China.

The six models suggested by the CCP's intellectuals show that some pluralist voices inside the CCP cadre emerged at a time when the CCP' was confronting the impasse of its rule while tackling a variety of domestic and foreign challenges. Some elements of certain models have been put into practice while some models have proven to be unfeasible in the Leninist system. At the same time, Xi's move towards a one-man rule proposed by his political counsel Wang Huning has confirmed the full embracement of the first model, thereby putting aside any space of deliberation and experiments of other models. Herein arise the questions of the motivation, scope and implications of such developments that mark an end of the 'two-term limit' of power transfer set up by Deng in order to prevent a return to totalitarian dictatorship during the Mao era.

The emergence and consolidation of one-man leadership

The years 2017 and 2018 mark a historical shift in China's political developments that bring back old rules of power transfer in the CCP senior leadership circle. In October 2017, the 19th National People's Congress (NPC) adopted 'Xi Jinping Thought on Socialism with Chinese Characteristics for a New Era' in the CCP's *Charter*, giving Xi a status unmatched except by Mao and Deng. NPC's decision appeared to pave the way for Xi's 'perpetual presidency' after his second five-year term in office. Later, in March 2018, during the opening of its annual parliamentary session, the NPC decided to scrap the two-term limit for the state president and vice-president and allowed Xi to retain the presidency as long as he can and will. Also, the NPC has confirmed the sixty-nine-year-old Wang Qishan – the retired former anti-corruption head – to become vice-president, thereby breaking the norm of age limit in nominating senior cadres to a new five-year term. In short, Xi has laid cards on the table and decided to break the collective party decision-making norm in the post-Deng era.[20]

Reactions and explanations vary following Xi's move towards one-man rule. Domestic sympathizers and Western admirers regard such a grand measure of reform as a guarantee for political stability of the CCP's rule. For them, China under Xi now feels strong enough to demonstrate a successful China model and 'to express itself in terms of its foreign policy and its international position' by putting aside Western values regarded as 'emotional private enjoyment'.[21] For instance, Xi has aggressively claimed China's territorial ownership in the South China Sea and is ready to challenge the US dominance in Asia. China also has begun to challenge the US leadership in the fields of military, technology and space affairs.[22]

In comparison, worrying and opposing voices consider China as being in jeopardy due to the three transformations China faces today (i.e. its changing role becoming a 'feisty competitor', the debt problem and its ageing population),[23] coupled with many uncertainties Xi's move has triggered. Critics raise their concerns with such a shift that not only threatens past painstaking efforts to institutionalize peaceful party and government leadership transitions every ten years. They also view Xi as becoming 'the most dangerous rival' against an open society, whose policy of social control suffocates vibrant forces in economy and society and subdue the destiny of individuals to the party state's interests.[24] In particular, observers consider Xi's move as an exposure of the consequences of the fierce, often bloody power struggle inside the CCP dating back to Mao's era. The shift from one-party rule to one-man rule obviously reveals CCP's failure to institutionalize power transfer of political leadership, leaving Xi no other choice than the overturning of the existing rules and taking the risk of possible backlash from his potential political rivals.[25] Ultimately, such a move has proved to be a key survival strategy for Xi to fight against coups and assassination bids and to restore the CCP's legitimacy, as its elite leadership has fallen prey to concurring corrupt factions which have profited from the state-led economic boom, while fighting against each other for power maintenance (Mahalingam 2017; Shu 2018).

A close look at the specific circumstances and scope of Xi's move towards one-man rule unveils the real face of the past collective elite rule, Xi's motivation and its implications. We recall the legitimacy-based theory of institutional change mentioned above which is deduced from mutually reinforcing economic, sociopolitical, or historical factors (Variant 3, see 'Tracing China's development model: New institutional and constructivist approaches as a theoretical framework'). Viewed from this prism, we assume that, following the third view mentioned above, Xi's power concentration involves a political instinct for survival and is the natural consequence of CCP's failure to institutionalize its power transfer since Mao. His decision to scrap the term limit of presidency serves to restore the unity of the government and the CCP's political legitimacy.

To be sure, empirical and comparative studies show that one-party rule is the most resilient system when compared with other types of authoritarian regimes (military regime and one-man rule). The reason for its durability lies in its institutional arrangements (e.g. the existence of congress of party representatives or/and political central committee) that can carefully balance a power system among different factions of the party while exercising its power. Within this system, as no single faction can attain a political monopoly, consensus emerges in terms of the regulation of power- and profit-sharing among the ruling class' different factions. Once consolidated, such collective rule cannot be easily challenged or divided by external forces. As emphasized by Shu (2018), this is the real face of an 'elite rule', which has ensured China's political stability in the past decades. At the same time, its collective power- and profit-sharing can lead to virulent collective corruption, as no single faction is willing to undertake disciplinary measures to break up the chains of mutual cover-up. The CCP increasingly is trapped in a state of inertia. It therefore becomes unable to cope with its structural governance problems and to address the rising tensions and frustrations between the ruling class and the ruled. Being a fresh designated successor, Xi witnessed in 2008 how Hu lost control of solving the CCP's governance problems, caught not only in the ruthless power struggle between Hu's faction and Jiang's faction but also in a vicious circle of collective corruption (Shu 2018).

Three driving forces have shaped Xi's authoritarian approach based on tactic, political and strategic calculations. The first and foremost force is a political instinct to eliminate political rivals. Similar to the violent bloody power struggles of the past (dating back to Lin Biao, Liu Shaoqi and Hua Guofeng during the Mao era and later Hu Yaobang and Zhao Ziyang during the Deng era), Xi too has allegedly survived several attempted coups and assassinations between 2012 and 2015, planned by his rivals (i.e. Zhou Yongkang and Bo Xilai from the faction protected by the former president Jiang). After those incidents, friends close to Xi noticed his determination to 'clean up the Communist Party', to clean up the Chinese hierarchy's abuses of power and corrupt behaviour'.[26] Later, Zhou and Bo were under investigation due to their corrupt behaviour (for details, see Chapter 5). As Xi has broken the balanced power- and profit-sharing rule, there is no way back for him to have compromises with other rival factions, not to mention to consult with them concerning the successor question. Secondly, Xi wants to prevent any scenario that would see the collapse of the CCP rule; he wants to consolidate control and to restore the CCP's legitimacy through vigorous reform measures. These measures include ideological campaigns at all levels by deifying the CCP's historical mission to make China great again and by cultivating a cult of personality surrounding Xi, the recruitment of reform-minded members, and the introduction of new institutional units aimed to suppress critical voices and political rivals, also in the name of anti-corruption campaigns. For instance, in rebuilding the Standing Committee, Xi has recruited five new members in October 2017 who are either can-do reformers or adept at coping doing business and financial issues. Observers interpret such personnel arrangements as a significant sign of Xi's new focus on trade and economic issues in the forthcoming trade quarrels with the United States after the phase of power consolidation during his first term.[27] Thirdly, Xi has accelerated China's foreign political influence activities through multiple channels, including the launching of the BRI as well as cultural promotion (e.g. via more than 500 Confucius institutes in foreign countries) and media propaganda work which also serves as a means of facilitating espionage. China's assertive foreign policy is guided by the concept of 'united front' and directed by the State Council Information Office and CCP Central Committee Foreign Affairs Commission. Praised as 'magic weapons', the assertive foreign policy strives to influence overseas Chinese and China-friendly representatives who will effectively 'influence, subvert, and if necessary, bypass the policies of their governments and promote the interests of the CCP globally' (Brady 2017: 3; Hoover Institution 2018). The ultimate purpose of this aggressive foreign policy is to extend China's global influence and to expand its economic and military agenda, thereby enhancing the CCP's domestic legitimacy and Xi's rule at home.

The implications of Xi's policy are fourfold. The scrapping of the term limit gives him time and space to consolidate his control and to reorganize the CCP's rule. The ensuing institutional change and expansionist agenda abroad have helped the party state to restore and to maintain its legitimacy, thereby ensuring the PRC will be able to outlast the former Soviet Union while preparing for the celebration of its 70th anniversary in October 2019. Promoting a cult of personality and enhancing social control via modern information technology signify a clear farewell to any prospects of democratic deliberations in terms of the development of a vibrant civil society and the establishment of democratic institutions. Under Xi, China experiences a fundamental change from an opening reformist country towards a surveillance bottlenecks state, in which even in the higher education system, the ideological work now determines *everything*. This may have already limited free academic research and exchanges between Chinese students and academics and their international counterparts.[28] Xi has full control of the CCP's members and the people behind him to pursue the China Dream and he certainly will do his best to justify his rule through best performance. Nevertheless, the high degree of power concentration has created its own bottlenecks. Officials become 'unsure how to execute policies or afraid to deviate from top-down demands'[29] and society becomes subordinated to the will of the new emperor. It constantly finds itself in a state of fear and anxiety. The declining economic growth, accompanied by uncertainties, resulted, in part, from Xi's rule and the US–China trade quarrels may provide occasions for social discontent and tensions in a highly suppressive party state. The fourth implication of Xi's policy is that China's extensive foreign influence activities have changed the power constellation in the international system. They mark the rise of authoritarian regimes now being able to counter the spread of democracy and to provide an attractive template for the diffusion of authoritarianism.

Conclusion and discussion: Does democracy still have a chance in China?

This chapter has highlighted the functioning of a China model of institutional change. The intertwining structural and legitimacy-related factors decisively shape the institutional change in China's Leninist state-party system. While collective elite rule in the post-Deng era provided political stability and allowed concurring voices to help the CCP to address a variety of external and domestic challenges, it delegitimized itself by its own virulent corrupt behaviour. This occasion provided a facilitating moment for Xi to step in and to take a full grip of power. As such, the change from a consensual elite rule to one-man rule is the result of crisis management. Xi further uses historical narratives to glorify the CCP's mission to bring China back to the central stage of world politics, justifying the legitimacy of such a one-man rule. Under Xi, the CCP can reassure its permanent arbitrary power *beyond* the PRC's constitution. The institutional change herein has demonstrated the dynamic of China's special characteristics in regulating the state–society relationship, in which society is required to be obedient towards the party state, just like the ancient Chinese society did towards its emperors. However, the drastic move towards a one-man rule reveals the continuing anxiety and paranoia in China's ruling circles that have haunted the CCP since the collapse of the Soviet Union.

What can be the outcomes and impacts of such a shift towards dictatorship in China? The question of the China puzzle reappears, with which Western opinion in the past often got China wrong through the recurring warning that China would eventually hit the wall if it does not become a democracy. In order to better understand China, Martin Jacques' suggestion to question the appropriateness of a Western paradigm and to recognize China as both a civilization state and a nation-state may be a good starting point to consider China differently, while discussing the impacts of Xi's strong leadership and the prospects of democracy in China.[30]

Reflecting upon the 'third wave of democratization' (Huntington 1991) in the 1990s, Herbert Kitschelt (1993: 413–14) revises three fundamental theoretical premises for explaining regime change. First, while conventional thinking has been preoccupied with identifying structural 'preconditions' of democratization (i.e. economic development, property rights, class configurations, cultural patterns, and state institutions), Przeworski et al. (2000) find that economic development does not generate democracies but democracies are much more likely to survive in wealthy societies. Therefore, one can instead pay attention to the process of political interaction and bargaining between stalwarts of an existing non-democratic regime, reform elites and outside democratic challengers. One assumption of revisionist thinking is that the process of transition is a better predictor of eventual regime outcomes than structural preconditions that precede the advent of liberalization. Secondly, whereas conventional thinking insists on the importance of democratic norms and orientations as preconditions of democratization, new approaches argue that popular democratic commitments are the result, not the prerequisite of democratization. Democracy is the contingent outcome of conflicts that depends on actors' initial resources, not their values. Hence, the key factor leading to the emergence and consolidation of democracy is not legitimacy, but the absence of alternatives to democracy that significant political actors view as feasible and preferable. Thirdly, in rejecting the pessimism of structural and normative analyses of preconditions to democracy, authors like Przeworski (1991) favour the use of game-theoretic tools to throw light on the timing of democratization and concern with the cognitive mapping of strategic situations and a 'hermeneutics' of strategic interaction that has often been neglected by conventional game theory.

In synthesizing the revised theoretical premises, following Daron Acemoglu and James Robinson (2005: viii), two favourable circumstances for democracy can be identified: (1) when there is enough social unrest in a non-democratic regime that cannot be defused by limited concessions and promises of pro-citizen policies. The outbreak of social unrest, in turn, depends on the living conditions of the citizens in the given non-democracy, the strength of civil society, the nature of the collective action problem facing the citizens in non-democracy, and the functioning of non-democratic political institutions that determine what types of promises made by the elite appear to be credible; (2) when the costs of democracy anticipated by the elite are limited, so that they are not tempted to use repression to deal with the discontent of citizens. These costs may be high when inequality is high, when the assets of the elite can be taxed or redistributed easily, when the elite have a lot to lose from a change in economic institutions and when it is not possible to manipulate the form of the nascent democratic institutions to limit the extent to which democracy is inimical to the interests of the elite. Moreover, these factors influence whether, once created, democracy is likely to survive. For instance, greater inequality, greater importance of land and other easily taxable assets in the portfolio of the elite, and the absence of democratic institutions that can avoid extreme populist policies all are more likely to destabilize democracy.

In other words, Acemoglu and Robinson's approach to democratization stresses not only the role of crises, but also the importance of social unrest, the threat of revolution and generally the de facto power of those without de jure political power in inducing a transition to democracy. And their approach finds support in the historical experience of systemic change both in Latin American and in China. The Latin American experience with democratization supports the notion that the threat of revolution and social unrest was important and is broadly consistent with the comparative statistics with respect to inequality (Acemoglu and Robinson 2005: 53–6). The change of dynasty from one emperor to another in Chinese history also demonstrates the crucial role of crises and social unrest. There is one famous Chinese proverb: If you don't get the heart of peasants, you'll lose the power, as the threat of peasant revolution will become real. The Chinese elite know well this inherent logic of their history. Furthermore, contrasting experiences highlight the significance of uncertainty and contingency of democratization, and therefore also choice, and even leadership (Gourevitch 1993). The early democratic experiment undertaken by the first republic in East Asia, namely, the Republic of China (ROC) under the Sun Yet-Sen and Yuan Shi-Kai regimes in the post-1911 period provides an example for the way democratic institutions can be kidnapped by local militia elite groups. Later, the dream of democracy turned out to be a nightmare of civil wars and instability, aggravated further by the Japanese invasion between 1931 and 1945.

The illustration of the China model as well as the analysis of the six institutional models demonstrate that reform-minded voices within the CCP are ready to adopt certain democratic elements with civil society's participation. For them, a well-tailored democratic design should serve as an exit strategy for the CCP to address social discontent and tensions and to remain in power. Nonetheless, the emergence of pluralist voices in the Chinese society during the post-Deng era has signified the beginning of the disfranchisement between the state and the party. In their second round of the East Asia Barometer surveys conducted in nine countries in 2006 and 2007, Shin and Cho (2010) find that the majority of East Asians do not equate democracy exclusively with political freedom. Their finding is illuminating: the prevalence of substantive or *communitarian* conceptions of democracy is one important characteristic of the cultural democratization unfolding in East Asia. That said, it is possible to imagine, in case of the emergence of crisis situations triggered by widespread social unrest as a radical response against the slowed bottleneck state, the power vacuum in a post-Xi era could well provide chances for experimenting a Chinese style of democracy with strong communitarian elements.

Regarding theoretical implications, the case of China explicitly defeats the hypothesis of the role of economic development and property rights as a prerequisite for democratization. Still, we observe a strong degree of interdependence between structural factors and legitimacy/trust governance (Variant 4), which had facilitated the launching of a series of institutional reforms, well managed by the CCP elite during the Jiang's and Hu's presidencies. Furthermore, in the Chinese context, evidence will be needed to explore if the causal autonomy of structural factors (Variant 2) alone can cause institutional change in terms of the role of social unrest and the threat of revolution.

Notes

1 His book was published in 2013, just after Xi's coming to power. Cited in Palmer (2018).
2 Mitchell and Clover (2018); Palmer (2018).
3 Wang Qishan, former anti-corruption chief, summerized Xi's speeches during the CCP's 19th Congress and argued that the advocacy for the 'indiscriminate' separation of party and government affairs in the past had led to the weakening of the party's leading role. Cited in Mai (2017).
4 Martel (2018).
5 Ibid.
6 Millions of people have already signed up in this publicly endorsed government surveillance system. As noted by Botsman, there are two reasons for explaining citizens' voluntary participation in this system. First, citizens might fear reprisals if they decide not to join this system. Secondly, there is a lure of gaining special privileges through the reward of being trustworthy on Sesame Credit. For instance, if their score reaches 600 and beyond, they can have a variety of special offers including getting a fast-tracked application to a coveted pan-European Schengen visa (at 750). See Botsman (2017).
7 Wang Shuqin from the Faculty of Philosophy and Social Science at Capital Normal University in China regards the moral standards the system assesses and financial data as a bonus to establish a faithful system. Cited in Botsman (2017). In a similar manner, the Chinese science fiction writer Cixin Liu regards the SCS as a necessary mechanism to prevent the outbreak of irrational behaviour of the mass in the digital world. See Freund (2019: 13).
8 Johan Lagerkvist, a Chinese internet specialist at the Swedish Institute of International Affairs, and Rogier Creemers, scholar specializing in Chinese law and governance at the Van Vollenhoven Institute at Leiden University, observe the disquieting development of this surveillance system in China. Here cited in Botsman (2017).
9 Sources based on a casual talk in February 2019 between the author and her house doctor, whose daughter's company based in Hamburg had recruited a Chinese intern for several months in 2018/19.
10 See Deuber (2019: 2), Osnos (2016).

11 Said Shi Yinhong based in Renmin university. Here cited in Perlez (2017).

12 See Deuber (2019).

13 Despite some efforts to investigate murder, cannibalism and destruction during Cultural Revolution following the failure of the Great Leap Forward, the CCP continues to suppress remembrance and historical reckoning of the era and its excesses. For instance, a retired cadre from the province Guangxi showed AFP his unpublished manuscript and stated: 'In 10 years of catastrophe, Guangxi not only saw numerous deaths, they were also of appalling cruelty and viciousness.' In small towns such as Wuxuan, residents decide to suppress the history of cruelty and cannibalism which was not caused by economic reasons, but by 'political events, political hatred, political ideologies, political rituals', said X. L. Ding, a Cultural Revolution expert at the Hong Kong University of Science and Technology. Here cited in Agency France Press (AFP) (2016). See also Wong (2016), Schrittmatter (2018).

14 See 'Environmental activism in China. Poison Protests. A Huge Demonstration over a Chemical Factory Unnerves Officials', 20 August (2011).

15 Sources based on an internal document of a CCP's think tank (1999/2000).

16 Cited in Perlez (2017). A former college professor, Wang was recruited by Jiang Zemin after the pro-democracy movement erupted on Tiananmen Square. Since then, he has been successful in climbing the ladder of Beijing's brutal politics and is regarded as 'the brain behind three supreme leaders', said Yun Sun, a China expert at the Washington-based Stimson Center. See Perlez (2017).

17 See Huang (2015).

18 As noted by Huang (2008), Lenovo is the most prominent product of what is known as 'round-trip' FDI: 'foreign' capital that is first exported from China and then imported back into China. The true contribution of China's open-door policy is not just about allowing foreign entry, but also about allowing Chinese exit. It enabled some of China's own indigenous entrepreneurs to find an escape valve from a very bad system.

19 In November 1987, an *Organic Law of Village Committees* was adopted by the Standing Committee of the NPC. Its implementation began in 1989, which stipulated that the chairman, vice-chairmen and members of village committees should be directly elected by the residents of the village.

20 Said Andrew Polk at Trivium, a Beijing-based consultancy. See Mitchell and Clover (2018).

21 In his book *China's Future*, Frank Sieren emphasizes China's exceptional capacity in tackling diverse challenges with its authoritarian rule. See Osterhammel (2018).

22 Martin Jacques, author of the global bestseller *When China Rules the World: The Rise of the Middle Kingdom and the End of the Western World*, sees China setting up an excellent example for developing countries to get rid of dependency and poverty, cited in Mogul (2018). See also *The Economist* (2014).

23 George Magnus, author of the new book, *Red Flags: Why Xi's China is in Jeopardy*, warns that the BRI initiated by Xi could leave the participating countries in debt. See Mogul (2018).

24 Kevin Carrico observes that there have been many steps backwards under Xi. Cited in Mitchell and Clover (2018). George Soros, the founder of the Open Society Foundations, regards Xi as the most dangerous rival for an open society. See Zick (2019: 3).

25 Observers like Susan Shirk note that Xi's move risks a backlash from other ambitious politicians. He behaves more like Mao than one originally thought. Cited in Buckley (2017).

26 Cited in *China uncensored staff* (2012), see the bibliography below. Based on another source Boxun, Zhou and Bo as rivals planned to take down Xi by killing him and performing a coup d'état. Bo fell in early 2012 due to a murder case in which his wife was involved and due to a corruption accusation against him. After the failed plots, the former security Caesar Zhou was first put under house arrest and later accused of corruption. See Boxun (2013).

27 See Buckley (2017), Mogul (2018).

28 Based on the author's personal observation while contacting a Chinese cooperation partner based in Beijing. For further observations on China's fundamental change, see Strittmatter (2019: 24–31).

29 Buckley (2017).

30 See EN 22.

Bibliography

Acemoglu, Daron and James A. Robinson, '*Economic Origins of Dictatorship and Democracy*, Available at books.google.com (2005).

Adler, E., 'Seizing the Middle Ground: Constructivism in World Politics', *European Journal of International Relations*, 3 (3) (1997), pp. 319–63.

Agency France Press (AFP), 'How Political Hatred during Cultural Revolution Led to Murder and Cannibalism in a Small Town in China', *South China Morning Post (SCMP)*, 11 May (2016). Available at https://www.scmp.com/news/china/policies-poli tics/article/1943581/how-political-hatred-during-cultural-revolution-led (accessed 5 January 2019).

Ahlers, Anna and Gunter Schubert, *Participation and Empowerment at the Grassroots. Chinese Village Elections in Perspective* (Plymouth: Lexington Books, 2012).

Aoki, Masahiko, Hyung-ki Kim and Masahiko Okuno-Fujiwara (eds.), *The Role of Government in East Asian Economic Development*. Comparative Institutional Analysis (New York: Oxford UP, 1996).

Bergstein, C. Fred, et al., *China's Rise: Challenges and Opportunities* (Washington: Institute for International Economics and the Center for Strategic International Studies, 2008).

Botsman, Rachel, 'Big Data Meets Big Brother as China Moves to Rate Its Citizens', *WIRED*, 21 October (2017). Available at https://www.wired.co.uk/article/chinese-gover nment-social-credit-score-privacy-invasion (accessed 1 January 2019).

Botsman, Rachel, *Who Can You Trust?: How Technology Brought Us Together – and Why It Could Drive Us Apart* (London: Penguin Portfolio, 2017).

Boxun, 'Xi Jinping Had Two Attempts Directed at Him by Zhou Yongkang', 3 December (2013). Available at https://en.boxun.com/2013/12/05/xi-jinping-experienced-two-a ssasination-attempts-by-zhou-yongkang/ (accessed 12 January 2019).

Brady, Anne-Marie, *Magic Weapons: China's Political Influence Activities under Xi Jinping*, Paper presented at the Conference on 'The Corrosion of Democracy Under China's Global Influence', supported by the Taiwan Foundation for Democracy, hosted in Arlington Virginia USA, 16–17 September (2017).

Braithwaite, Valerie and Margaret Levi, *Trust and Governance* (New York: Russell Sage Foundation, 1998).

Buckley, Chris, 'Xi Jinping Unveils China's New Leaders but No Clear Successor', *The New York Times*, 24 October (2017). Available at https://www.nytimes.com/2017/10/24/ world/asia/xi-jinping-china.html (accessed 27 September 2018).

Bueno de Mesquita, B., *The Logic of Political Survival* (Cambridge, MA: MIT Press, 2003).

Callahan, William A., 'National Insecurities: Humiliation, Salvation and Chinese Nationalism,' *Alternatives: Global, Local, Political*, 29 (2) (2004), pp. 199–218.

Chan, Anita, Stanley Rosen and Jonathan Unger, 'Students and Class Warfare: The Social Roots of the Red Guard Conflict in Guangzhou,' *The China Quarterly*, 83 (1980), pp. 397–410.

Chen, Fanyu, 'Xi Jinping Becoming Emperor? China's Institutional Change: Developments and Effects,' (2018). Available at www.whogovernstw.org (accessed 18 October 2018).

Chen, Jie and Yang Zhong, 'Why Do People Vote in Semi-Competitive Elections?' *The Journal of Politics*, 64 (1) (2002), pp. 178–97.

China uncensored staff, 'Speculation of Assassination Attempt on Xi Jinping' (2012). Available at http://www.chinauncensored.com/index.php/real-china/548-speculati on-of-assassination-attempt-on-xi-jinping (accessed 10 January 2019).

Chow, Gregory C., 'Economic Reform and Change in China,' *Annals of Economics and Finance*, 5 (2004), pp. 127–52.

Chu, Yun-Han, Larry Diamond, Andrew J. Nathan and Doh Chull Shin (eds.), *How East Asians View Democracy* (New York: Columbia UP, 2008).

Cohen, Jerome A. *When will China Realize a Society of Rule of Law?* (2012). Available at www.usasialaw.org.

Collier, Michael. *Explaining Political Corruption: An Institutional-Choice Approach*. Paper presented at the 40th Annual Convention, ISA, Washington, D.C. February 16–20 (1999).

Ding, Shuei-Liang, *Debating the Chinese Model*. Hong Kong: Social Sciences Academic Press/Boyuan Foundation (2009).

Deuber, Lea, 'Pekings Neue Stärke,' *SZ*, 5/6 January (2019).

Easton, D., *A Systems Analysis of Political Life* (Chicago: University of Chicago Press, 1965).

Fewsmith, Joseph, *China since Tiananmen*. The Politics of Transition (Cambridge UP, 2001).

Freund, Nicholas, 'Ich kenne die Masse besser als viele Intellektuelle,' *Süddeutsche Zeitung (SZ)*, 4 January (2019).

Frey, Bruno S., *Politico-Economic Models and Cycles*. Diskussionsbeiträge des Fachbereichs Wirtschaftswissenschaften der Universität Konstanz, No. 83 (1976).

Gewirtz, Julian, *Unlikely Partners: Chinese Reformers, Western Economists, and the Making of Global China* (Cambridge, MA: Harvard UP, 2017).

Gilley, Bruce, 'Legitimacy and Institutional Change: The Case of China,' *Comparative Political Studies*, 41 (3) (2008), pp. 259–84.

Gong, Gerrit W., *Memory and History in East and Southeast Asia* (Washington DC: CSIS Press, 2001).

Gourevitch, Peter A., 'Democracy and Economic Policy: Elective Affinities and Circumstantial Conjunctures,' *World Development*, 21 (8) (1993), pp. 1271–80.

Guo, Baogang and Dennis Hickey, *Dancing with the Dragon: China´s Emergence in the Developing World* (Plymouth: Lexington Books, 2010).

Guo, Yingjie. *Cultural Nationalism in Contemporary China: The Search for National Identity Under Reform*. Routledge Studies on China in Transition (2003).

Halper, Stefan, *The Beijing Consensus: How China´s Authoritarian Model will Dominate the 21st Century?* (New York: Basic Books, 2010).

Hasenkamp, Miao-ling, *Universalization of Human Rights? The Effectiveness of Western Human Rights Policies towards Developing Countries after the Cold War*. With Case Studies on China (Frankfurt am Main: Peter Lang, 2004).

Hasenkamp, Miao-ling Lin, 'Transitional Justice in East Asia: Searching for Justice between the Global and the Local', in Anja Mihr, Gert Pickel and Susanne Pickel (eds.), *Handbook for Transitional Justice* (Springer VS, 2018), pp. 495–522 (in German).

He, Weifang, 'The Role of Public Intellectuals', *Economic Observer*, 18 April (2006).

Hoover Institution, *Chinese Influence & American Interests. Promoting Constructive Vigilance*. Report of the Working Group on Chinese Influence Activities in the United States, co-chairs Larry Diamond and Orville Schell (Stanford, California, 2018).

Huang, Y. and D. Yang, *Journal of Chinese Political Science*, 7 (1/2) (2002), pp. 19–46.

Huang, Yasheng, *Capitalism with Chinese Characteristics: Entrepreneurship and the State* (Cambridge: Cambridge UP, 2008).

Huang, Yufan, 'Xi Jinping Adviser Has Long Pushed for Strong Leadership', *Sinosphere/ the New York Times*, 29 September (2015). Available at https://sinosphere.blogs.nytim es.com/2015/09/29/china-president-xi-jinping-advisor-wan-huning/?mtrref=undefine d&gwh=E2F837A2DB48055F992052D034C74570&gwt=pay (accessed 13 January 2019).

Huntington, Samuel P. *The Third Wave: Democratization in the Late Twentieth Century* (Norman: University of Oklahoma Press, 1991).

Immergut, Ellen M. 'The Theoretical Core of the New Institutionalism', *Politics and Society*, 26 (1) (1998), pp. 5–34.

Inglehart, R. and C. Welzel. *Modernization, Cultural Change, and Democracy: The Human Development Sequence* (Cambridge: Cambridge UP, 2005).

Kato, Junko, 'Institutions and Rationality in Politics - Three Varieties of Neo-Institutionalists', *British Journal of Political Science*, 26 (4) (1996), pp. 553–82.

Katznelson, Ira and Barry L., Weingast, 'Intersections Between Historical and Rational Choice Institutionalism', in Ira Katznelson and Barry L. Weingast (eds.), *Preferences and Situations: Points of Intersection Between Historical and Rational Choice Institutionalism* (New York: Russell Sage Foundation, 2007).

Kelly, David, 'Social Movements in Urban China', *China Brief*, The Jamestown Foundation, February 15 (2006).

Kingston, Jeff, 'National Humiliation: China Still Vanquishing, Suppressing Ghosts of Past', *The Japan Times*, 14 September (2013). Available at https://www.japantimes.co.jp/o pinion/2013/09/14/commentary/national-humiliation-china-still-vanquishing-suppre ssing-ghosts-of-past/#.XDP3wC2X9TY (accessed 7 January 2019).

Kitschelt, Herbert, 'Comparative Historical Research and Rational Choice Theory: The Case of Transitions to Democracy', *Theory and Society* 22 (1993), pp. 413–27.

Kojima, Kiyoshi, 'The "Flying Geese" Model of Asian Economic Development: Origins, Theoretical Extensions, and Regional Policy Implications', *Journal of Asian Economics* 11 (2000), pp. 375–401.

Kwan, Chi Hung, *The Rise of China and Asia's Flying Geese Pattern of Economic Development: An Empirical Analysis Based on US Import Statistics*. The Research Institute of Economy, Trade and Industry (RIETI) Discussion Paper Series 02-E-009 (2002), pp. 1–17.

Lee, Hong Yung, *The Politics of the Chinese Cultural Revolution: A Case Study*. Berkeley: University of California Press (1978).

Levi, Margret, 'Modeling Complex Historical Processes with Analytic Narratives', in Renate Mayntz (ed.), *Akteure, Mechanismen und Modelle. Zur Theoriefähigkeit makro-sozialer Analyse* (Frankfurt am Main: Campus Verlag, 2002), pp. 108–27.

Levitsky, Steven and Lucan A. Way, 'Elections Without Democracy: The Rise of Competitive Authoritarianism', *Journal of Democracy*, 13 (2) (2002), pp. 51–65.

Lieberman, Robert C., 'Ideas, Institutions, and Political Order: Explaining Political Change', *The American Political Science Review*, 96 (4) (2002), pp. 697–712.

Lipset, Seymour Martin, 'Some Social Requisites of Democracy: Economic Development and Political Legitimacy', *American Political Science Review*, 53 (1) (1959), pp. 69–105.

Liu, Qianqian, 'China's Rise and Regional Strategy: Power, Interdependence and Identity', *Journal of Cambridge Studies*, 5 (4) (2010), pp. 76–92.

Mahalingam, V., 'Xi Jinping's Fight against Coups and Assassination Bids', *Indian Defence Review*, 19 August (2017). Available at http://www.indiandefencereview.com/spotlights /xi-jinpings-fight-against-coups-and-assassination-bids/ (accessed 25 January 2019).

Mahoney, J. *The Legacies of Liberalism: Path Dependence and Political Regimes in Central America*. Baltimore: Johns Hopkins UP (2001).

Mai, Jun, 'The "One Simple Message" in Xi Jinping's Five Years of Epic Speeches', *South China Morning Post*, 3 November (2017). Available at https://www.scmp.com/news/ china/policies-politics/article/2118170/xis-epic-speeches-can-be-summed-one-sim ple-message-says (accessed 9 December 2018).

Martel, Frances, 'Xi Jinping Urges "Unity of Thinking" and End to "Vulgar" Internet in Propaganda Conference', *Breitbart.com*, 22 August (2018). Available at https://www. breitbart.com/national-security/2018/08/22/xi-jinping-urges-unity-thinking-end-vulgar-internet-propaganda-conference/ (accessed 9 December 2018).

Meyerson, Harold, 'A Flawed American Political Model Aids China', *Washington Post*, 31 March (2010).

Mitchell, Tom and Charles Clover, 'China's Xi Jinping Shocks Rivals with Plan to Scrap Term Limit', *Financial Times*, 25 February (2018). Available at https://www.ft.com/ content/1508d632-1a3f-11e8-aaca-4574d7dabfb6 (accessed 15 October 2018).

Mogul, Priyanka, 'China's "New Era" under Xi Jinping: Progress of Jeopardy?' *Asia House*, 9 October (2018). Available at https://asiahousearts.org/china-xi-jinping-progress-jeopardy/ (accessed 1 January 2019).

North, Douglass, *Institutions, Institutional Change, and Economic Performance* (Cambridge: Cambridge UP, 1990).

Onuf, N., 'A Constructivist Manifesto', in K. Burch and R. A. Denemark (eds.), *Constituting International Political Economy* (Boulder: Lynne Rienner, 1997).

Osnos, Evan, 'The Cost of the Cultural Revolution, Fifty Years Later', *The New Yorker*, 6 May (2016). Available at https://www.newyorker.com/news/daily-comment/the-cost-of-the-cultural-revolution-fifty-years-later (accessed 27 December 2018).

Osterhammel, Jürgen, 'Wie man gegen die Schwerkraft regiert', *Frankfurter Allgemeine Zeitung (FAZ)*, 19 December (2018). Available at https://www.faz.net/aktuell/feuille ton/buecher/themen/frank-sieren-und-kai-strittmatte-schreiben-ueber-china-159463 91.html (accessed 23 December 2018).

Ostrom, Elinore, *Governing the Commons, The Evolution of Institutions for Collective Action* (Cambridge: Cambridge UP, 1990).

Palmer, James, 'China Becomes Officially a Dictator: Xi Jinping Declares Himself as a Life-Long President', *International Chronicles: Interactive Forum of Political Culture*, 5 March (2018). Available at http://www.theinternationalchronicles.com/2018/03/05/ china-officially-becomes-a-dictatorship-xi-jinping-declares-himself-president-for-life/ (accessed 16 November 2018).

Peerenboom, Randall, *China Modernizes: Threat to the West or Model for the Rest?* (Oxford UP, 2007).

Perlez, Jane, 'Behind the Scene, Communist Strategist Presses China's Rise', *The New York Times*, 13 November (2017). Available at https://www.nytimes.com/2017/11/13/world/asia/china-xi-jinping-wang-huning.html (accessed 6 January 2019).

Perlez, Jane, 'Xi Jinping Pushes China's Rise Despite Friction and Fear', *New York Times*, 22 October (2017). Available at https://www.nytimes.com/2017/10/22/world/asia/chin a-xi-jinping-global-power.html?action=click&module=RelatedCoverage&pgtype=A rticle&region=Footer (accessed 1 January 2019).

Petersmann, Ernst-Ulrich, 'The Future of the WTO: From Authoritarian "Mercantilism" to Multilevel Governance for the Benefit of Citizens?' *Asian Journal of WTO & International Health Law and Policy*, 6 (1) (2011), pp. 45–80.

Przeworski, Adam, *Democracy and the Market: Political and Economic Reforms in Eastern Europe and Latin America* (Cambridge: Cambridge UP, 1991).

Przeworski, Adam, Michael E. Alvarez, Jose Antonio Cheibub and Fernando Limongi. *Democracy and Development Political Institutions and Well-Being in the World, 1950–1990*. Cambridge Studies in the Theory of Democracy (Cambridge: Cambridge UP, 2000).

Quade, Elisabeth A., 'The Logic of Anticorruption Enforcement Campaigns in Contemporary China', *Journal of Contemporary China* 16 (50) (2007), pp. 65–77.

Roland, G., 'Understanding Institutional Change: Fast-moving and Slow-moving Institutions', *Studies in Comparative International Development* 38 (4) (2004), pp. 109–31.

Schrittmatter, Kai, *Die Neuerfindung der Diktatur. Wie China den digitalen Überwachungsstaat aufbaut und uns herausfordert* (München: Piper, 2018).

Schubert, Gunter, 'Herrschaft, Vertrauen und Legitimität in der VR China', *China Aktuell*, 2 (2006), pp. 5–39.

Scott, W. Richard, 'The Changing World of Chinese Enterprise: An Institutional Perspective', in Anne S. Tsui and Chung-Ming Lau (eds.), *The Management of Enterprises in the People's Republic of China* (Springer Science + Business Media, LLC, 2002), pp. 59–78.

Shepsle, Kenneth A., 'Studying Institutions: Some Lessons from the Rational Choice Approach', *Journal of Theoretical Politics*, 1 (1) (1989), pp. 131–47.

Shi, Tianjian, 'China: Democratic Values Supporting an Authoritarian System', in Yun-Han Chu, Larry Diamond, Andrew J. Nathan and Doh Chull Shin (eds.), *How East Asians View Democracy* (New York: Columbia UP, 2008).

Shi, Tianjian, 'Village Committee Elections in China: Institutionalist Tactics for Democracy', *World Politics* 51 (3) (1999), pp. 385–412. doi:10.1017/S0043887100009126.

Shih, Chi-Yu, *Collective Democracy: Political and Legal Reform in China*. Hong Kong: The Chinese UP (2000).

Shin, Doh Chull and Youngho Cho, 'How East Asians Understand Democracy: From a Comparative Perspective', *Asien*, 116 (2010), pp. 21–40.

Shirk, Susan L., *The Political Logic of Economic Reform in China*. California Series on Social Choice and Political Economy(Oakland, CA: U of California P, 1993).

Shu, Sijien, 'Xi-Constitution Predicts Radical Change without A Preparatory Committee', 4 March (2018). Available at https://www.storm.mg/article/407426 (accessed 26 September 2018).

Skocpol, T., *States and Social Revolutions: A Comparative Analysis of France, Russia, and China* (Cambridge, UK: Cambridge UP, 1979).

Smith, Rogers M., 'If Politics Matters: Implications for a "New Institutionalism,"' *Studies in American Political Development*, 6 (1992), pp. 1–36.

Spruyt, Hendrik, 'The Origins, Development, and Possible Decline of the Modern State', *Annual Review of Political Science*, 5 (2002), pp. 127–49.

Strittmatter, Kai, 'Sieben Sachen (Seven Things)', *Süddeutsche Zeitung Magazin*, Nr. 5, 1 February (2019).

Strittmatter, Kai, *Wie Die Neuerfindung der Diktatur. Wie China den digitalen Überwachungsstaat aufbaut und uns damit herausfordert*. München: Piper Verlag (2018).

The Economist, 'What China Wants', 24 August (2014). Available at https://www.economist.com/news/essays/21609649-china-becomes-again-worlds-largest-economy-it-wants-respect-it-enjoyed-centuries-past-it-does-not (accessed 20 September 2018).

Thelen, Kathleen, 'How Institutions Evolve: Insights from Comparative Historical Analysis', in J. Mahoney and D. Rueschemeyer (eds.), *Comparative Historical Analysis in the Social Science* (Cambridge/UK: Cambridge UP, 2003), pp. 208–40.

Thelen, Kathleen, 'The Explanatory Power of Historical Institutionalism', in Renate Mayntz (ed.), *Akteure, Mechanismen und Modelle. Zur Theoriefähigkeit makro-sozialer Analyse* (Frankfurt am Main: Campus Verlag, 2002), pp. 91–107.

Thelen, Kathleen and Sven Steinmo, ,Historical Institutionalism in Comparative Politics', in Sven Steinmo et al. (eds.), *Structuring Politics: Historical Institutionalism in Comparative Analysis* (New York: Cambridge UP, 1992).

United Nations Conference on Trade and Development (UNCTAD), *The Asian Developmental State and the Flying Geese Paradigm*. Discussion Papers No. 213 (New York and Geneva: United Nations, 2013).

Wade, Robert, *Governing the Market: Economic Theory and the Role of Government in East Asian Industrialization* (Princeton UP, 1990).

Wang, Yuanyuan and Jing You, 'Corruption and Firm Growth: Evidence from China', *China Economic Review* 23 (2) (2012), pp. 415–33.

Whiting, Susan H., *Power and Wealth in Rural China: The Political Economy of Institutional Change* (Cambridge: Cambridge UP, 2001).

Wong, Catherine, 'We Must Confront Our Dark Past of the Cultural Revolution to Avoid Repeating It, Says Chinese Novelist Yan Lianke', *SCMP*, 9 May (2016). Available at https://www.scmp.com/news/china/policies-politics/article/1942609/we-must-confront-our-dark-past-cultural-revolution (accessed 5 January 2019).

Wu, Alice, 'China Must Lay to Rest Its Victim Mindset Over "Century of Humiliation"', *South China Morning Post*, 5 July (2015). Available at https://www.scmp.com/comment/insight-opinion/article/1831982/china-must-lay-rest-its-victim-mindset-over-century (accessed 7 January 2019).

Yu, Jianxing, Jun Zhou and Hua Jiang, *A Path for Chinese Civil Society: Exploring China's Model of Development: A Case Study on Industrial Associations in Wenzhou, China* (Lanham, MD: Lexington Books, 2012).

Yuan, Zaijun, *The Failure of China's Democratic Reforms* (Plymouth: Lexington Books, 2011).

Zheng, Yongnian, *Globalization and State Transformation in China*. Cambridge Asia-Pacific Studies (Cambridge UP, 2004).

Zhu, Zhichang, 'Institutional Change and Strategic Choice: Debating the 'Stage-model' of Strategy in Emerging Economies', *Asia Pacific Business Review*, 24 (3) (2018), pp. 371–88.

Zick, Tobias, 'Ein Mann mit Feinden (A Man with Many Enemies)', *SZ*, 26/27 January (2019).

3

China's provincial leaders of communist propaganda

Liang Qiao

Introduction

In recent years, many China watchers increasingly have paid attention to the issue of China's leadership transitions in connection with its increasing economic power and authoritarian system. On the one hand, they have observed that the Chinese Communist Party (CCP) appoints its provincial leaders very cautiously as they are in charge of China's provincial economies and nationwide economic growth is one of the CCP's top priorities in governing China. These cadres are the centre's representatives to a regional government and its people. But some of today's China regional leaders will be the next top leaders of the country. While scholars argue that the CCP has sought sustained economic growth to gain public support and to justify its rule of China (Shih et al. 2012), they may have ignored the fact that GDP growth is not the only argument that the CCP has used to justify its rule. The CCP tries to convince its people that the benefit of obeying the regime comes with comprehensively improved life quality in return (Yan 2012). Besides political leadership, the CCP is also responsible for people's social well-being (Thornton 2012). Therefore, the work of the CCP's propaganda officials plays a crucial role in dressing up the party as the strongest player that is also the ruler. Whatever the party does, the propagandists need to publicize it. The propaganda organs of the communist party not only handle the CCP's public relations issues, but also are responsible for the people's ideological education (Brady 2002). It is not until the propaganda department of the party broadcasts about it that we will know what the party has achieved or done.

This study points out that the CCP centre manages China's provincial propaganda work by managing career advancements of a provincial chief of communist propaganda (*shengwei xuanchuan buzhang* 省委宣传部长). Moreover, as the propaganda sub-system is an indispensably important department of a provincial CCP committee, provincial propaganda chiefs' career paths are also different by region. Officials who are in charge of regional economies are easier to evaluate, because regional growths are more direct measurement of their work. For propaganda chiefs, the study argues that they are also evaluated differently, even in a much less obvious way – that is different provinces in China have different propaganda priorities.

This study shows that by controlling its provincial propaganda leaders, the CCP governs Chinese people's awareness of the party-state regime and people's aspiration towards political modernization after decades of sustained economic development and industrialization. Democracy, representation and freedom of speech have not yet come to Chinese society. Many argue that it is because China does not have a middle class that demands the transition (Nathan 2016); instead, the regime created large number of privileged governmental officials because the regime commands the most powerful financial tools (Dickson 2012). It is because the propaganda control is all over the society with surveillances everywhere that the state makes people watch, look at, listen to, read and believe what the state wants them to watch, look at, listen to, read and believe. Even with the middle-class population growing, many from the middle class choose to obey for they do not know about other options. Career mobility of the provincial chiefs of communist propaganda is a fine example of a mechanism of the CCP's political control. This study examines career mobility in order to understand how the state controls the propagandists' careers to control their propaganda work; and by controlling the provincial propaganda work, the state controls the Chinese society.

Studying provincial political elites in China

Today's Chinese provincial governments focus more on the regional economy than the Marxist ideological teachings. That is because the CCP centre promotes the idea that the CCP does not only provide the Chinese people with the integrity and dignity of the nation but also with greatly improved life quality. Scholars argue that Chinese media are no longer solely influenced by the CCP's propaganda; and propaganda control over the society can no longer be compared to its prime in the Mao Zedong era (Latham 2000). But as ideological teaching remains to be crucial for the CCP to unite all its cadres and the entire bureaucracy, as a matter of fact, provincial cadres who are in charge of propaganda work in China still occupy very prominent posts.

Previous studies on Chinese regional leaders heavily concentrate on the top-tier leaders of China's provincial or municipal governments. Compared to cadres who work in specialized departments and organs of China's provincial governments, governors and provincial party secretaries deal with more important decision-makings, such as general economic development projects which require much more comprehensive leadership skills. As a result, provincial party secretaries and governors are not only older of age, but also with more years of governing experiences that the majority of them are meanwhile members of the CCP Central Committee. In the hierarchy of Chinese bureaucracy, top tier of provincial leaders (party secretaries and governors) are more likely to be promoted as central leaders than provincial departmental chiefs. Also, bio information of provincial party secretaries and governors is more available to scholars who conduct such research. And with many years of leadership experiences and services to the CCP, profiles of the provincial top leaders are more known to the public. In fact, for a lower-ranked cadre in the CCP's national or provincial political systems, little publicized information or media coverage can help people find out about him. And many lower-ranked cadres do not provide clearly detailed entries on their bios such as educational background and employment history. With such difficulty in gathering enough facts for empirical studies, China scholars prefer to establish their causalities on more reliable data sources. When you have a higher ranked provincial leader, who has been under the public's eyes for years with a more polished résumé and is next in line to be chosen to fill in a central leadership post, it is understandable that research on the career path of this Chinese provincial leader attracts more readerships.

Moreover, previous studies on Chinese regional leaders' careers are not fully aware of the locational differences on leaders' career mobility patterns. Scholars argue that industrial provinces in China are more important for being the economic engines of the country. Hence, governing the more urbanized cities and industrialized provinces has become crucial not only to provincial leaders but also to the central government. Thus, some scholars argue that the better economic performance a province or a region has, the greater chance for its regional leaders to get promoted by the centre (Bo 2002). The successes of the market economy, private ownerships and entrepreneurs have all become challenging issues to the CCP leadership, as political recruitment is no longer the shortcut to higher social classes. As pointed out by Li and Bachman, becoming a mayor of a municipality has often been a 'stepping stone' to other higher political posts in China, as in recent decades cities have taken on a much greater importance than under Mao's regime (Li and Bachman 1989). Yet, rapid urbanization in China has raised many new challenges to Chinese authorities in the past few decades: environmental sustainability, exhaustion of natural resources, relentless real estate projects and community development, the welfare and livelihood of the laid-off state-owned enterprises' workers, wages and medical cares for tens of millions of migrant workers, education for lower income families, and the politically urgent task of dealing with the resistance and protests of citizens against governmental policies and regulations.

These issues caused by China's rapid economic growth for the past three decades can hardly be solved or relieved solely through economic means. The answer can be simple: as the state-led economic growth is heavily politicized, it also requires some changes of the regime or at least the way the regime pushes its regional leaders to achieve more smashing GDP growth rates. Especially massive urbanization projects nationwide have caused more frequent popular uprisings and collective actions against the government's land policies. Local government's push of urbanizing and industrializing rural China aims at boosting its local GDP growth with real estate sales and building polluting factories for more local revenues (Hsing 2006). But only by examining China's top-tier provincial leader's career movement does not reveal all these small steps towards the regime change. We need to look closer or from a different angle. For instance, studies show that the rising importance of environmental protection in provincial China has put more weight on China's provincial bureau chiefs of environmental protections even though many of these environmental chiefs were not trained for saving the environment. Only one-fourth of environmental bureau chiefs have environmental backgrounds while the rest of them were from other professional sections. Candidates who are most likely to be appointed as provincial environmental bureau chiefs are those who can meet province's policy priorities and provincial leaders' own interests (Kosta 2013).

Although scholars have argued that more and more Chinese regional leaders are being moved not only to different locations, but also to different professional fields (Brosgaard

2012); the more conventional way of analysing Chinese regional leaders' political mobility has been examining a regional leader's economic performance and his factional ties with one or more of the higher ranked CCP leaders (Choi 2012). This study makes different argument on the latter point of view of regional leaders' political mobility. In the first place, to consider a provincial party secretary or a governor's overall performance, regional economy is the most direct and visible indicator that shows the leader's skills of making people's livelihood better. But measurement for a province's social development remains ambiguous and indirect, while the social impact is subtle and long lasting. On the other hand, factional politics does matter in Chinese politics either historically or contemporarily. While studies try to utilize various methods in gauging factional factors on provincial leaders' political mobility, sooner or later it will come to the point that the CCP is seeking a leader who can defend and extend its rule as China's solely dominant political force and also ideologically affirmative, but not anyone who is economically capable but selfishly protective to his protégés. As Brodsgaard (2007: 82) points out, 'Researchers do not take Chinese administrative concepts seriously, claiming that the key to an understanding of how China works is not official concepts, but informal practices and networks.' By and large, factional analysis needs to be combined into scholars' research along with other determining factors of leaders' characteristics. The ultimate player of 'the game of the throne' is the CCP, thus, we try to understand the regime by studying its cadre appointment and succession system, not the other way round.

Furthermore, currently the CCP party-state regime is still capable of controlling the people and the society of China in various ways. It is gradually being decentralized, but not being dismantled. Speaking of the party's provincial governance, it is up to the CCP centre to choose the means and the time of playing a 'consultative' authority than an autocracy. For instance, when the news media in China are being more commercialized, it was the regime that decided to do so, not that it was forced to do so. And nationwide propaganda organs of the party still have heavy control over the press. Scholars argue that such consultative authoritarianism, which merges the regulatory-state idea of a relatively autonomous civil society collaborating with the state to solve social problems, is to protect the society from interest groups and social instability (Teets 2013). Also, the way that local people's congresses are being managed serves as a system of division of power under the Party's supervision. Yet the consultative model of governance, where party takes others' opinion into consideration once in a while, 'could be seen as a promising sign of development towards a more participatory form of governance; it also underlines the limits of reform and the determination of the Party not to share more power than it finds necessary' (Almen 2013: 254). However, it is still the party that controls the ultimate power where it holds its cadres under the protection from objections to their performances. And decisions such as personnel arrangements of China's provincial government are more of the consultative output, not consultative decision-making. So to speak, the cadre appointment system is not consultative, because the public is not involved in any of the decision-makings.

Overall, previous studies on Chinese provincial leaders have not provided satisfactory answers for the following questions. First, if the primary criterion for promoting governors and provincial party secretaries is the provincial economic growth, what is the criterion for promoting provincial second-tier political leaders such as provincial propaganda chiefs? Do the same rules apply, or propagandists have other qualifications to meet for getting promoted? Secondly, when provincial top-tier leaders get promoted, giving that the majority of them are already members of the CCP Central Committee, many of them become central leaders with much higher apparatus; but for second-tier leaders such as provincial propaganda chiefs, which ones of them, or, those with what curriculums, get a great leap upwards in the party's political hierarchy to fill a more significant post? Does the CCP centre choose its provincial chief propagandists the same way it chooses its governors and party secretaries?

Last but not the least, for the provincial chief propagandists, who are in charge of the provincial 'thought work (思想工作)', what would be the indicators of their professional performance? In other words, if the centre relies on provincial GDP growths to promote provincial party secretaries and governors, what performance does it want to see from provincial propaganda chiefs? As we know that economic development is something much more visible and can be promoted through certain means (i.e. governmental projects, infrastructures, FDIs, etc.) within a shorter period of time (before a provincial leader finishes his two five-year terms), what is the strong suit of the propagandists that the centre is particularly interested in? Moreover, scholars of comparative politics have long been arguing that a well-accomplished market economy nurtures better civil society with pro-democracy middle class (Lipset 1959). And the wealthier provinces of China do come with significantly higher literacy rates and longer life expectancy; the question is, does the propaganda work become less essential to the local government since it focuses more on the economy? And, do the chief propagandists of the more developed provinces of China enjoy less promotional advantages compared to that of governors and party secretaries of these provinces as these are economically advanced parts of China but not measured by thought work accomplishments? If so, do all the provincial chiefs of communist propaganda departments receive equal promotional opportunities for they are evaluated by the CCP centre's ideological indicator (if there is one) but not by the scale of provincial economy? These questions have not been thoroughly studied neither by scholarship of comparative politics nor by Chinese political scientists. This study at present intends to lead scholarly arguments to this direction by providing more empirical evidence.

Regional differences and provincial CCP propaganda chiefs' career mobility

But why the propagandists? Why do they matter to the regime and to the Chinese society? One may argue that whenever the regime seeks power to strengthen itself, why not invest in military forces or infrastructures because soft power building can be rather costly and slow. In fact, scholarship of Chinese politics has discovered the trend that in recent decades, the party state of China is as much interested in investing in soft power building as in military strengths and artilleries. The CCP has noticed, pointed out by scholars that the impression of a superpower does not only come from economic and military hegemony, but also from cultural perception as well.

China's international image is associated with its political behaviour (Wang 2003). To the world, China's achievements (under the CCP's rule) in economic, political, and cultural development collectively make up the CCP's broader ideological programme of developing 'socialism with Chinese characteristics' (Edney 2012). Meanwhile, when China is seeking diplomatic successes outside the country, domestic governance and political stability can also boost its confidence among other great powers (Zhao 1998). Thus, both internationally and domestically, the party views its propaganda work as very essential to its ruling successes and the regime's longevity. Though foreign propaganda work and domestic ideological control are different practices, the party's top propaganda chiefs make the rules for both. In consequence, the director of the Central Department of Propaganda is considered as a very important political figure in the CCP, for the department is a well-organized bureaucratic hierarchy and controls enormous political, social and economic resources (Shambaugh 2007).

Unlike economic growths, which became a great emphasis of the CCP only in late 1970s, ideological control has always been an essential part of the CCP. For a socialist state, communism is primarily a belief system of revolution and social reconstruction. Since the late years of Deng Xiaoping era, especially under Jiang Zemin's leadership as the general secretary of the CCP, the party has gradually switched its ideological concentration from the orthodox Marxist approach to the more governance-based single-party rule of China; as pointed out by scholar, the CCP enjoys its 'performance legitimacy' rather than calling for continuous communist revolutions (Cai and Zhu 2013).

Furthermore, as China's economic achievement has been basically state led, so have its social problems. Scholars have found that among all the political dissatisfactions of the people in China, the regime is the most sensitive to the ones calling for collective action or merely potential thought of it (King et al. 2013). Thus, stability, in other words, the rule of the party, is the primary priority to the CCP's ideological management of the society. Scholars have further pointed out that the CCP's propaganda work in recent decades has not been in decline; instead, the Central Department of Propaganda has strengthened its organization to fit in the updated political situations of China (Shambaugh 2007: 58; Edney 2012: 913). Therefore, provincial CCP propagandists of China deal with two main tasks in their daily work: to keep administrative control over the press to control Chinese people's social life, and to keep ideological control over the governmental officials and party cadres to unify their thoughts and to carry out the CCP centre's important policies. This study here does not evaluate the CCP's propaganda work system over China; instead it shows how the party is evaluating the party's provincial propaganda chiefs in order to promote some of them. So to speak, this study intends to find out what qualifications or characteristics a provincial chief propagandist needs to get promoted? As propagandists normally are not in charge of economic policy making, are they actually affected by China's regional socioeconomic differences? Therefore, by sampling Chinese provincial chiefs of CCP propaganda in the 2000s, this study's empirical evidence answers the two research questions below.

First, given similar personal and professional background, are propaganda chiefs of the developed provinces being considered differently from those of the underdeveloped provinces? Previous studies on popular support to authoritarian regimes show that under an authoritarian regime, the more educated the citizens are, the less likely they would support the regime. And strongest support for authoritarianism comes from citizens who are with moderate education and perception to the regime, but not with sophisticated educational background to think critically of the governmental propaganda and indoctrination (Geddes and Barbara 1989). In addition, a more recent study on China's case suggests that the highly educated Chinese are generally not persuaded by state media's political messages (and the state media are under the Central Department of Propaganda's control); while in the less developed rural China the overall support for the communist regime is rather high (Kennedy 2009). In other words, according to scholars, in the more developed provinces of China, where conditions for education, social welfare and information technology are better off, people tend to believe less in the party state's propaganda and patriotic broadcasting. However, it does not mean the people of the developed Eastern China are less frequently involved in the state propaganda; it only means that many of them have the freedom to choose what to believe. And the agenda of the party propaganda may not be affected by the people's reception of it. And the provincial chiefs of the CCP propaganda departments nationwide all work in the bureaucratically similar systems of ideological education. The locations of the chief propagandists should not affect their career priority, whether they are in the developed provinces or not. In fact, as the internet has become a main platform for Chinese people to exchange information and ideas, the party state controls the media altogether, either foreign or domestic, to keep the society politically stabilized (Liu 2011). If so, unlike other governmental heads in a provincial government, the provincial chief propagandist's work should be evaluated based on his counterparts' performance across the country who hold the same post. Yet, the propaganda chief's career future can still be limited by his location. Despite of the specialized functions of propaganda work, the provincial government's overall governance and economic contribution concern the CCP centre the most. Much is said, the study here argues that a provincial CCP propaganda chief's career mobility is affected by the overall performance of the provincial government; even though the propaganda department is not directly responsible for achieving economic successes.

Secondly, compared to their counterparts in the rest of China with similar personal and professional background, are propaganda chiefs of ethnic minority-concentrated provinces being considered equally for promotional opportunities? Previous studies have found that propaganda work still plays a very important role in the CCP's governance of China in the twenty-first century, yet, they have only provided with the more generalized studies of the propaganda work and media control nationwide. As a matter of fact, in most provinces of China, the CCP's cadres are promoting the regime's ruling legitimacy by claiming its success in economic growth. In regions where Chinese ethnic minorities historically reside, the party state promises the people not only with better economy and welfare, but also with respect to the local people's religious and national traditions in exchange for their political endorsement.

The CCP controls China's geographically remote but politically important regions, including Hong Kong and Macau, by establishing elaborate and strong local party organizations and nomenclature system (Burns 1990). Although the five ethnic provincial units (Xinjiang, Tibet, Inner Mongolia, Ningxia and Guangxi) are the so-called 'autonomous administrative regions', they all have highly similar local CCP committees with provincial party leaders directly appointed by the CCP centre. And the propaganda branches of the local party committees are also similarly organized as they are in other provinces of China. In recent years, local ethnic resistance to the CCP's rule has been more frequently exposed to both domestic and international media. Especially the growing numbers of collective actions, from protests to violent riots among ethnic Tibetans and Uyghurs, have attracted continuous international reportages on the CCP's regional governance in these provinces which are considered by the party state as negative publicities to the administration. Despite the fact that local economies flourished in both Xinjiang and Tibet as the result of the contemporary government-led development,[1] the rising dissatisfactions emerge and spread towards the CCP's strengthened control. Thus, though with economic achievements, which rely on the state government's investments and beneficial policies, the government is still having difficulty in consolidating its rule in China's ethnic minority regions. Governing these regions, as emphasized by China's top leaders themselves, is a crucial matter that is domestic and international, religious and ideological, and, political and cultural.[2] And the primary solution, according to the leaders, is to 'greatly strengthen the Marxist nationalistic values and the party's policies for the minorities to the people and CCP cadres of all ethnicities'.[3] Moreover, scholars argue that in recent crisis management in ethnic minority regions, the Chinese government communication becomes 'persuasive and manipulative' (Chen 2012). Propaganda work in ethnic minority provinces is thus given extra importance for defending the regime's belief system and nationalism. Studies also show that the government's media control and cyber-censorship over ethnic minority provinces are stricter (Greitens 2013).

Data and methods

Data

This study has sampled 288 provincial chiefs of the CCP propaganda departments from the year 1998 to 2011 (Table 3.5). All thirty-one provincial units of China are included; and case selections in each province are evenly distributed. The great difficulty, however, is that unlike a provincial administration, provincial propaganda chiefs' bios and other personal information is not regularly released to the public. As these propagandists work for the party, it is not lawfully necessary for them to disclose certain information. But this study has tracked down the CCP centre's and provincial committee's monthly personnel arrangement reports during the time period, and recorded the information that this study needs to complete the database.[4] Among the 288 chief propagandists, 55.9 per cent of them (n=161) were the first directors of provincial propaganda work; and 44.1 per cent of them (n=127) were deputy directors.[5] One distinct feature of the most Leninist political parties is that to determine a party cadre's supremacy compared to other cadres, it does not matter what his post is in the administration or the legislation or a state-owned enterprise, it only matters what his post is in the party (Clark 2013). It is also true for Chinese provincial chief propagandists. The majority of the first directors sampled by this study were provincial party committees' standing members (51.0 per cent, n=147). But many deputy governors had not gained the standing membership on provincial committees. In fact, some first directors of propaganda were deputy governors; and when they were appointed as propaganda chiefs, they were also chosen to be standing members on provincial party committees. Hence, leaving deputy governorship to become first propaganda director was a promotion in their career. It is a proof that propaganda work has never been underestimated by the CCP to strengthen its rule that it chooses the best or the most experienced cadres of its.

In addition, some scholars argue that attending professional training programmes at local or central party schools help promote a cadre's political career. Because they receive relevant trainings (the performance argument); and get to know important people in the circle (the factionalism argument) (Pieke 2009). Thus in estimation of propaganda chiefs' promotional likelihood, this variable is coded. So is some other professional background information of the propagandists sampled.

Rankings of provincial economies can be found at China's National Statistics Bureau's website. By using phrases such as 'rich' or 'developed' provinces, this study refers to provinces that have much greater economic performances according to the ranks; while 'poor' or 'underdeveloped' provinces are those ranked relatively much lower by the government.

Estimations

The logistic regression analysis models of CCP provincial chief propagandists' political mobility are as follows:

Model 1: The likelihood that a Chinese provincial propaganda chief will be promoted to the central government after his provincial service is associated with the following independent variables and control variables: his age, gender (male=1, female=0), college education, his ethnicity (Han Chinese or not), current working location (East, West, Middle, or Northwest of China), whether his current region is a rich province (or not), whether this is an ethnic minority autonomous province (or not), whether it is the official's hometown province (or not), he attended colleges or universities (or not), he is the first director (or not), he is the deputy director (or not), he is a provincial CCP standing committee member (or not). Moreover, he worked as non-propaganda bureaucrat in a local or regional government before (or not), he worked in the central government before (or not), he worked in the press (newspapers and TV stations, etc.) before (or not), he worked in other propaganda offices before (or not), he worked full-time for the Communist Youth League nationwide before (or not). How long he served as provincial propaganda chief? All the above independent variables – except the propagandist's age and years of services – are operationalized as dummy variables.

Model 2: The likelihood that a Chinese provincial propaganda chief will remain or be transferred to serve in the provincial government in Eastern China's developed provinces is associated with independent variables and control variables of Model 1. All the above independent variables are dummy variables, except the official's age and number of years in service as provincial chief propagandist.

Model 3: The likelihood that a Chinese provincial propaganda chief will be promoted not only to the central government, but also be appointed as a minister (or a deputy minister) of the central government immediately after his provincial post is associated with the independent variables and control variables of Models 1 and 2. All the above independent variables are dummy variables, except the official's age and number of years in service as provincial chief propagandist.

Model 4: The likelihood that a Chinese provincial propaganda chief will receive a promotion within three years of his appointment is associated with the independent variables and control variables of Models 1, 2 and 3 and his current working location in China. Except age and number of years in service as the chief, all variables are dummy variables.

In addition, in order to examine the propagandists' probabilities of receiving promotions and levels of promotions, by controlling the relative risk reduction (the RRR option), this study also deploys two multinomial regression analytic models:

Model 5: The likelihood that a Chinese provincial propaganda chief will be promoted to the central government (as a minister, a deputy minister or a ministerial post) is associated with the following independent variables and control variables: his age, college education, his ethnicity (Han Chinese or not), whether his current region is a rich province (or not), whether this is an ethnic minority province (or not), he is the first director (or not), he is the deputy director (or not), he is a provincial CCP standing committee member (or not). Moreover, he worked in a local or regional government before (or not), he worked in the central government before (or not), he worked in the press (newspapers, TV stations, etc.) before (or not), he worked in other propaganda offices before (or not), he worked full-time for the Communist Youth League nationwide before (or not). How long he served as provincial propaganda chief? All the above independent variables – except the official's age and years of service in propaganda chief post – are operationalized as dummy variables.

Model 6: The likelihood that a Chinese provincial propaganda chief will be promoted as a top-tier provincial leader (provincial party secretary, governor or vice provincial party secretary) is associated with independent variables and control variables of Model 5. All the above independent variables are dummy variables, except the official's age and number of years in service as provincial chief propagandist.

In the analysis, a situation characterized by no change of post is coded as '0', promotion to provincial leadership is coded as '1', and promotion to central government is coded as '2'. The purpose of deploying multinomial regression models is to analyse the official's likelihood to be promoted to a higher political system.

Findings

(1) Provincial chiefs of propaganda who were promoted to the central government immediately after their provincial service were those who were directors of provincial propaganda, served in Central China, or in an ethnic minority

province. But this prediction is successful only at a lower level of statistical significance (Table 3.1). Other variables coded by this study do not have significant influence on the results.

(2) Provincial propaganda chiefs who continued serving in Eastern China were those who were deputy directors of propaganda, had central government working experiences, worked in propaganda offices elsewhere before and who previously worked in Eastern China's developed provinces. Though this prediction is successful only at a lower level of statistical significance, it suggests that officials who work in the developed provinces are more likely to stay in these regions. However, for officials from the underdeveloped parts of China, either they do not receive great promotion, or they may find it difficult to get out the underdeveloped regions. Officials from Northwestern China, where it is the least developed in the country, have little chance getting promoted (Table 3.1).

(3) Provincial chiefs of propaganda who were appointed as ministers or ministerial level official in the central government immediately after their provincial service were those who had local government leading experiences, led propaganda work in Eastern China or Central China, worked in a developed province or an ethnic minority province and worked in his hometown province. This finding suggests that before a cadre is chosen to lead the central government, he needs sufficient knowledge of local governance in China, either as a local leader or head of a specialized administrative organ (Table 3.1).

(4) Multinomial regression models show that compare to propaganda chiefs who got promoted to provincial leaders (base outcome=1), those who got promoted to the central government (base outcome=2) were officials who had Youth League working experiences, had worked in the central government before his provincial services and served in a developed province (Table 3.2). The results show that officials with the Communist Youth League background are not limited by their locations; they receive promotions anyway either to provincial leadership or to work in the central government. But they are more likely to get promoted if they serve in a more developed province of China given that they also have factional ties or personnel connections with the Communist Youth League officials nationwide. But compare to propaganda chiefs with the League background and serving in Eastern China, propaganda chiefs in ethnic minority provinces, which are the underdeveloped part of China, are not in a fair competition that they may need to try harder to get promoted.

(5) Logistic regression analysis shows that for provincial chief propagandists who received promotion within three years of their appointment were those who had working experiences in the press, worked in other propaganda offices before and served in a developed province, or in an ethnic minority province. He was from Central or Western Chinese provinces. Given the nature of Chinese politics, getting a promotion in three years as provincial leaders or higher is a rapid promotion indeed. This also shows that propaganda officials with relevant professional experiences are more likely to be considered by the centre for filling the post (Table 3.3).

(6)   Descriptive statistics also shows that among the 100 propaganda chiefs in Eastern
      China's developed provinces observed by this study, 94 per cent of them (n=94)
      were CCP cadres had ever served in Eastern provinces before. In other words,
      to these ninety-four propaganda chiefs, they may not have stayed in the same
      province through their entire political career, but they were actually chosen from
      the developed Eastern half of China. It shows that for cadres who did not start
      their career in these provinces, it can be difficult for them to get in (Table 3.4).

Further discussion: China's provincial leaders and propaganda chiefs under Xi Jinping

When Xi Jinping became the General Secretary of the CCP in 2012, some of the structural contents of the CCP politics had been changed over the past five years. During his first five-year term as the CCP General Secretary and the president of China, Xi severely tightened his control over Chinese political and even social life. Many of the provincial propaganda chiefs sampled by this study are still in power in Chinese regional politics from 2012 to 2017. Under Xi Jinping's leadership, he emphasized the importance of communist ideology and a stronger leadership of the Communist Party. Xi's famous anti-corruption campaign, by taking down thousands of top-ranked CCP cadres from Politburo members to deputy chairmen of China's armed forces, gained him superior popularity and popular support from the Chinese society. As this study suggests, the legitimacy of the ruling single party does not only come from GDP growth or anti-corruption actions against its own officials, but also is very dependent to the regime's propaganda machine to make a lively show about it. There is no doubt that Xi and his propaganda chiefs have tried whole-heartedly to promote the regime's ruling legitimacy by convincing the Chinese people that Xi Jinping is the chosen leader that fits to rule. More importantly, not only at central level, but in provincial politics, cabinet reshuffles have Xi's personal ideas written all over them by choosing the loyal regional leaders who carry out Xi's ideological preaching and personal orders without giving second thought. Many China watchers have pointed out that the most recent anti-corruption actions taken by Xi Jinping and his close allies who occupy posts on the CCP Politburo do not just purge those fallen cadres of CCP who were corrupt; instead, these fallen cadres were taken down because they did not obey the new leader promptly. What's more, it was the CCP's national propaganda machine at work that convinced the Chinese audience that these were the corrupt leaders and they were rooted out to keep the regime pure and healthy.

In October 2017, the Communist Party of China (CPC) held its 19th National Congress in Beijing by hosting more than 22,000 party delegates and cadres coming from all parts of China. During this national congress session, as expected, Xi Jinping successfully resumed his second five-year term as the General Secretary of the CCP. He will, in the Chinese national legislative session of March 2018, keep serving as president of China. Two things from the 19th CCP National Congress were noteworthy and are highly relevant with this study presented here. First, more provincial leaders were recruited into the party's central leadership. For those who now run the central government of China, nearly all of them have very solid and mature leadership experiences in China's provincial politics. Obviously, loyalty to General Secretary Xi Jinping (now officially known to all as 'the core' of the CCP leadership) is an even more crucial credential in search of the leaders. Secondly, alongside his ambitious national revival blueprint in nearly all the sectors of socioeconomic life in China, what drew much more attention was Xi's own newborn ideological sub-system known as Xi Jinping's thoughts on socialism with Chinese characteristics in the new era. Officially, Xi and his close allies are converting their practices of governing China into a new ideology along with what are now known as Maoist and Deng Xiaoping theory. Here, this study suggests that China's provincial propaganda chiefs will play more important roles. Their still overpower many other branches of the bureaucracy.

With economic achievements and improved social development, the CCP still intends to keep ideological reins on the market economy with communist party's propaganda to ensure that the reform would not in reality midwife a potential political competitor. Yet, just as the socioeconomic development of China is vastly uneven nationwide, provincial chiefs of communist propaganda are not being equally favoured by the centre. It is not because the less favoured are the less loyal to the regime; still, they are being treated differently by the regime. What is more, if the regime is not fair or just to all of its regional political elites, can it be fair or just to its entire people living in all parts of China? In the more developed provinces, where flourishing market economy brings recognition for liberty and democracy, the party's propaganda control and thought work have not loosened at all; while in provinces with mixed ethnic views on Chinese nationalism and with political dissatisfactions, the regime's ideological education is cautious but affirmative. Therefore, this study suggests that the economic performance of the promotion logic only represents part of the regime's plan in controlling its regional political elites. The real motivation, for focusing on economy and building the nation-state at the same time, is, in fact, political. Only when the regime needs to strengthen its influence on provincial governance and to tighten the party's ideological rein, propaganda directors of these regions will be more likely to get promoted.

Xi Jinping values the role played by communist propaganda both domestically and internationally. Moreover, Xi presses the urgency of telling China's own story and the self-confidence China must have when facing diverged paths towards political and economic development in future decades. Many of the so-called universal values are being dismissed by the CCP's rule over the Chinese society for the past few years. It is possible that with years of success in media control and ideological education, the CCP has managed to direct the mass communication for but not against its willingness. This study at present is only an experimental step in figuring out the CCP's propaganda mechanism by unfolding its personnel arrangements of China's provincial propaganda chiefs. It is important to rule out the role played by the propaganda chiefs in Chinese politics and society: they do not always directly rule the country, but they are crucial for the CCP to sustain its rule.

Note: This study is supported by National Social Science Fund of China (No. 16CZZ021).

Appendices

Table 3.1 Logistics Regression Analysis

| | (1) | (2) | (3) |
	Central Government After	East After	Minister After
age	1.003	0.933	1.017
	(0.0363)	(0.0589)	(0.0424)
sex	0.660	1.172	0.557
	(0.380)	(1.793)	(0.446)
hometown	0.448*	0.286	0.222**
	(0.170)	(0.191)	(0.111)
nonhan	0.460	1	0.517
	(0.441)	(.)	(0.631)
provhead	8.529**	2.160	1.793
	(6.998)	(5.278)	(2.059)
vphead	2.511	0.0618**	3.248
	(1.576)	(0.0649)	(2.415)
standmember	0.754	0.0155	3.702
	(0.503)	(0.0394)	(3.951)
league	1.546	0.521	1.728
	(0.570)	(0.367)	(0.827)
localexp	0.512	0.372	0.234**
	(0.226)	(0.304)	(0.115)
centrexp	2.664*	0.212*	2.184
	(1.233)	(0.159)	(1.186)
pressexp	0.469	1.101	1.185
	(0.195)	(0.734)	(0.531)
propabef	0.860	15.68**	1.346
	(0.332)	(14.81)	(0.595)
length	1.343***	0.745	1.557***
	(0.113)	(0.121)	(0.157)
fromwest	0.618		
	(0.465)		
noweast	0.223	392.1**	0.0427***
	(0.179)	(789.7)	(0.0394)
nowwest	0.266	0.411	0.633
	(0.227)	(0.785)	(0.513)
nownorest	1.331	1	2.696
	(1.292)	(.)	(2.796)

Table 3.1 (Continued)

	(1)	(2)	(3)
	Central Government After	East After	Minister After
nowmid	0.0493**	0.664	0.0734**
	(0.0480)	(1.435)	(0.0729)
richreg	2.286	0.544	7.918**
	(1.516)	(0.718)	(5.822)
minzureg	3.384	3.796	1.542
	(2.257)	(7.302)	(1.133)
fromeast		3.081	
		(3.265)	
N	287	252	287

Exponentiated coefficients; Standard errors in parentheses
$^*p < 0.05$, $^{**}p < 0.01$, $^{***}p < 0.001$
Source: Author's Database.

Table 3.2 Multinomial Logistics Regression Analysis

	(5)			(6)		
	Promotion Level			Promotion Level		
	0	1	2	0	1	2
age	1	0.914*	0.900	1.111	1.015	1
	(.)	(0.0406)	(0.0520)	(0.0642)	(0.0430)	(.)
sex	1	1.515	3.109	0.322	0.487	1
	(.)	(1.101)	(3.104)	(0.321)	(0.362)	(.)
hometown	1	0.183***	0.111***	8.974***	1.638	1
	(.)	(0.0895)	(0.0708)	(5.701)	(0.722)	(.)
nonhan	1	0.392	0.229	4.374	1.713	1
	(.)	(0.359)	(0.347)	(6.648)	(2.188)	(.)
provhead	1	2.065	1.264	0.791	1.633	1
	(.)	(1.615)	(1.626)	(1.018)	(1.813)	(.)
standmember	1	8.250*	22.40*	0.0447*	0.368	1
	(.)	(6.840)	(28.54)	(0.0569)	(0.385)	(.)
league	1	1.930	11.94***	0.0838***	0.162***	1
	(.)	(1.009)	(7.869)	(0.0552)	(0.0729)	(.)
localexp	1	1.569	2.604	0.384	0.603	1
	(.)	(0.707)	(1.622)	(0.239)	(0.283)	(.)
centrexp	1	7767522.5	39318572.2	2.54e-08	0.198***	1
	(.)	(4.99481e+09)	(2.52833e+10)	(0.0000164)	(0.0932)	(.)
pressexp	1	2.951	7.469**	0.134**	0.395*	1
	(.)	(1.658)	(5.175)	(0.0928)	(0.173)	(.)

(*Continued*)

Table 3.2 (Continued)

		(5)		(6)		
		Promotion Level		Promotion Level		
propabef	1	2.861*	3.817*	0.262*	0.749	1
	(.)	(1.281)	(2.247)	(0.154)	(0.316)	(.)
length	1	1.087	1.292*	0.774*	0.841	1
	(.)	(0.111)	(0.166)	(0.0995)	(0.0768)	(.)
fromwest	1	0.195	0.188	5.315	1.036	1
	(.)	(0.257)	(0.292)	(8.262)	(0.945)	(.)
fromeast	1	0.194	0.121	8.243	1.600	1
	(.)	(0.258)	(0.179)	(12.17)	(1.270)	(.)
nowwest	1	7.867	3.590	0.279	2.191	1
	(.)	(11.02)	(5.615)	(0.436)	(1.771)	(.)
noweast	1	14.17	3.196	0.313	4.435*	1
	(.)	(21.84)	(5.177)	(0.507)	(3.349)	(.)
richreg	1	0.929	8.326	0.120	0.112**	1
	(.)	(0.879)	(9.283)	(0.134)	(0.0853)	(.)
minzureg	1	1.184	3.948	0.253	0.300	1
	(.)	(1.082)	(4.649)	(0.298)	(0.243)	(.)
N	287			287		

Source: Author's Database.

Table 3.3 Logistics Analysis of Chinese Provincial Propaganda Chiefs Who Received Promotion in Three Years

	(4)
	Promotion in Three Years
age	0.955
	(0.0354)
sex	1.548
	(1.008)
nonhan	196954.4
	(151316387.8)
han	169923.1
	(130548662.6)
provhead	8.034*
	(7.482)
vphead	1.959
	(1.009)

Table 3.3 (Continued)

	(4)
	Promotion in Three Years
standmember	0.128*
	(0.118)
league	1.242
	(0.534)
localexp	2.446
	(1.170)
centrexp	0.568
	(0.279)
pressexp	2.996*
	(1.299)
propabef	3.234**
	(1.325)
fromeast	0.0885*
	(0.0972)
fromwest	0.00359***
	(0.00588)
fromnorest	0.0191*
	(0.0371)
frommid	0.000362***
	(0.000760)
noweast	0.922
	(0.890)
nowwest	58.73**
	(89.51)
nownorest	4.302
	(5.868)
nowmid	1151.8***
	(2356.2)
richreg	82.21***
	(86.52)
minzureg	11.23*
	(11.01)
N	287

Exponentiated coefficients; Standard errors in parentheses

* $p < 0.05$, ** $p < 0.01$, *** $p < 0.001$

Source: Author's Database.

Table 3.4 Propaganda Chiefs in Eastern Chinese Provinces with Eastern Working Experiences (1998–2011)

	Current in Eastern China		
Worked in Eastern China before	**No**	**Yes**	**Total**
No	169	6	175
Yes	18	94	112
Total	187	100	287

Source: Author's Database.

Table 3.5 Headcounts of Provincial Chief Propagandists' Career Advancements

	Provincial Propaganda Chief (Yes = 1, No = 0)		**Total**
Level of Promotion	**0**	**1**	**N/A**
None	35	18	53
Provincial Leader	68	99	167
Ministerial Post	24	44	68
Total	127	161	288

Source: Author's Database.

Notes

1 In 2011, provincial GDP per capita growth rate was 5 per cent in Shanghai, 8 per cent in Guangdong, 11.3 per cent in Tibet and 10.7 per cent in Xinjiang. Unemployment rate was 3.5 per cent in Shanghai, 2.5 per cent in Guangdong, 3.2 per cent in Tibet and 3.2 per cent in Xinjiang. Source: http://data.stats.gov.cn, accessed October 7, 2013.
2 Jintao (2005).
3 Zemin (1992).
4 These personnel reports, month by month and year by year, can be retrieved from a number of provincial government's websites; and the *People's Daily* (http://www.people.com.cn) and Xinhua News Agency (http://www.xinhuanews.net) also publish and archive nationwide personnel appointments reports.
5 It should be noted here that first director's information is more available as they are relatively higher ranked. Many deputy directors' bio information is not available and not released even after years of his employment in the government. For cases such as a deputy director also chairs another governmental branch (i.e. some deputy propaganda chiefs were also chiefs of provincial cultural bureau), he is coded as a propaganda chief in this study. Because a provincial propaganda chief is ranked higher than a provincial culture official.

Bibliography

Almen, Oscar, 'Only the Party Manages Cadres: Limits of Local People's Congress Supervision and Reform in China', *Journal of Contemporary China*, 22 (80) (2013), pp. 237–54.

Bermeo, Nancy G., 'Democracy and Lessons of Dictatorship', *Comparative Politics*, 24 (3) (1992), pp. 273–91.

Brady, Anne-Marie, 'Regimenting the Public Mind: The Modernization of Propaganda in the PRC', *International Journal*, 57 (4) (2002), pp. 563–78.

Brodsgaard, Kjeld Erik, 'China studies in Europe', in *China-Europe Relations* (Routledge, 2007), pp. 49–78.

Brodsgaard, Kjeld Erik, 'Politics and Business Group Formation in China: The Party in Control?' *The China Quarterly* 211 (2012): 624–48.

Burns, John P., 'The Structure of Communist Party Control in Hong Kong', *Asian Survey*, 30 (8) (1990), pp. 748–65.

Cai, Yongshun and Lin Zhu, 'Disciplining Local Officials in China: The Case of Conflict Management', *The China Journal*, 70 (2013), pp. 98–119.

Chen, Ni, 'Beijing's Political Crisis Communication: An Analysis of Chinese Government Communication in the 2009 Xinjiang Riot', *Journal of Contemporary China*, 21 (75) (2012), pp. 461–79.

Choi, EunKyong, 'Patronage and Performance: Factors in the Political Mobility of Provincial Leaders in Post-Deng China', *The China Quarterly*, 212 (December 2012), pp. 965–81.

Clark, William A., 'Khrushchev's "Second" First Secretaries: Career Trajectories after the Unification of Oblast Party Organizations', *Kritika: Explorations in Russian and Eurasian History* 14 (2) (2013), pp. 279–312.

Dickson, Bruce J., 'Revising Reform: China's New Leaders and the Challenge of Governance', *China: an International Journal* 10 (2) (August 2012), pp. 34–51.

Edney, Kingsley. 'Soft Power and the Chinese Propaganda System', *Journal of Contemporary China*, 21 (78) (2012), pp. 899–914.

Geddes, Barbara and John Zaller, 'Sources of Popular Support for Authoritarian Regimes', *American Journal of Political Science*, 33 (2) (1989), pp. 319–47.

Greitens, Sheena Chestnut, 'Authoritarianism Online: What Can We Learn from Internet Data in Nondemocracies?' *P.S.: Political Science and Politic* (April 2013). DOI:10.1017/S1049096513000346.

Herman, Edward S., 'The Propaganda Model: A Retrospective', *Journalism Studies*, 1 (1) (2000), pp. 101–12.

Hollins, T. J., 'The Conservative Party and Film Propaganda between the Wars', *The English Historical Review*, 96 (379) (1981), pp. 359–69.

Hsing, You-Tien, 'Land and Territorial Politics in Urban China', *China Quarterly*, 187 (September 2006), pp. 575–91.

Huang, Yasheng, *Capitalism with Chinese Characteristics* (New York: Cambridge UP, 2008).

Jintao, Hu, 'At the Central Conference of Ethnic Affairs (Zai Zhongyang Minzu Gongzuo Huiyishang de Jianghua)', *Xinhua News Agency*, 27 May (2005), Available at http://new s.xinhuanet.com/newscenter/2005-05/27/content_3012700_5.htm (accessed 7 October 2013).

Kennedy, John James, 'Maintaining Popular Support for the Chinese Communist Party: The Influence of Education and the State-Controlled Media', *Political Studies*, 57 (2009), pp. 517–36.

King, Gary, Jennifer Pan and Margaret E. Roberts, 'How Censorship in China Allows Government Criticism but Silences Collective Expression', *American Political Science Review*, 107 (2) (May 2013), pp. 326–43.

Kostka, Genia, 'Environmental Protection Bureau Leadership at the Provincial Level in China: Examining Diverging Career Backgrounds and Appointment Patterns', *Journal of Environmental Policy & Planning*, 15 (1) (2013), pp. 41–63.

Latham, Kevin, 'Nothing but the Truth: News Media, Power and Hegemony in South China', *The China Quarterly*, 163 (September 2000), pp. 633–54.

Lee, Charlotte, 'Party Selection of Official in Contemporary China', *Studies of Comparative International Development* (2013), DOI: 10.1007/s12116-013-9132-0.

Li, Cheng and David Bachman, 'Localism, Elitism, and Immobilism', *World Politics* 42 (1) (1989), pp. 64–84.

Lin, Tingjin, 'The Promotion Logic of Prefecture-Level Mayors in China', *China: An International Journal*, 10 (3) (2012), pp. 86–109.

Lipset, Seymour Martin, 'Some Social Requisites of Democracy: Economic Development and Political Legitimacy', *American Political Science Review*, 53 (1) (1959), pp. 69–105.

Liu, Serena, 'Structural of Information Control in China', *Cultural Sociology*, 5 (3) (2011), pp. 323–39.

Mickiewicz, Ellen, 'The Modernization of Party Propaganda in the USSR', *Slavic Review*, 30 (2) (1971), pp. 257–76.

Nathan, Andrew J., 'The Puzzle of the Chinese Middle Class', *Journal of Democracy*, 27 (2) (2016), pp. 5–19.

Pieke, Frank N., *The Good Communist: Elite and State Building in Today's China* (Cambridge: Cambridge UP, 2009).

Quade, Elizabeth A., 'The Logic of Anticorruption Enforcement Campaigns in Contemporary China', *Journal of Contemporary China*, 16 (50) (2007), pp. 65–77.

Schram, Stuart R., 'The Party in Chinese Communist Ideology', *China Quarterly*, 38 (June 1969), pp. 1–26.

Shambaugh, David, 'China's Propaganda System: Institutions, Processes and Efficacy', *The China Journal*, 57 (2007), pp. 25–58.

Shih, Victor, Christopher Adolph and Mingxing Liu, 'Getting Ahead in the Communist Party: Explaining the Advancement of Central Committee Members in China', *American Political Science Review*, 106 (1) (2012), pp. 166–87.

Teets, Jessica C., 'Let Many Civil Societies Bloom: The Rise of Consultative Authoritarianism in China', *The China Quarterly* 213 (2013): 19–38.

Thornton, Patricia M., 'The New Life of the Party: Party-Building and Social Engineering in Greater Shanghai', *The China Journal*, 68 (2012), pp. 58–78.

Tsai, Wen-Hsuan and Nicola Dean, 'The CCP's Learning System: Thought Unification and Regime Adaption', *The China Journal*, 69 (January 2013), pp. 87–107.

Wang, Hongying, 'National Image Building and Chinese Foreign Policy', *China: An International Journal*, 1 (1) (2003), pp. 46–72.

Wu, Guoguang, 'Command Communication: The Politics of Editorial Formulation in the People's Daily', *The China Quarterly*, 137 (March 1994), pp. 194–211.

Yan, Xiaojun, '"To Get Rich Is Not Only Glorious": Economic Reform and the New Entrepreneurial Party Secretaries', *China Quarterly*, 210 (June 2012), pp. 335–54.

Zemin, Jiang, 'At the Central Conference of Ethnic Affairs (Zai Zhongyang Minzu Gongzuo Huiyishang de Jianghua)', *State Ethnic Affairs Commission*, 23 July 2005 (1992), http://www.seac.gov.cn/art/2005/7/23/art_3094_69842.html (accessed 10 October 2013).

Zhao, Suisheng, 'A State-Led Nationalism: The Patriotic Education Campaign in Post-Tiananmen China', *Communist and Post-Communist Studies*, 31 (3) (1998), pp. 287–302.

Zheng, Yongnian and Guoguang Wu, 'Information Technology, Public Space, and Collective Action in China', *Comparative Political Studies*, 38 (5) (June 2005), pp. 507–36.

Zhiyue, Bo, *Chinese Provincial Leaders: Economic Performance and Political Mobility since 1949* (Armonk, NY: M.E. Sharpe, 2002).

Zhu, Jiangnan, Jie Lu and Tianjian Shi, 'When Grapevine News Meets Mass Media: Different Information Sources and Popular Perceptions of Government Corruption in Mainland China', *Comparative Political Studies*, 46 (8) (2013), pp. 920–46.

4

Politics of representation and the changing meanings of rule of law in contemporary China

Ceren Ergenc

Introduction: Rising authoritarianisms globally

Since the global financial crisis in 2007, the world has witnessed a series of backlashes against political liberalism in the form of refugee crises coupled with anti-immigrant racism, the rise of white supremacist rhetoric in multicultural societies, ethnic clashes as well as mass riots. Governments responded with increasing authoritarianization across the world. Trump in the United States, Duterte in the Philippines, Modi in India, Erdogan in Turkey, Orban in Hungary are often referred to as the symbols of the resurgent populist authoritarianisms, globally speaking. Brexit, the rise of the far right in continental Europe and the mass riots in Brazil are examples of similar sociopolitical phenomena.

These populist authoritarian leaderships are responses to global structural changes such as the global financial crisis in 2007. The neoliberal order promotes a free-market approach yet refers back to the modern state to insulate social and political conflict through constitutional and legal changes (Bruff 2014). The end result is the modern state becoming a less democratic entity regardless of the regime type.

Neoliberalism is often seen as an economic system with free market as its operating rationale. However, it has contained 'the necessary evils of governmental rule' (Peck 2008: 7) from the very beginning. It was what the Western Camp of the Cold War had to offer; therefore, it had to be defended with the political tools of states and trans-state actors. That was the case even when shrinking of the state was suggested as a solution to the 1978 oil crisis in the Western camp. In short, neoliberalism is a political economic ideology, and the political dimension of it is not necessarily defined by political liberalism. The rising populist authoritarianisms, therefore, are not necessarily an exception to the system but they have their roots in the system:

> Neoliberalism is, both in principle and in practice, '... compatible with, and sometimes even productive of, authoritarian, despotic, paramilitaristic, and/or corrupt state forms and agents within civil society'. (Brown 2003: 2)

However, there are differences between the rise of authoritarianism around the world in the earlier stages of neoliberalism in the 1980s and today. Authoritarianism can also be observed in the reconfiguring of state and institutional power in an attempt to insulate certain policies and institutional practices from social and political dissent (Bruff 2014: 116; Jessop 1985). The consequence is the otherization of those who cannot survive in an austerity regime in order to pre-emptively eliminate/discourage social discontent and dissent. White supremacy and anti-immigration sentiments are among those consequences.

The repertoires of containing dissent and constraining social forces changed from direct suppression to the use of already existing institutions such as unions and legal aid clinics to discourage and disorient the political agenda of the dissenting social forces. The neoliberal state shifts from consent production to coercion when it is unable to deliver prosperity and employs tools of 'legally engineered self-disempowerment' (Bruff 2014). Citizens are deprived of their citizenship rights given the security concerns at the macro level.

While there are identifiable trends in the new stage of authoritarian neoliberalism, there is considerable variegation in practices across the world and over time. There is a wider context to each local case and as Koch (2013) puts it, authoritarian (neoliberalism]) should be analysed as a set of practices, an approach that allows contradictions.

The rise of neoliberal authoritarianism is often associated with the rise of China. For example, China's BRI is claimed to promote or encourage authoritarian regimes given its non-conditionality clause. This chapter argues that China's domestic politics, rather than foreign policy, might set an example for the disempowering practices of the most recent stage of authoritarian neoliberalism with its use of legal means.

Rule of law was an important goal for the reformers and social forces in reform-era China, and it was achieved to a large extent. The current administration is known to use the existing stage of rule of law and legalization to discourage collective rights movements while encouraging protection of individual rights. Contemporary China witnesses an amalgamation of political and legal in order to discourage collective/ organized social discontent (Gallagher 2017). Law is seen as a decollectivized and individualized tool of citizen appeasement. To confirm Peck and Theodore and Koch above, both continuity and change in institutions and ideas coexist in contemporary China.

Economic, legal and social reforms since the 1980s have affected the Chinese society and its relations with the state. Decentralization of economic policies empowered both local officials and created new social forces such as business people (Zheng 2002), new middle classes (Goodman 2014) and informally and flexibly employed workers (Chen 2004). The extensive codification of laws provided individuals and groups with the legal means to pursue their own interests and defend their rights through institutionalized channels. Facing a more assertive society, the state responded to the need for political participation and representation with a project of 'administrative democracy' in the Hu Jintao era and the principle of 'ruling the country with law' in the Xi Jinping era.

The administrative democracy is a new government project that mostly involves different mechanisms that would enable citizens to participate in policy making.

Besides, the consultative and legislative institutions, in an attempt to redefine their roles against the executive within the political system, started to strengthen their relationship with their constituencies. The non-institutionalized forms of political participation and representation have become prevalent in China, and the changing dynamics in the political system and society also transform the existing institutions.

The emphasis on the governance by law in the Xi Jinping era signifies yet another turn in the state–society relations in present-day China. There is an unchanging emphasis on legality in reform-era China since the Jiang Zemin era when most of the current laws were codified. The current president Xi Jinping also repeatedly praises ruling the country according to law. However, the understanding of rule of law has changed over time. The reform and transition of legal institutions and practices is pertinent to the debates on political participation and representation in China.

The changes in the understanding of rule of law by the state elite changes how political participation and representation are practised in China since the latter's institutions are mostly informal and flexible. This chapter argues that the current understanding of rule of law encourages an individualized legal relationship with the state through channels such as Administrative Litigation courts in order to prevent collective interest representation and public interest advocacy which has the potential to organize citizen action.

This chapter will first introduce the formal and grassroots mechanisms of political participation and the ideas behind them. Then, it will introduce the history of ideas that shape rule of law and legal institutions in reform-era China. It concludes with a discussion on the prospects of political participation and representation in present-day China.

From Weiquan to Weiwen: Politics of representation in China

Studies on political representation mostly focus on electoral systems while studies on collective action and deliberative democracy focus on participation processes but this chapter aims to demonstrate that public participation and political representation are inherently related and define one another. This is particularly the case in China because in an electoral system, deliberative mechanisms are not expected to be universally representative (Cai 2009) but in the absence of formal electoral representation, however, representation in other participatory mechanisms is burdened with expectations their institutional designs cannot carry (Ergenc 2014). The following section will introduce the representation system in China's formal and informal political participation institutions. The aim of the section is to demonstrate how the existing institutions shape state–society relations and affect regime legitimacy.

Formal representation systems

The People's Congresses (PC) and People's Political Consultative Conference (PPCC) and its committees are two institutions that constitute the legislative in the dual political system of China. National People's Congress (NPC) is the national-level legislative organ and there are provincial, prefecture and county level PCs. PPCC is an organ that provides policy consultation and supervision and it has provincial, prefecture and county level committees.

The PPCC was established in 1945 as a de facto platform for GMD and CCP to discuss the post-war arrangements for the newly established Chinese nation-state. Consequently, the Political Consultative Assembly held in 1946 hosted representatives of the United Front member parties for a pluralist decision-making process. The PPCC acted as the de facto legislative organ between 1949 and 1954 and promulgated the first constitution of PRC. While the PPCC left its legislative powers to NPC in 1954, it continues to act as a venue for the representation of United Front parties, minorities, women, youth, workers and professional groups (Chen 2015) and as advisory legislative organ. The NPC took over the main legislative role in 1954 but always convenes at the same time with the PPCC and the regular meetings of these two representative institutions are referred as 'Twin Meetings'.

Albeit having different institutional capacities and missions, both the NPC and PPCC suffer from the control of the CCP in a similar way: their policy-making power is curbed and reduced to providing consultation and information to the CCP, and helping the CCP to incorporate different social sectors into the regime (Yan 2011). Being largely inactive and ineffective for most of the history of modern China prior to the reform era, the NPC and PPCC have been trying to reinvent themselves as institutions with more influence in the reform era.

The PC elect their delegates in a multi-level system and, according to the constitution, it has legislation, supervision, policy-providing and propaganda in its job definition. As legislation is monopolized by the Party and the government, the NPC compensates this inability with an emphasis on its supervisory and consultative role. The NPC delegates choose to focus on specific issue areas to supervise the conduct of the executive and also to provide policy recommendations. These delegates might have a descriptive relationship with the issue area they choose to specialize on. For example, a delegate with worker background develops expertise in labour relations. Alternatively, delegates might have a symbolic relationship with their constituents as in the case of intellectuals who take up issues because they have scholarly knowledge on them.

The PPCC delegates are selected according to the representativeness of their constituents. A solid portion of them are representatives from the mass organizations such as trade unions or the women's federation, and United Front parties. The PPCC used to be a venue that would mingle the communist and non-communist community influentials, but it has broadened its representative inclusiveness to include opinion leaders from all categories such as the arts and sports worlds, students and disabled citizens.

The NPC is an organ with legislative authority because its members are elected, even if indirectly, whereas the PPCC is a consultative organ without the power of decision-making (Yan 2011: 75). Despite these legal and institutional differences, the solution they find in practice to claim an existence in the political system is to act like delegates or messengers of their constituents to the state. This is particularly the case at the local level where the pressure to reproduce the mass line and to reinforce the legitimacy of the Party is higher. The local PCs and PPCC committees do not enjoy the access and capacity to influence their central branches have regarding policy innovation. Their membership is dominated more by the CCP members and the entire representation system is under stricter surveillance of the local Party leaders. Therefore, there is not much room left for the PC and PPCC representatives alike to conduct their legislative and consultative duties. The only opening they have to demonstrate their presence in the local political network is to act as advocates of their constituents. The relatively small size of the localities in which the NPC and the PPCC have branches enables them to establish close contact with the populace and to utilize the traditional social networks to reach first-hand information about their constituents.

The PPCC's institutional design is to promote the representation of affected interests even if interest-holders are not organized, or the civic association that claims representation of them is already included in the PPCC. The official role of the PPCC is legislative and policy consultation but the PPCC members try to add supervision among their tasks following the revival of the organization in the reform era. Chinese scholars acknowledge that the People's Congress and the Western parliamentary system are based on similar premises with regards to political representation. They also have differences, yet these differences are still defined within Western theories of representation (Jing 2007).

The main difference lies in the difference in perceptions of the Western and Chinese scholars on the legitimacy of representation (Jing 2007). The system that China's People's Congress is modelled after is different from the Western liberal tradition because the NPC's theoretical roots are based on the Paris Commune. The NPC's main principles merge executive and legislative powers into one (议行合一), retain a class-based nature of democracy (民主的阶级性) and maintain the continued leadership of the Party. This institutional design is modelled after the Leninist party system in which the executive has a significant influence over the legislative (Pfeffer 1976).

The historical class base of the Leninist party system was changed with the Three Representatives Theory of Jiang Zemin in 2002. The economic development of the 1980s and 1990s created new social forces such as highly skilled white-collar professionals and medium-level entrepreneurs. Commonly referred as the new middle classes of China (Goodman 2014), these cleavages proved to be the force behind China's rapid economic advancement. However, the economic policies that would enable their goals disadvantaged the urban workers and peasants who were the core basis of the CCP. Stuck between the new entrepreneurial class and the working class, Jiang Zemin decided to shift the Party's representative claim in favour of the former.

The aforementioned Three Represents Theory states that the party state of China represents (1) the advanced productive forces, (2) China's advanced culture and (3) the fundamental interests of the largest majority of the Chinese people. The advanced productive forces refer to the abovementioned occupational groups such as engineers, corporate professionals, and academics, and medium- and large-scale entrepreneurs (Lewis and Xue 2003). China's advanced culture refers to Chinese Han nationalism as a unifying discourse. The largest majority of the Chinese people referred in the third Represent are the traditional social base of the Party state such as workers, migrant workers, peasants and army veterans. The Three Represents Theory aims to transform this social base from 'broad masses to a broad market' (Lewis and Xue 2003). In other words, the classes and social cleavages that are not among the 'advanced productive forces' would be treated as the potential consumers of China's growing economy.

The realignment of the representative relationship between state and society required new institutions and venues for individual and collective interest representation and rights advocacy besides the PC and PPCC. The next section will introduce these new mechanisms.

Collective interest representation in participatory policy-making mechanisms

The previous section described the formal representation systems in the Chinese political regime. The NPC and the PPCC are the main focus of the scholarship on political representation in China. However, representation in organized interest groups or participatory politics also play an important role in China as both formal institutions (NPC and PPCC at both central and local levels) and grassroots platforms both try to circumvent the dominance of the CCP in legislation and policy making.

The central government of China initiated a series of administrative reforms to compensate for the limited political reforms. Citizen participation in public administration has become part of the official reform agenda in China since the early 2000s. Administrative and legislative public hearings are among the earlier examples of such institutionalized public participation. They are often noted as venues for political representation and participatory policy making in print and online media.

There is considerable literature on participation in local politics in China. Most of these works focus on rural developments, as these cases are more grassroots and therefore assumed to better reveal the changes in the state–society relations than their urban counterparts (O'Brien and Li 2006; Oi and Walder 1999; Fewsmith 2006). Among these rural administrative reforms are village elections, chamber committees and township councils. These rural administrative mechanisms involve the rural residents directly in the decision-making process.

The new urban administrative mechanisms, on the other hand, are first initiated by the central agencies and are held by local governments with considerable flexibility that leaves room for localized arrangements. The centrally initiated urban innovations in governance preclude decision-making power but provide extended processes of deliberation. Public hearings (听证会) and public meetings (旁听会) are among the practices of 'deliberative democracy with Chinese characteristics' besides informal political participation in urban China such as campaigning, boycotting and protesting (Shi 1997; Goldman 2005; He 2014; Leib and He 2010; Fishkin et al. 2010; Peerenbaum 2002).

The implementation of these deliberative administrative practices turns into a learning process for all parties involved and changes the ways in which citizens/society relate to the state organs. The motivations and experience of the participants, rules and procedures that provide these practices with a legitimate degree of transparency and predictability, and the efficiency of the process, all contribute to the evolution of state–

society relations. They provide all parties involved with certain political attributes such as sense of entitlement to the right and responsibility to participate in political decision-making.

Public hearings have been criticized and dismissed by both the Chinese public and scholars of political science and public policy. The Chinese public calls public hearings 'rubber stamp' performances that attempt to create the perception of justice, inclusiveness and transparency but fail to achieve any of them. The main reason why the Chinese public is not content with public hearings is the limited public access given the small number, and seemingly random selection of participants and the lack of decision-making power. Scholars, on the other hand, place their analyses of public hearings in the broader public policy regime and point out that in the lack of accompanying democratic institutions such as formal representation systems and checks and balances among institutions that would supervise the policy-making process, public hearings fail to effectively influence the policy-making process.

An area in which citizens play an important role as stakeholders is the implementation of policies. As the real success of policy making is only tested on the ground, the evaluation and re-making of a policy as well as its supervision at the implementation become important phases. Citizens step up to the stage mostly at this phase by providing the officials with feedback about the implementation and evaluation of their policies. In this sense, delegates of the local PCs and representatives of the PPCCs play a similarly significant role.

The localness of the community leaders establishes a closer contact with the passive citizens that the discourse-setting national opinion leaders cannot maintain. Public hearings thus empower local community leaders whereas online media creates national opinion leaders. National-level opinion leaders remain anonymous to passive citizens, either because they do not reveal their identities on online forums or their language is too distant to the masses as in the case of critical intellectuals. Therefore, there is a two-stage empowerment in local politics: participatory politics (which includes, or at least overlaps with, elite politics of the PCs and PPCC committees and community governance institutions such as neighbourhood committees) empower the community influentials and these local leaders empower the passive citizenry through social networks.

Convinced of their right to participate, citizens search for strategies to enhance their capacity to participate. Participants use sources readily provided to them during the meetings and also manipulate them to better serve their ultimate goals. They also employ methods that are available to them such as media publicity, legal codes and their social networks. The broader public also tries to maximize the outcome of public hearings by creating publicity about the issue to be discussed in a hearing before the meeting is held. They also screen the participant profile to ensure their representativeness. Lastly, they follow up with the decisions that come out the meetings. Media also plays a role in the collective civil effort to constrain official behaviour in public hearings in particular. Some of the national and local media enlist correspondents specialized in public hearings to cover them, analyse them and create publicity about them. All in all, it is a collective, yet uncoordinated, civil action to transform public hearings into a political representation tool. It is not a wholesale social movement but one of the phenomena that is cited when one talks about changing state–society relations in contemporary China (Ergenc 2014).

Debates on representation: From mass Line to Weiquan

Unlike electoral representation whose legitimacy lies in the grassroots, for China, the Party is at the heart of the system and the nature of the representation is 'rational-revolutionary' (规律-使命式代表). Hence, the People's Congress system is also influenced by the spirit of the Chinese political system (中国国情的制约) (Jing 2007). The CCP endorsed a system of 'three-in-one/trinity'(三位一体) in the reform era. This system unites leadership of the party, the ownership of the system by the masses (当家作主) and the rule of law.

While the political regime did not formally change in China, the nature of the institutions has changed over time. For instance, collective interest representation and rights advocacy evolved from the class-based mass line of the Mao era to individual rights protection (*weiquan*) of the post-Mao era in China. Consequently, the evolution of the perceptions about citizens' rights and collective interests changed the expectations about the formal representation institutions and participatory policy-making mechanisms.

The main difference between parliamentary representation and Marxist/Leninist representation is that the former is based on elections and the latter is based on class background. According to the Marxist-Leninist 'progressive' representation theory (先进性代表理论), progress comes through class struggle. The proletariat is the most progressive element in the society and the workers' consciousness is only economic; they need propaganda and training in political consciousness by Marxist intellectuals. Therefore, the Mass line (群众路线) and People's Congress systems are based on different premises. Mao combined them in two pillars: (1) discourse-production; (2) policy making. According to Jing (2007), this division of labour worked well during state-building period but it fell short of a working system afterwards.

Mass line is shared ideological correctness. The formulation and implementation of mass line requires willing support of the masses since, theoretically speaking, they are the ultimate source of authorization for the Party. The mass campaigns are the tools to include the masses and obtain their consent to both the ideological meta-discourses and public policies. This dual process would lead the masses and the elite alike towards a shared imagination of revolutionary ideal.

The notion of a shared and uncontested definition of 'collective good' differentiates the Mass Line from the liberal theories of representation in the West since liberalism conceives collective interest as an aggregation of individual interests. In a liberal world view, by definition, there is no greater good than the summation of individual needs and demands. On the contrary, for Rousseau and Burke as well as Mao, there is a collective good greater, and more important, than the summation of individual needs and demands; and in an ideal society, individuals should be willing to give up their interests for the greater good of the society (Frakt 1979: 700).

Mass Line allows little room to expression of individual interests and even individualized participation. The mass campaigns of the Mao era were geared towards reaching an understanding of the common good/ objective truth collectively. There are mass organizations to represent special interest groups in the society such as women and students; however an individual's interest is not borne out of their private conditions but is an outcome of the structural conditions around them (Wang 2014).

The transition from mass line to collective interest representation and citizens' right advocacy happened with the marketization of the economy and the emergence of social actors who define their individual and group interests as separate from that of the state (Zheng 2002). The language of interests entered the Chinese lexicon in the 1980s and the 1990s witnessed the development of many platforms of collective interest advocacy. Rights consciousness in China is also a direct consequence of this process as well as the codification of the legal system in the 1990s. The administrative laws that were promulgated during the late 1980s into early 2000s opened the doors for administrative litigation cases in which the citizens could sue the officials for wrongdoings. Likewise, this package of administrative laws and the new criminal law enabled lawyers to act as defence attorneys. Private law companies rapidly sprung up especially in the big cities.

While the 'ordinary lawyers' (Givens 2014) were taking up administrative litigation cases across the country, a series of high-profile cases helped frame this legal transformation as the 'Rights Protection Movement' (维权 *weiquan*). The Weiquan movement started with the infamous incident of a migrant journalist's death by beating in the hands of the local police in Guangzhou as a part of the measures taken to control the illegal immigrant population. The local media soon picked up the story and initiated a public campaign to follow up the case, but the local government shut down the local media and arbitrarily arrested the editors and the family attorney of the deceased migrant journalist. This event triggered reactions from all over the country and justified the position of attorneys, the advocacy of legal scholars and interrogative journalists' position in society. It also created an environment conducive to greater accountability and legality as it proved that the government is afraid of bad publicity and would adhere to legal norms in order to ensure legitimacy in the eyes of the public. The Weiquan principles were soon widely accepted across the society. Many citizen groups such as environmental groups, homeowners, professional groups and migrant workers used the rights protection discourse in their public interest advocacy cases.

The promulgation of the Administrative Litigation Law (ALL) in 2009 provided a solid foundation for Weiquan struggles. The ALL enables citizens demand rectification of state wrongdoings and compensation for their losses in the courts. There has been a steady increase in the ALL cases in the courts since the first drafting of the law. The ALL connects social movements and legal activism in contemporary Chinese society.

The increased use of laws and legal institutions in rights activism raises the question of how the legal system shapes and interacts with collective interest representation and public advocacy in China. There are different interpretations of how rule of law is understood and practised in China. The following section will first introduce the debates on rule of law and then describes the changes in how it is practised in the reform era.

Changing meanings of the rule of law in China

The rule of law is officially one of the pillars of the political regime in the reform-era China but there was a form of rule of law in the Mao era as well. The rule of law of the Mao era was based on socialist legality and the rule of law of the post-Mao era is based on liberal legality. There are discussions on whether the current state of rule of law in China should be defined as a procedural rule of law (thin rule of law) or pluralist rule of law (thick rule of law) (Peerenboom 2002: 16). These debates indicate that there have been changes in the nature of the rule of law even during the post-Mao era China. Therefore, it is crucial to understand the changing meanings of rule of law in order to understand the interrelationship between rule of law and politics of representation in contemporary China.

Rule of law 'in the new era'

There are several turning points that changed how participation and representation are perceived and practised in China since the official endorsement of the Three Represents Theory in 2002. The SARS crisis that shook China in 2003 had an important outcome. That is, for the first time in modern Chinese history, a legal investigation was conducted and the officials found responsible for mishandling the crisis were asked to resign. Later that year, at the Third Plenum of the 16th Party Congress, China's premier Hu Jintao took the idea into his agenda. He quoted Mencius, a third-century BC disciple of Confucius on 'taking the people as the foundation of governance' (*minben*,民本) and coined the term 'people centred' (*yirenweiben*, 以人为本), which meant in the context governing people for the people. These developments, followed by the arrest of CEOs of several SOEs on corruption charges in 2004 and 2005, have created an understanding in China that now there was precedence for accountability.

The 2003 SARS crisis empowered the civil society and led to an increase in the ROL consciousness. The 2008 Wenchuan earthquake, however, triggered a clampdown on the empowered civil society. The fact that most of the victims were in public buildings and that the local government did not allow the media and the non-governmental sector into the disaster area to conceal this fact raised many questions about both the capacity and accountability of the Chinese state (Repnikova 2017; Johnson 2018). The public criticism towards the state regarding the obstruction of non-governmental disaster relief efforts and media censorship turned into a broader challenge to the existing regime reaching its peak with the democracy call known as the 'Charter '08' signed by public intellectuals later in 2008.

The fact that the public discontent with the lack of state capacity and accountability had the potential to turn into a collective action against the regime eventually led to an increase in the restrictions on the non-governmental sector in China. The clampdown was far from being systematic, as the Hu Jintao administration otherwise witnessed a relatively freer public space similar to the early Deng Xiaoping era. The emergence of a relatively free public sphere was more of initial reaction to the growing societal discontent amplified with the backlash by public intellectuals as in the case of 'Charter '08', an open letter calling for political change in China signed by 303 Chinese intellectuals. The Xi Jinping era, however, furthered the narrowing of the public space in a more systematic way. On the one hand, the arrest of human rights lawyers and public intellectuals intimidated the public opinion. On the other hand, there were structural changes in the practice of the legal system that affected collective interest representation and public advocacy in China.

There are different takes on how to interpret these changes. Some scholars focus on the changes within the legal system and how these would shape the political regime while others point out the ways in which law is instrumentalized in political struggles. The former approach concludes that the legal system is undermined in the Xi Jinping era while the latter approach warns that putting political process into legalist frameworks helps the state to 'depoliticize' collective interest representation and rights advocacy actions.

Legal scholars warn against the use of law for political mobilizations even though some agree that there are various interpretations of what qualifies as rule of law in a regime. The 2000s witnessed a scholarly debate between legal scholars who claimed that rule of law is not a mere set of laws that citizens abide. It is also a set of values that provide the political regime with normative actions of a liberal democracy (e.g. Lubman 2011). Others pointed out that the rule of law that reinforces liberal values is a thick description of rule of law and it is better to judge the political regimes with a thin, procedural definition of rule of law (Peerenboom 2002). The latter group views China as having a rule of law since the late 1990s.

More recently, however, Xi Jinping's use of law (or the legal language) for political ends is often criticized. For instance, Carl Minzer, who previously sided with Peerenboom (2002), now thinks what we observe in China is a turn against the law (2013). The use of ALL that was first promulgated in 1997 by ordinary citizens has gradually increased. The increase in the use of the ALL took a particularly sharp turn during the early years of Xi Jinping's tenure (Wang and Liu 2019; Givens 2014). Even when the 'ordinary lawyers' lose most of their cases and taking up ALL cases is not the wisest career decision, there is still a clear upward trend in individual ALL cases. These are all individual cases, because as soon as there is a group representation, it becomes legal activism due to the way the state treats the complainants and their attorneys.

The reason was that Xi Jinping encouraged dissenting citizens to sue the local governments individually instead of committing collective action (for instance, see new forms of grassroots participation and activism in Fu and Distellhorst (2018), previously mentioned by Ergenc 2014). Therefore, there was a relative increase in the ALL cases won by citizens. However, Minzer (2013) warns that the lawyers and judges are still intimidated to act against the local state. Lawyers and judges lost the autonomy they enjoyed to a certain extent in the Hu era. Moreover, in the later stages of Xi Jinping's leadership, Minzer (2013) observes, there is a turn towards mediation, which practically means a turn back to the mass line understanding of collective interest representation. In other words, legal mediation is not used in favour of the interest representation and negotiation of the social classes and cleavages but as a medium of arbitration to eliminate dissenting voices.

Political scientists, contrary to legal scholars, do not focus on the procedural correctness of the rule of law. Political scientists look at the issue areas where rule of law is maintained and for what political ends. Gallagher (2017) looks at how law is instrumentalized in labour relations by the state and observes that the state encourages the workers to seek justice within the legal system.

While it is possible to correct the individual wrongdoings in the courts, channelling collective interest representation and public interest advocacy into individualized legal cases reduced what is otherwise a collective issue into individual citizens' problems and therefore atomized the citizens. The same attitude renders collective bargaining rights ineffective by delegitimizing asking beyond the legal minimum. It eliminates the unions as agents of collective interest representation. Dimitrov (2016) points out that the rule of law is upheld pragmatically in China. The government sees that rule of law is upheld in few selected issue areas related to economics such environmental law and intellectual property rights law, but not in government accountability. Thornton (2013) also seconds that *Not in My Backyard (NIMBY)*environmental activism cases without a broader agenda are successful in ALL courts. Therefore, Dimitrov's (2016) analysis confirms that rule of law is relevant for the CCP in maintaining power and wealth.

These changes in the interpretation and implementation of rule of law even within the same leadership generation are explained with the subordination of law to ideology within the Leninist party-state regime (Creemers 2018). It is therefore expected that rule of law is practised unevenly in different times and regarding different issues (Dimitrov 2016). Authors agree that the Chinese state operates to achieve power for the party state and wealth for the Chinese nation (Lewis and Xue 2003; Creemers 2018; Kojima 2015), and these two goals shape the ideology of the state. Kojima (2015) identifies Marxism Leninism Mao Zedong Thought, autocratic developmentalism and nationalism as three dominant ideologies that the CCP has carried forward to pursue power and wealth. Xi Jinping's recent turn towards using the law to eliminate politically rival factions within the party and the bureaucracy while maintaining social control through individualized legal representation can be seen as the latest stage of the law serving the greater political purpose of the state. As Creemers (2018) points out, however, that does not mean total lawlessness or corruption in the legal sphere. Citizens still, and more than in the past, use law to solve their disputes with the state, and even the top leadership feels obliged to refer to the constitutional framework in their actions as exemplified in the 2018 constitutional change that abolished the presidential term limit.

Discussion: Rule of law without representation?

Resistant to comply with the democratization and post-socialist transition processes, the future prospects of the political regime in China is hotly debated. Most China watchers seem to concur with the resilience of the current regime with structural adjustments (in reference to Nathan 2002). However, the direction and nature of the structural adjustments are without a consensus. The reason for this is disagreement over the definition and the scope of certain processes and institutions pertinent to the regime legitimacy and state capacity in China.

This study holds that the state of rule of law in China is politically determined; therefore, it is crucial to understand the changes in the politics of representation over decades in socialist China. In the early years of the PRC, the party state represented the proletariat and therefore the political representation was class based. In the post-Mao years, a more pluralist representation of political and social interests replaced the single-class-based representations. Classes and cleavages in the society found new venues and channels to voice their demands, to pursue their interests and to advocate their rights. The nature of rule of law also shifted from a two-tier socialist rule of law to a procedural rule of law based on the protection of basic rights and liberties.

The post-Mao years can be divided into two periods after the establishment of rule by law and the promulgation of most of the laws by the 1990s. The Rights Consciousness movement made use of the newly established laws and the environment conducive to a pluralist understanding of rule of law for public advocacy purposes. The increasing number of collective interest representation events in the 2000s, however, let the government change the understanding of political participation and representation. In order to constrain opportunities for collective action, citizens were encouraged to go to courts to solve their rights and interest-related disputes. Moreover, new systems such as community governance system were introduced to individualize collective participation mechanisms.

To conclude, the changes in the uses and purposes of rule of law in China can be explained with the dynamics in the politics of representation. Societal actors such as rights advocacy activists and workers' committees use legal framework to push their political agendas. Conversely, the state uses legal venues to overcome the citizen strategies and prevent collective action. The prospects for the future of the political regime in China lie in this interaction between political processes and legal frameworks.

Bibliography

Brown, Wendy, 'Neo-liberalism and the End of Liberal Democracy', *Theory & Event*, 7 (1) (2003), doi:10.1353/tae.2003.0020.

Bruff, Ian, 'The Rise of Authoritarian Neoliberalism', *Rethinking Marxism*, 26 (1) (2014), pp. 113–29.

Cai, Dingjian, *Zhongguo zou xiang fa zhi 30 nian, 1978–2008 (China's journey toward the rule of law: legal reform, 1978-2008)* (Beijing Shi: She hui ke xue wen xian chu ban she, 2009), Beijing

Chan, Anita, *China's Workers Under Assault: The Exploitation of Labor in a Globalizing Economy* (Armonk, NY: M. E. Sharpe Inc., 2001).

Chen, Jie, *Popular Political Support in Urban China* (Woodrow Wilson Center Press, 2004).

Chen, Minglu, *Local Governance: The Roles of the People's Congresses and the People's Political Consultative Conferences in Handbook of Handbook of the Politics of China*, ed. D. S. G. Goodman (Cheltenham, UK: Edward Elgar Publishing, 2015), pp. 104–16.

Creemers, Rogier, *Party Ideology and Chinese Law* (9 July 2018). Available at SSRN: https://ssrn.com/abstract=3210541.

Dimitrov, Martin K., 'Structural Preconditions for the Rise of the Rule of Law in China', *Journal of Chinese Governance*, 1 (3) (2016), pp. 470–87.

Ergenc, Ceren, 'Political Efficacy through Deliberative Participation in Urban China: A Case Study on Public Hearings', *Journal of Chinese Political Science*, 19 (2) (2014), pp. 191–213.

Fewsmith, Joseph, *China since Tiananmen: From Deng Xiaoping to Hu Jintao*. 2nd ed. (New York: Cambridge UP, 2006).

Fishkin, J., B. He, R. Luskin and A. Siu, 'Deliberative Democracy in an Unlikely Place: Deliberative Polling in China', *British Journal of Political Science*, 40 (2) (2010), 435–48.

Frakt, Phyllis M., 'Mao's Concept of Representation', *American Journal of Political Science*, 23 (4) (1 November 1979), pp. 684–704. doi:10.2307/2110802.

Fu, Diana and Greg Distelhorst, 'Grassroots Participation and Repression under Hu Jintao and Xi Jinping', *The China Journal*, 79 (January 2018), pp. 100–22.

Gallagher, Mary, *Authoritarian Legality in China: Law, Workers, and the State* (Cambridge: Cambridge UP, 2017).

Givens, John Wagner, 'Sleeping with Dragons? Politically Embedded Lawyers Suing the Chinese State', *Wisconsin International Law Journal*, 31 (3) (2014), pp. 101–40.

Goldman, M., *From Comrade to Citizen: The Struggle for Political Rights in China* (Cambridge, MA: Harvard University Press, 2005).

Goodman, David S. G., *Class in Contemporary China* (Cambridge: Polity Press, 2014).

He, Baogang, *Rural Democracy in China: The Role of Village Elections* (Hampshire and New York: Palgrave Macmillan, 2007).

He, Baogang, 'Deliberative Culture and Politics: The Persistence of Authoritarian Deliberation in China', *Political Theory*, 42 (2014), pp. 58–81, C1-1.

Horsley, Jamie, 'The Rule of Law: Pushing the Limits of Party Rule', in Joseph Fewsmith (ed.), *China Today, China Tomorrow: Domestic Politics, Economy and Society* (Lanham, MD: Rowman & Littlefield Publishers, 2010), pp. 51–68.

Jessop, B., K. Bonnet, S. Bromley and T. Ling, 'Thatcherism and the Politics of Hegemony: A Reply to Stuart Hall', *New Left Review*, 1st ser., 153 (September–October) (1985), pp. 87–101.

Jing, Yuejin, 'The Theory of Representation and Chinese Politcis: A Comparative Analysis (代表理论与中国政治 - 一个比较视野下的考察)', *Social Science Research*, 3 (2007), pp. 16–21.

Johnson, Ian, *After-Shocks of the 2008 Sichuan Earthquak, New York Review of Books*, 9 May 2018, https://www.nybooks.com/daily/2018/05/09/after-shocks-of-the-2008-sichuan-earthquake/ (accessed 25 November 2019)

Koch, Natalie, 'Field Methods in "Closed Contexts": Undertaking Research in Authoritarian States and Places', *Area*, 45 (4) (2013), pp. 390–95.

Kojima, Kazuko, *Ideology of the Chinese Communist Party in Handbook of Handbook of the Politics of China*, ed. D. S. G. Goodman (Cheltenham, UK: Edward Elgar Publishing, 2015), pp. 42–56.

Leib, Ethan J. and Baogang He, *The Search for Deliberative Democracy in China*. 1st ed. (New York: Palgrave Macmillan, 2010).

Lewis, John W. and Xue Litai, 'Social Change and Political Reform in China: Meeting the Challenge of Success', *China Quarterly*, 176 (December 2003), pp. 926–42.

Lubman, Stanley. 'Don't Overlook China's "Ordinary" Lawyers', China Real Time Report. *The Wall Street Journal*, 31 August (2011). Available at http://blogs.wsj.com/chinareal time/2011/08/31/dont-overlook-chinas-ordinary-laywers/.

Minzner, Carl F., 'China at the Tipping Point? The Turn Against Legal Reform', *Journal of Democracy*, 24 (1) (2013), pp. 65–72.

Nathan, Andrew J., 'Authoritarian Resilience', *Journal of Democracy*, 14 (1) (2003), pp. 6–17. doi:10.1353/jod.2003.0019.

O'Brien, Kevin J. and Lianjiang Li, *Rightful Resistance in Rural China*, 1st ed. (Cambridge UP, 2006).

O'Brien, Kevin J. and Suisheng Zhao, *Grassroots Elections in China*. 1st ed. (London: Routledge, 2010).

Oi, Jean and Andrew Walder, *Property Rights and Economic Reform in China*. 1st ed. (Stanford: Stanford UP, 1 August 1999).

Peck, Jamie, Remaking laissez-faire. Progress', *Human Geography* 32 (1) (2008), pp. 3–43.

Peerenboom, Randall, *China's Long March toward Rule of Law* (Cambridge: Cambridge UP, 2002).

Pfeffer, Richard M., 'Mao and Marx in the Marxist-Leninist Tradition: A Critique of "The China Field" and a Contribution to a Preliminary Reappraisal', *Modern China*, 2 (4) (1976), pp. 421–60.

Pitkin, Hanna F., *The Concept of Representation* (Berkeley: University of California Press, 1972).

Repnikova, Maria, *Media Politics in China: Improvising Power Under Authoritarianism* (New York: Cambridge University Press, 2017), 271 pp.

Thornton, Patricia, 'The Advance of the Party: Transformation or Takeover of Urban Grassroots Society?' *China Quarterly* (2013), 213, pp. 1–18.

Shi, Tianjian, *Political Participation in Beijing* (Cambridge, MA: Harvard University Press, 1997).

Yan, Xiaojun, 'Regime Inclusion and the Resilience of Authoritarianism: the Local People's Political Consultative Conference in Post-Mao Chinese Politics', *The China Journal*, 66, (2011), p. 53.

Wang, Shaoguang, 'Daibiaoxing Minzhu yu Daiyixing Minzhu (Representative and Representational Democracy)', *Open Times* (2014), https://www.readingthechinadre am.com/wang-shaoguang-representative-and-representational-democracy.html (accessed 25 November 2019).

Wang, June and Sida Liu. 'Ordering Power Under the Party: A Relational Approach to Law and Politics in China', *Asian Journal of Law and Society*, 6 (1) (2019), pp. 1–18.

Zhao, Suisheng, *Debating Political Reform in China Rule of Law vs. Democratization* (Armonk, NY: M.E. Sharpe, 2006).

Zheng, Yongnian, 'Interest Representation and the Transformation of the Chinese Communist Party', *The Copenhagen Journal of Asian Studies*, 16 (2002), pp. 57–85.

5

Eliminating and raising tigers and flies

The paradox of China's anti-corruption campaign

Miao-ling Lin Hasenkamp

Introduction

Corruption rewards inefficiency; it harms economic development and social trust. In the Chinese context, corruption shows a different face: multifaceted and complex, ready to defy such conventional wisdom. Observers describe it as the 'East Asian paradox' (Wang and You 2012; Wedeman 2006). Not only is corruption deeply interwoven with processes of economic reform. Several studies show how corruption constitutes an important venue that counterbalances local resistance to reforms (Sands 1989; Yu 2008; Trinh 2013). Dong and Torgler (2010) even identify a *positive* relationship between corruption and economic development, 'which is driven primarily by the transition to a market economy'. Corruption-related behaviour in different forms is also needed in many informal social relations (*guanxi*) due to shortage of supplies of services or goods (e.g. the necessity of paying a bribe in order to have a good doctor in China's crowded medical facilities or to get into good schools).[1]

The downsides are manifold. Virulent corruption violates social norms and influences citizens' attitudes towards the government and its institutions (Licht et al. 2007; Eek and Rotstein 2005; Newton 2006). Ordinary Chinese citizens often find themselves becoming victims of corruption either found in unsafe food or in rising housing prices resulting from, for instance, a deal between a local government and a shady businessman. Furthermore, the proliferation of elite networks among entrepreneurs and state officials has seen its best days in ruthlessly stealing public goods for personal rent-seeking (Osburg 2018). As a result, Beijing lost control in curbing collective corruption and mounting social discontent and tensions have gradually eroded the CCP's legitimacy to rule.

In view of this crisis of governance, since November 2012, President Xi Jinping has given the anti-corruption agenda top priority. In comparison with the CCP's early clean-action campaign, Xi's vigorous crackdown has left both civilian and military 'tigers' (notably the former security boss Zhou Yongkang and Xi's former political rival Bo Xilai), 'cats and flies' at all levels taken down and getting punished. A 2018 report issued by the Ministry of Supervisor and Central Discipline Inspection Commission claimed to have tackled 406,000 cases between January and September, leaving 387,000 employees and party members receiving punitive measures.[2] In particular, the establishment of the National Supervision Commission (NSC) in March 2018 has transformed China's previous dual-track anti-corruption system into a centralized one, marking the decreasing political influence of local leaders (Deng 2018). Beijing also has extended its overseas campaign by launching such projects as 'Sky Net' and 'Fox Hunt' in order to hunt down fugitive venal officials. According to a China's top anti-graft watchdog, till June 2017, 2,873 fugitives had been captured from over 90 countries and regions which helped recover some $130 million. In 2016, over 1,000 fugitives were brought back to China for justice. Several commentators praised President Xi's efforts being 'a very good reference for other Communist parties', whose success can ensure 'China's sustained development' and lead to 'increasing prosperity and national credibility'.[3]

Some old and new questions arise: To what extent is the phenomenon of corruption in China different from other countries? What is the relationship between the ongoing economic reform, corruption and anti-corruption in reform China? How can this link be explained with the existing theory of corruption? What are the effects and implications of Xi's crackdown at both domestic and transnational levels? This chapter adopts a combination of neo-institutional economic approaches, cultural norms, social capital and leadership theory to decipher this specific relationship in China. It recurs to primary and secondary sources and aims to explore new terrains of theorizing corruption and to explain the dilemma the Chinese government faces between its anti-corruption crackdown measures and economic reforms including progressive regulations at the financial market. This chapter presents three arguments:

Argument 1: Corruption in China involves a *specific* paradox with many tensions. Corruption and economic development are two sides of one coin, shaped by vertical leadership and informal social networks with utility-forging holes.

Argument 2: Anti-corruption efforts under Xi have served to reorganize the CCP's rule and helped it to restore its legitimacy. Nonetheless, due to the lack of an independent institutionalized check-and-balance system, the level of corruption turns out to be a matter of subjective acceptance and adaptation, as long as it follows cultural rules found in the interaction between economic and non-economic activity and its costs do not disturb the profit-sharing of economic development. Ultimately, anti-corruption efforts become a powerful political instrument for President Xi in eliminating his political rivals and launching rigorous governance reforms towards a totalitarian rule.

Argument 3: Facing the rise of global anti-corruptionism (Sampson 2015), the gradual approach of China's involvement in transnational anti-bribery campaign, however, may constitute a tipping point for China to introduce innovative anti-corruption mechanisms. They may prove to be decisive for incremental reform of the rule of law and social attitudinal change.

To follow our arguments, the chapter is divided into three sections. The first section constructs a theoretical framework with four parameters (economic, cultural and social capital, institutional and leadership) that are supposed to highlight the specific relationship of corruption, economic development and anti-corruption in China. The second section analyses the anti-corruption crackdown under Xi and explores its transnational links and implications. The final section summarizes the findings and gives some theoretical and practical reflections derived from our examination.

Corruption, anti-corruption efforts and economic reform in China: Exploring their links

Varied studies from different disciplines (political economy, policy analysis, economics, sociology, organization studies, social psychology and cultural anthropology) have provided in-depth insights into the causes, types, features and effects of corruption in different contexts. From an economic and political perspective, 'corruption' is generally defined as distortion of public goods resulted from the diversion of state resources by officials into funding private benefits. The World Bank Group (2012) calls corruption 'the abuse of public office for private gain'. In the post-Enron period, corruption is defined in a broader and stricter way: For Transparency International (2009), corruption involves 'the abuse of entrusted power for private gain'. International Conventions such as the United Nation (UN) Convention and the Organisation for Economic Cooperation and Development (OECD) Convention as well as the Council of Europe also cover bribes, kickbacks, embezzlement, misappropriation of property and obstruction of justice.[4] Vito Tanzi defines corruption as 'the intentional non-compliance with the arms-length principle aimed at deriving some advantage for oneself or for related individuals from this behaviour' (cited in Begovic 2005: 2). This definition provides a more sophisticated picture covering both economic and sociopolitical aspects. It contains three core elements: (1) the violation of the arms-length principle; (2) intentional bias; (3) the existence of some advantage. At least, this definition implicates certain forms of corruption (i.e. bureaucratic corruption and collective corruption, see Wedeman 2006) embedded in social interactions with expectations and obligations agreed among the involved individuals within certain political and social networks.

Particularly, the combination of economic, (neo)institutional and sociological approaches helps highlight the causes of corruption (i.e. the dilemma of institutional power in protecting transactions and (re)distributing resources, on the one hand, and the temptation of exploiting this power, on the other) as well as the role of norms and contextual factors in shaping and constraining corrupt behaviour (Lambrsdorff et al. 2005: 2–3; de Graaf 2007). Some studies show how weak public institutions and distortions in economic policies give rise to 'rent-seeking by public officials and the incubation of corrupt practices' (Ahmad et al. 2012: 277; Mo 2001). Others demonstrate how reinforcing factors (historical/colonial and social backgrounds and gender, educational, fiscal and economic factors) shape the scope of corruption (He 2000; Dong and Torgler 2010; Dong 2011). Dong and Torgler (2010) find that in the Chinese context, provinces with great anti-corruption efforts, higher educational attainment,

Anglo-American historical influence, 'greater openness, more access to media, higher relative wages of government employees and a greater representation of women in the legislature are markedly less corrupt'. Furthermore, organizational scholars adopt a macro-social perspective and regard corruption as a process of 'a gradual institution of misbehaviour which contributes to legitimizing behaviour and socializing others into it in such a way that it gradually becomes normalised', what Ashforth and Anand (2003, here cited in Breit et al. 2015: 319ff) call a 'culture of corruption'. In addition, social capital research has highlighted correlations between social trust, tolerance and respect, happiness in individual life, better working democratic institutions, more open economics, greater economic growth, and less crime and corruption both at individual and societal level (Rothstein 2013: 1010–11).

Overall, the growing literature on corruption has enriched our understanding of the various ways in which the abuse of power is performed, why corruption takes place and who it involves, and how it can be deterred and prevented. At the same time, as noted by Breit et al. (2015: 321ff), corruption research is often motivated 'by normative description and analyses of corruption' and tends to oversimplify its complexity. As a result, a creative engagement of theorizing corruption might have been long overdue. Efforts are still needed to examine the underlying causes and mechanisms as well as the circumstances of reinforcing factors in enhancing or deterring corruption. Against the backdrop of President Xi's ongoing anti-corruption campaign, a re-examination of corruption in China famously known as the 'East Asian paradox' or 'double paradox' (Wedeman 2012) may provide a timely occasion to explore new terrains for theoretical approaches. We turn to both well established and less known theoretical approaches and adopt four parameters that may give us a nuanced account of corruption in China with both theoretical and practical implications. These parameters are interrelated and involve economic, cultural and social capital, institutional and leadership ones. Whereas economic and (neo)-institutional parameters provide an institutional choice analytic frame in which rational individual choices are shaped by rules, mechanisms and factors defining the structure of expected costs and benefits (Vannucci 2015: 2; Collier 2002: 3), the cultural and leadership parameters look particularly at the differences in cultural traditions, social norms and networks, political opportunistic costs and individual moral preferences at the societal and leader level.

The reasons for the adoption of these parameters as an analytic frame are threefold. First, the analytic capacity of neo-institutional economics and sociology lies in their common concern of highlighting from inside the corrupt relationship. Both approaches underline the role of norms, trust and reciprocity in economic transactions. While there are no clear-cut boundaries between New Institutional Economics (NIE) and New Economic Sociology (NES), their different views of the role of institutions prove to be complementary. For NES, institutions are socially constructed, whose underlying normative preconditions as well as the formation of networks and relationships constrain the free choice of individuals. As noted by Lambsdorff et al. (2005: 6), all action (including economic one) 'is socially situated, and cannot be explained by individual motives alone; it is embedded in ongoing networks of personal relations rather than carried out by atomised actors'. In comparison, NIE pays attention to institutional preconditions/setting that facilitate corrupt transactions. For NIE, institutional arrangements are used to minimize transaction costs and to safeguard transactions against opportunistic behaviour. Hence, institutions are created to maximize the benefits of economic action. NIE's concern is then to examine how institutions emerge, how they are designed and evolve as a 'consequence and result of maximising behaviour', and thus, lastly, 'how they economise on transaction costs' (Lambsdorff et al. 2005). Secondly, a cultural and social capital parameter helps highlight the different and elusive face of 'corruption' in the Asian/Chinese context, as corruption occurs often in the form of graft, which, as part of social interactions understood as *quanxi*, has its own social meaning and function. Derived from the social norm 'reciprocity', it is associated with a moral dimension and legal culture which may be demonized in the West as 'immature, primitive, backward, subjective and irrational', compared with Western laws which are seen as 'developed, modern and advanced, objective and rational' (Lindsey 2002, cited in White 2006: 4). The strength of this parameter lies in its explanatory capacity in illuminating the relationship (either in correlation or a causal one) between cultural differences, social norms/social capital, interiorized values and corruption. It also upholds the importance of the quality of social capital and the ethics of a given network in shaping the scope and form of corruption (Callahan 2005; Tantardini and Garcia-Zamor 2015). Thirdly, a close view of China's top-down reform efforts intertwined with the emergence and development of virulent corruption as well as the ensuing anti-corruption campaign reveals the central role of leadership in contributing to the phenomenon of structural corruption. The existing leadership literature from organizational studies in general shares the view that a strong centralized leadership normally tends to nurture corruption and that shared leadership backed by the concept of balance of power 'can provide a buffer against corruption' (Pearce et al. 2008: 354). Meanwhile, the role of leadership in fostering or reducing corruption in the Chinese context may prove to be at best elusive. The inclusion of a leadership perspective in the combined economic-institutional and cultural approaches provides powerful tools in explaining the paradox of the CCP's rule between power maintenance, tolerance towards corruption and crackdown efforts against 'evil' corruptors.

The four parameters are supposed to explain the relationship between economic development, corruption and anti-corruption efforts during China's reform era. The following paragraphs sketch the underlying assumptions and approaches and highlight the empirical relevance and limitations of each parameter.

The economic parameter

The economic parameter emphasizes that corruption is the outcome of rational individuals' choice to deviate from laws and/or informal norms for the pursuit of their self-interest. Corrupt exchanges in the form of a principal-agent-client model at the micro level can be briefly described as follows: following the theory of individual utility maximizing, an individual will be involved in corruption 'in a world of scarce resources' (Rose-Ackerman 1978: 5), imperfect information and many risks if for him 'the benefits associated with the act are expected to outweigh the costs' (Soreide 2014: 26). Three prerequisites are necessary while defining corruption as an 'abuse of entrusted power': (1) delegation of decision-making power from the principal/ the truster to another actor (the agent) for pursuing the principal's interests; (2) the trust-giving or betrayal of trust, internalized rules and incentives, the control of agent's actions, supervision and enforcement mechanisms due to 'asymmetric information'. Corruption occurs when an agent decides to have an exchange with a corruptor and the latter will obtain confidential information and have access to resources the corruptor would otherwise not be entitled to; (3) In such a corrupt exchange, the agent receives as a reward money or other valuable resources (Collier 2002: 4; Vannucci 2015: 7–8).

Driven by such economic incentives, according to Heidenheimer (2017) and Gordon White (1996, here cited in He 2000: 245), there exist three categories of corruption, which can also be found in the Chinese context: (1) 'Black corruption', whose practices include graft, bribe, embezzlement, extortion, smuggling, tax evasion, etc. These practices constitute an important part of economic crimes whose purpose is to increase personal wealth. (2) 'Grey corruption' involves the misuse of public power, in which leaders of public institutions use their power to increase the revenue of their institutions and improve the situation of their staffs. Carl Friedrich (1972) regards such practices as corrupt, as they damage the interests of the excluded groups, institutions and the general public. (3) Practices of 'white corruption' can be identified in a variety of informal *guanxi* and networks including both nepotism and favouritism found for instance in the personnel recruitment and promotion. They apply and interpret laws in a way that benefit their relatives and friends. Based on the principle of reciprocity, such practices usually are accepted and expected, as the maintenance of such networks is considered as essential for receiving and giving favourable treatments at both public and private level. Nonetheless, such practices are condemned by those excluded, although they would hardly hesitate to engage in such practice 'should they have an opportunity to do so' (He 2000: 245).

The explanatory strengths of an economic parameter lie in its capacity to explore the relationship between economic development, corruption and anti-corruption. From a macroeconomic perspective, Graeff and Svendsen (2013: 2829ff) show damaging effects of corruption upon economic wealth, as 'corruption in itself means that resources end up in the wrong places and not in socioeconomically optimal investments'. As such, corruption entails higher transaction and control costs economic actors have to invest which will bind resources to non-productive purposes (see also Vian 2008). Moreover, one observes that corruption in general is higher in poor countries. The 2009 *Transparency International Corruption Perceptions Index (CPI)* showed that the ten least corrupt countries (such as New Zealand, the Netherlands and Canada) had an average real GDP per capita of $36,700. In comparison, the ten most corrupt countries (such as Haiti, Turkmenistan and Afghanistan) had an average real GDP per capita of $5,100' (cited in Bai et al. 2014). In particular, several studies have explored the circumstances under which corruption has negative effects upon firm growth and anti-corruption has effects upon economic development (for details see the section 'Corruption and anti-corruption as driver of economic growth in reform China?'). Evidence also shows a strong correlation between the degree of market liberalization and expected reduced corruption (Lin et al. 2018). In underdeveloped financial market, corruption proves to be an important mediator to get things done. Lin et al. (2018: 1ff) point out that corruption can boost shareholder value in *less* regulated financial markets. As institutions support market transactions that work poorly, for investors and shareholders, influencing officials 'can be the only way to access essential resources'. In such cases, corruption becomes grease payments which firms must pay to build 'connections' with officials that lubricate 'bureaucratic gears' to 'get things done' (Fisman 2001; Wei 2001; McMillan and Woordruff 2002, here cited in Lin et al. 2018: 1). Despite of the strengths of the economic variable to highlight the relationship between corruption, economic development and anti-corruption, it often falls short of providing convincing explanations *why* economic incentives may not induce corrupt behaviour. The tools provided by a cultural and social capital help address this weakness.

The cultural and social capital parameter

The cultural and social capital parameter assumes that corruption is related to the functioning of endogenous cultural norms, ethical preferences, the forms of social capital at individual and collective levels (Licht et al. 2003; Callahan 2005; Tavits 2005; Baquero 2015; Vannucci 2015). For Licht et al. (2003: 6), corruption, together with the rule of law and accountability, constitutes 'social norms' of governance. These norms specify behaviour seen 'as desirable or legitimate in the shared view of societal members and whose violation elicits at least informal disapproval' (Cialdini and Trost 1998; Cooter 1998, here cited in Licht et al. 2003). Ethical standards derived from these norms have been labelled in different ways in the literature on corruption: moral costs in economic theory, cultural norms in comparative politics, quality of social capital, and ethical preferences in networks which provide a compelling perspective in elucidating the relationship between corruption, economic development and anti-corruption. 'Moral cost' can be understood as normative barriers found in an agent's preferences and identifications with the public organization's values and purposes. As noted by Vannucci (2015: 11), the higher the moral cost for an agent, the stronger he/she will psychologically suffer and feel guilty in case of infringement, 'perceived as a betrayal of public trust, independently from its detection'. In particular, derived from several empirical examinations, scholars suggest to look at the forms and quality of social capital and the ethics of each network's inside/outside distinction that foster or reduce corruption (Callahan 2005; López and Santos 2014; Baquero 2015). Following Nahapiet and Ghoshal (1998: 243ff), social capital theory assumes that 'networks of relationships constitute a valuable resource for the conduct of social life' in providing their members with 'the collectivity-owned capital, a "credential" which entitles them to credit, in the various sense of the word' (Bourdieu 1986: 249, here cited in Nahapiet and Ghoshal 1998). Much of this social capital 'is embedded within networks of mutual acquaintance and recognition' (Nahapiet and Ghoshal 1998) and has many different attributes and forms. For the clarification of virulent corruption in China, we suggest to look at the structural/organizational and relational dimensions of social capital whose distinction lies in the consideration of the macro and meso perspectives (Nahapiet and Ghoshal 1998; Tantardini and Garcia-Zamor 2015). Whereas structural/organizational social capital concerns the pattern of networks between actors or units, relational social capital focuses on the particular relations people have, such as trust, respect, friendship and *yi-chi* (brotherhood in the Chinese context) that influence their behaviour (Nahapiet and Ghoshal 1998: 244). Corruption and political scandals, as research shows, can have strong effect on citizens' attitudes towards leaders, governments and political institutions (Bowler and Karp 2004; Seligson 2002, cited in Newton 2006: 2). Following social capital theory, there is 'a virtuous circle of high trust, well established social institutions, good government, and strong popular political support, which then helps to sustain social trust between citizens, foster community and civic participation, and encourage collective activity for the common good' (Newton 2006: 9ff). The combination of circumstances suggests that 'a mixture of high or rising social capital and poor government performance may cause political support to fall' (Newton 2006). As such, social trust is a core component of relational social capital and is normally used as a key indicator of it. Social trust between citizens contributes to economic growth and efficiency in market economics, stable and efficient democratic government, the equitable provision of public goods, social integration, cooperation and harmony.[5]

While exploring the relationship between social capital and corruption, four core principles of social networks and economic outcomes along both dimensions of social capital are worth mentioning here. The first principle involves norms and network density. As noted by Granovetter (2005: 33–5ff), norms are 'shared ideas about the proper way to behave; density is the proportion of the possible connections among those nodes that are actually present' (Granovetter 2005: 34ff). The denser a network is, the more unique paths can be found along which information, ideas and influence can travel between any two nodes. It follows that greater density facilitates the acceptance of ideas about proper behaviour, which 'also renders deviance from resulting norms harder to hide and, thus, more likely to be punished'. The second principle underlines the advantage of weak ties, as more novel and unique information flows to individuals through weak than through strong ties (Granovetter 2005: 34–5). Furthermore, Burt (1992) upholds the strategic advantage of 'structural holes' which involve the way different parts of networks are bridged. Within these holes, individuals enjoy 'with ties into multiple networks that are largely separated from one another'. Finally, attention is paid to the interpenetration of economic and non-economic action. Following Granovetter (2005: 35ff), when economic and non-economic activities are intermixed, 'non-economic activity affects the costs and the available techniques for economic activity'. Such mixing of activities (i.e. 'social embeddedness' of the economy) means 'the extent to which economic action is linked to or depends on actions or institutions that are non-economic in content, goals or processes'. They include for instance social networks, culture, politics and religion (Granovetter 2005).

In other words, the cultural and social capital parameter provides insight into the effects of culture and social capital upon economic and political performance, effects which are at best ambivalent and depend upon the forms and quality of social capital. On the one hand, social capital increases the efficiency of social action found in those networks with weak ties or structural holes. For López and Santos (2014: (1), 'the universalistic trust (linking and bridging social capital) constitutes a positive social capital that is negatively linked to corruption'. Graeff and Svendsen (2013: 2829) also find that in the European context, 'the augmentation of positive social capital could work as an effective counterforce to corruption, even if it does not compensate for the economic loss caused by corruption'. On the other hand, trust (bonding) rooted in particularistic nodes can constitute a negative social capital which is related to the *uncivil* social capital of corruption, ethnocentrism and sectarianism (Nahapiet and Ghoshal 1998: 245; López and Santos 2014; Tantardini and Garcia-Zamor 2015: 599). López and Santos (2014) further find out that if cultures are characterized of favouring 'the legitimation of dependency relations and the formation of closed particularistic groups (power-distance and community factors)', they 'create a breeding ground for the development of these amoral rent-seeking structures'. The consequences are, as found in the culture of corruption, high economic costs resulting from 'rent-seeking' of many off-the-books transactions to carry on normal production of goods and services. Further consequences include the loss of social trust towards public officials and the entailed apathy of citizens regarding politics that can lead to an inertial state of governance with low stocks of social capital (Baquero 2015).

Meanwhile, in spite of the strengths of cultural arguments to unveil the structural and social embeddedness of corruption, they may easily become political instruments for local elites to defy external critiques in arguing that the involved cultural context (e.g. the Chinese context) has its own unique and uniform way of doing things and Western admonition for reform is a new form of cultural imperialism (Lindsey 2002, cited in White 2006).

The neo-institutional parameter

The neo-institutional parameter focuses on control mechanisms which 'allow the internal regulation of social interactions within corrupt networks, and their effects on individuals' beliefs and preferences' (Vannucci 2015: 18). Several studies have upheld the usefulness of institutional economics to develop a better understanding of why corruption occurs and the best policies to combat it (Collier 2002; Lambsdorff 2007). There are three different ways in elaborating an institutional analytic frame. The first one consists of 'both internal (agency) and external (structural) worlds' (Collier 2002: 3). The external world refers to the institutional (rule) structure that influences an agent's perceptions and decision-making (the internal world). Another way of elaborating a neo-institutional frame refers to the *informal* 'institutional framework', in which corrupt practices between agent and corruptor take place and several enforcement mechanisms may be applied to regulate such practices with sanctions attached to them (Vannucci 2015: 19). Lambsdorff (2007) argues that rather than being deterred by penalties, corrupt actors are more influenced by other factors such as the opportunism of their criminal counterparts and the danger of acquiring a reputation of unreliability. At stake is the value of 'the word given' between corrupt partners which, under certain circumstances, can positively shape the actors' moral preferences. Vannucci (2015: 20) observes for instance how 'personal or idiosyncratic sources of trust and loyalty towards counterparts can generate an ethical preference towards "integrity in corruption"', which constitutes a moral stance that to be trustworthy while managing bribes has already a value in itself. Driven by such moral conviction, first-party control occurs when the informal norms of corruption are violated and cause discomfort or feelings of guilt for those who have internalized their obligations in corrupt deals. If all partners share similar internalized norms and respect reciprocal trust, corrupt exchanges can be successfully maintained (Vannucci 2015).

A further way of elaborating an institutional frame is oriented towards policy choices. It adopts an integrated theory from political science and economics and makes a distinction between individualist and institutional approaches (Nas et al. 1986: 107ff; Thompson 2018). Corruption is regarded *both* as a process and as 'a product of individual and structural variables that interact to produce both positive and negative consequences' (Nas et al. 1986). The individualist approaches focus on '*quid pro quo* exchanges' (Thompson 2018) and include 'considerations such as greed and the likelihood of detection and prosecution' which may help suggest one set of policies for reducing corruption (Nas et al. 1986). At the institutional level, 'bureaucratic constraints, citizen participation, and the congruence of legal structures and social demands' all offer a competing set of concerns for examination. The strengths of the neo-institutional parameter dwell in its emphasis on the close connection between patterns of corruption and the legitimate functions of institutions. For Thompson (2018: 495), corruption has at best a contradictory function to fulfil: it 'benefits the institution while undermining it'. Hence, the neo-institutional parameter compellingly reveals the necessity to launch reforms which 'should be directed toward finding alternatives for the functions the corruption serves'. Nonetheless, both individualist and institutional approaches might have overlooked the role of self-interested or enlightened executive leadership which may prove to be the key to comprehensively understanding corruption.

The leadership parameter

The leadership parameter upholds the role of executive leadership (centralized or shared leadership) in reducing or fostering corruption. Derived from mainstream leadership theories from different perspectives (notably philosophical, psychological, organizational, behavioural ones), it helps illuminate how individual characteristics (i.e. leaders' responsibility disposition) in relation to other factors such as locus of control and Machiavellianism have influenced corrupt activity. To date, analysts have adopted leadership theories to explain and compare the influence of different types of leadership in shaping corporate management behaviour. Pearce et al. (2008: 354–5) summarize the results of three empirical studies and suggest that decentralized, shared leadership 'may indeed provide a more robust leadership system than relying only on leadership that is traditional, more centralized and vertical in nature' (Pearce et al. 2008: 355). Meanwhile, despite the broad application of leadership theories and recognition of their usefulness in identifying the circumstances and factors that shape corporate behaviour in top management teams, they have not yet been sufficiently considered in explaining executive corruption at political leadership level. China's case might well provide an opportunity to test the generalizability of the merits of shared leadership with positive organizational outcomes found in the existing literature. The detection of the real face of China's collective shared leadership system installed by the reform father Deng Xia-Ping (see section 'The Emergence and Consolidation of

One-Man Leadership' in Chapter 2) might demonstrate a countering example of the efficiency of shared leadership in fighting against corruption.

Most related to our purpose, the approaches and assumptions of three leadership theories are worth mentioning here. Behavioural theory as the first leadership theory focuses on the causes and effects of leaders' behaviour. Derived from motivation study, House and Howell (1992, here cited in Pearce et al. 2008: 355ff) distinguish two types of leaders with two distinct responsibility dispositions. Leaders with personalized power orientation and low responsibility disposition desire positions of power for the purpose of personal aggrandizement instead of pursuing the benefit of the collective (Conger 1990; Hogan, Curphy and Hogan 1994, here cited in Pearce et al. 2008: 355ff.). In contrast, leaders high in socialized need for power tend to have a high responsibility disposition. They exhibit 'greater integrity when confronted with ethical decision-making dilemmas' (Pearce et al. 2008: 355ff.) and will consequently be less likely to get involved in corruption. The second and third theories involve a transactional-transformational paradigm and highlight how leaders behave in a given institutional setting: either they are transactional (self-interested and culture-bounded) individuals/actors or ready to move beyond their self-interests for the good of the group, organization or society inspired by a transformational vision. As noted by Bass (1985, 1997), whereas transactional leaders work within the cultural constraints of the setting or organization, transformational leaders are motivated to change the context and the organization.

Supported by these three theories, we assume that, in China's party state, empowering leadership from above has created effective shared leadership. However, such leadership against the backdrop of increasing interdependence between politics and economics has also facilitated the building of concurring networks, in which leaders' high desire for their personal aggrandizement often outweighs their commitment to achieving objectives for the betterment of the collective entity. Due to a low level of responsibility disposition, the CCP's shared leadership becomes immersed in a perverse culture of corruption which has not only triggered an outcry of the loss of moral standards in society. It has also deteriorated the CCP's political legitimacy to rule.

In sum, the four parameters with their respective approaches and assumptions are deemed to provide tools for explaining the relationship between corruption, economic development and anti-corruption in the Chinese context. The following section is charged with two major tasks. It first identifies and analyses the specific characteristics of this relationship without ignoring its transnational link and implications. It also tests the applicability of the combined perspective with four parameters.

Corruption and anti-corruption as driver of economic growth in reform China? Recent developments and implications

Though Chinese corruption might have its own unique features, actors involved are not limited to employees in the public sector. They also include any Chinese state functionary engaging in public activities whose corrupt practices 'refers to both economic (embezzlement, misappropriation of public funds, and bribery) and disciplinary corruption (violation of social norms and the dereliction of duty) that are damaging to public interests' (Ko and Weng 2011: 359). Practices of the three categories of corruption mentioned above have sharply increased since the launching of its reform opening policy towards the end of the 1970s unto the post-Deng era. A close look at these phenomena reveals a high degree of interdependence of economic, institutional, cultural and social capital as well as leadership factors shaping the scope and content of corruption in reform China. Four characteristics can be identified in relation to the ensuing anti-corruption campaigns.

First, during its 1978 to late-1980s marketization reform, corruption had a political function to counter local leaders' resistance against reform measures. As observed in Trinh's case study (2013: 1ff), 'The opportunities for corruption that stemmed out of the reform process had counter-balanced the political anti-reform resistance coming from the local governments.' Local elites had been able to profit from gains from corruption which replaced lost privileges, 'regulated incentives, and created new forms of relationships that eventually allowed reforms to happen', thereby providing the process with much-needed momentum. As such, corruption has helped tie the gains of local leaders with those of the entrepreneurial class, 'resulting in a public-private network and a vested interest in the continuation of reforms' (Trinh 2013). With the opportunities opened for corruption, graft prevailed due to the growth-focused system which demands performance at all levels. Every official and party secretary is required to achieve high performance for securing promotion, thereby facilitating the establishment of a meritocratic system. In view of such virulent practices of graft, President Jiang Zemin therefore used structural reforms to keep it at bay. Deregulation and competitive measures were introduced towards state-owned enterprises (SOEs) and military business.[6] In spite of enhanced anti-corruption and market reform efforts, towards the end of the 1990s, China's rank and score in Internet Corruption Perception Index still rose from fifty-four (1996) to eighty-five (1998).[7]

Secondly, particularly viewed from the economic parameter, the relationship between corruption, economic growth and anti-corruption in China is at best complex and elusive. There exist at least three types of such relationships. The first one, as found in several studies (Wang and You 2012; Bai et al. 2014), involves a substitution relationship between the degree of financial regulation, corruption and firm growth in the private and state-owned firms. Bai et al. (2014) for instance find that 'the negative effect of growth on bribery is larger if firms are more mobile'. The study of Wang and You (2014ff) further confirms this relationship. In China's Southeast and Central regions, it appears that corruption has contributed to firms' growth in *underdeveloped* financial markets, which also led to fast economic growth. Hence, one expects that pervasive corruption deters firm growth 'where there are more developed financial markets'. Another type of relationship involves a positive correlation between anti-corruption efforts and economic growth. In the branch of Research and Development (R&D), Dang and Yang (2016: 39ff) detect positive effects of anti-corruption upon firm behaviour as intensive anti-corruption crackdown 'raises the cost of seeking for political bond and strengthens the incentive for firm innovation'. Different factors may play a crucial role in defining this *positive* correlation. They include the circumstances when (1) intensive anti-corruption crackdown is issued in politically connected firms; when it takes place (2) in those non-SOEs and (3) in provinces with more intense anti-corruption efforts; (4) in regions with a more developed market economy. In other words, specifically in the branch of R&D, the factors of the degree of political connection and marketization, the types of firms, and the heterogeneity of regions have shaped the relationship between anti-corruption and economic growth. In contrast, several empirical studies (Chen and Zhong 2017; Wang 2016) detect a negative relationship between anti-corruption and economic growth as the third type of this complex relationship. Wang's study (2016) shows the increasing centralized anti-corruption efforts have an adverse influence on investment growth, thereby curbing economic growth particularly at the provincial level. Visits made by the CCP's Provincial Committee of Discipline Inspection (PCDI) as an important initiative also have discouraged business registration, marking a probable trade-off in anti-corruption and economic growth (Chen and Zhong 2017: 1).

Thirdly, driven by governmental money-pouring measures particularly under President Hu Jintao, a culture of (executive) corruption with strategic holes in China came into shape through network-building between politics and economics. Viewed from the cultural, social capital and leadership parameters, the mutual rent-seeking behaviour and the power struggle among different political factions and business groups have left most anti-corruption measures inefficient, serving at best as political tools for the CCP to restore its political legitimacy. Due to the concern of the rising unemployment rate resulting from market reforms as well as the global financial crisis, Hu reversed Jiang's policy and purposefully poured money into big SOEs that 'could create a rapid increase of production'.[8] As government, party bureaucracies and SOEs increase, many senior cadres participated in managing lucrative side business. Concurring factions and interest groups (i.e. SOEs, big banks, the Party and government bureaucracies, local governments and the military) coordinated with or concurred against each other while making fortunes. In particular, their business relationships have been sustained through highly gendered practices such as male solidarity, brotherhood, paternalism, mutual aid and *yiqi* (honour or a sense of duty that defines personal relationship). Members of those networks are expected to maximize their profits, 'to put their brotherly relationship above all other commitments, sharing their success and using positions of power to the advantage of their associates' (Osburg 2018: 153). Consequently, some top leaders and their families were able to gain huge fortunes: For instance, between 2007 and 2012, the former security boss Zhou Yongkang reportedly accumulated a fortune of $145 billion (for details, see the following subsection); the former premier Wen Jiabao and his family obtained a fortune of $30 billion. In other words, the scale of executive corruption became astronomic and turned out to be out of control. Besides executive corruption, the results of extensive fieldwork reveal the micro-level operation of corruption resulting from guanxi-practices embodied in informal institutional mechanisms that facilitate the contracting process of corrupt exchange (Li 2011: 1). As argued by Li (2011), the participants of corruption view guanxi-practice as an alternative operating mechanism 'in which risk of exchange safety is controlled, and moral costs and cognitive dissonance are reduced'.

Fourthly, corruption proves to be a natural by-product of China's unprecedented economic miracle, as long as it has spurred, not stalled, growth. Following the logic of Deng's reform principles – good cats are those who catch mice, regardless of their colour (e.g. black or white), what some consider to be the weaknesses of China's economy have been its strengths. At least, with its state-controlled capitalism, the CCP's centralized authoritarian rule has set up an unusual development model, in which unbalanced growth 'isn't evidence of a looming risk so much as a sign of successful industrialization. Surging debt levels are a marker of financial deepening rather than profligate spending'.[9] In this respect, a tacit social contract between the Chinese government and its people appears to have fulfilled its mission in the post-Deng era: Derived from the lessons learnt from the 1989 Tiananmen crackdown, the Chinese people have been told to keep an abstinent position towards politics. As long as the CCP's leadership tackles a variety of challenges and improves the living standards of the majority, the people tolerate corruption within certain limits. The benefits of the CCP's authoritarian rule dwell in its adaptation and ability to rapidly correct course, including the adoption of anti-corruption measures. At stake is the central question of whether the party-state regime 'can strike the right balance between state intervention and market forces'[10] for the maintenance of its political legitimacy. Meanwhile, an Ipsos survey conducted in 2017 shows that the Chinese people are mostly concerned with the moral decay in their land.[11] Coupled with rising unemployment and debts, the loss of social trust, particularly towards corrupt party functionaries, has gradually cast a shadow upon the CCP's capacity to lead China.

Anti-corruption campaign: Past and recent developments under Xi and its political and transnational implications

A review of the CCP's past anti-corruption efforts reveals that they have been strongly shaped by highly interlinked economic, political, institutional and leadership concerns. Two features of such efforts can be identified. First, as noted by Quade (2007), 'serious attempts at anticorruption enforcement have been periodic in nature'. In explaining the timing of anti-corruption campaigns from 1981 to 1997, Quade detects a plausible correlation between changes in macroeconomic policy and the intensification of anti-corruption enforcement. There are four major anti-corruption campaigns, starting respectively in 1982, 1986, 1989 and 1993, which 'coincided with the end of an inflationary peak and the beginning of a macroeconomic austerity period'. As such, for Quade, the aforementioned anti-corruption campaigns had an economically driven function and were used 'primarily to combat economic overheating and not corruption itself'. Secondly, most anti-corruption campaigns have been a 'clean-up' action, 'seen as a kind of campaign-style enforcement, rather than enforcement by law' (Li 2010). Consequently, although the clean-up strategic action might have success in keeping corruption 'under control' in areas such as cadre control, self-purification and remedy, it remained limited to deter low-level corruption, but not high-level, high stakes corruption, and might even encourage inflation of the size of bribes and could hardly fix the fundamental problems embedded in the redistribution structure (Li 2010; Wedemann 2006).

With the coming to power of President Xi Jinping – who has made anti-corruption campaigns as one of his main goals – in November 2012, a new era has begun with a new focus on and appreciation of the strength of the 1980 Criminal Law of the People's Republic of China (PRC Criminal Law). In general, China's anti-corruption laws are stipulated in this *Law* which contains provisions on offences of bribery and corruption. Following modernization efforts in 1997, it is supposed to provide a vigorous legal framework in curbing and eliminating corruption. Derived from this strengthened legal framework, Xi's anti-corruption campaign has been undergoing institutional change serving first and foremost to purge corrupt networks controlled by 'big tigers' in the central government and to restore the CCP's legitimacy to rule. Unlike the previous anti-campaign efforts deemed as selective and largely limited to the investigation of local functionaries and businessmen (local 'flies'), Xi's strike is comprehensive and harsh. It involves not only investigations into *all* sectors of government including state functionaries at the ministerial/provincial level and top leaders within the CCP, the economy and the military, but also judicial, administrative and party discipline reforms with a preventive character (Transparency International 2018: 5–6). In his 2017 report to the National People's Congress (NPC), the Procurator-General of the Supreme People's Procuratorate (SPP) Cao Jianming noted that there were 47,650 persons charged for corruption or dereliction of duty; 10,472 state functionaries have been investigated and punished for taking bribes.[12] According to sources provided by China's SPP and Central Commission for Discipline Inspection, between 2012 and 2015, there is a continuing growth in the number of cades disciplined by party, which stands in a sharp contrast to the decreasing number of people prosecuted by the procuratorate.[13]

Famous cases involved the investigation and punishment of several big tigers including the former permanent committee member of the Political Bureau Zhou Yunkang (2007–12), Ling Jihua and Bo Xilai (the former party chief in Chongqing, who was famous for his campaign for red songs and clampdown on local snakeheads, mafia bosses and criminal leaders). Following network measurement and recursive selection models (Lu 2017: 5–7; 8–12), there exists strong evidence indicating that Xi's anti-graft strike does appear to be a political purge (Lu 2017: 11). The fall of Bo Xilai between 2012 and 2013 is a good example in giving his many enemies and leaders in the CCP good news and made their lives, 'despite its destabilising drama and surprise, in the end much easier in managing the horse-trading around the leadership transition in late 2012'.[14]

The extent to which Xi's anti-graft campaign has served as a political instrument still remains to be carefully compared in different cities at both central and local levels. Evidence shows at least several incompatible, contrasting multiple goals Xi's campaign might pursue. On the one hand, as all top CCP leaders share the consensus that 'the big tigers' have become regime troublemakers, the lack of self-protection practices across factions as well as factional warfare has helped Xi to justify his strike deemed as necessary disciplinary measures for the restoration of CCP's legitimacy. In particular, unlike the past campaigns, Xi's strike has centralized anti-corruption control through an institutional change from the past dual-track to a single anti-corruption agency model. As observed by Deng (2018: 58; 60–6ff), the establishment of NSC in 2017 upholds a party 'leading control system', in which local officials are now obliged to follow directions, principles and goals set up by the central government's measures including the following steps: (1) the centralization of control agencies; (2) the expansion of the party's Discipline Inspection Committees (DICs); (3) the creation of a balanced cooperative system between the NSC and DICs; (4) intentional vagueness while applying anti-corruption laws for the sake of party control; (5) clear top-down instructions while enhancing the party rule (Deng 2018: 66). A direct effect of such centralization efforts is the substantial decreasing influence of local party leaders in anti-corruption. On the other hand, analysts have doubted the real purpose of Xi's strike which obviously is not limited to a power struggle. In spite of Xi's claim in stating that the campaign was launched to 'meet people's demands' (Xi 2015, here cited in Lu 2017: 12), one cannot help avoid assuming that anti-corruption attracts public attention away from the pressure from slowing economic growth. A vicious circle appears to emerge in the midst of Xi's ongoing anti-graft strike. As found in several empirical studies, the CCP's centralized anti-corruption control system not only has some negative effects upon local economies (Lin et al. 2018; Chen and Zhong 2017; Lu 2017; Wang 2016). The CCP's increasing ideology-driven interventions in those SOEs as well as in private enterprises have slowed down investors' activities, thereby inducing a surge of the unemployment rate regarded as unprecedented in the post-Deng era.[15] In this regard, the outcry from the former president Jiang in admonishing Xi to rethink his harsh strike is deemed as an urgent warning against Xi's policy which might have already hurt the dearest bones of China's economy.

Meanwhile, since mid-2014, the global fight against transnational bribery has opened new perspectives for Xi to internationalize China's anti-corruption efforts. Analysts observe that, in spite of China's adoption of a gradual approach, whose weak legal framework falls short of implementing Article 16 (referring to criminal liability) anchored in the United Nations Convention Against Corruption (UNCAC), China's interests in and impact upon international cooperation in the field of anti-corruption is viewed as 'both a normative challenge to OECD standards and an opportunity for engaging China more effectively' (Lang 2017; see also Gintel 2013). The increasing involvement of China's companies (often SOEs) in transnational bribery has become a serious international problem. As shown in those large-scale infrastructure deals that mark China's development strategy both domestically and abroad, bribery has been prevalent. Also, China has become a popular hub for money laundering which has posed a significant challenge not only for OECD efforts to curb transnational bribery, but also for China's efforts 'to reign in the venality of its own bureaucracy' (Lang 2017: 4). A series of high-level cases undertaken by the US authorities recently reveal how China has continued to harbour 'common systematic bribery and nepotism schemes' (Wedeman 2014; SEC 2016, cited in Lang 2017: 4). It turns out to be that China's cooperation is essential for the global fight against transnational bribery. In several cases, European states have begun to cooperate with China on extradition, joint policy action and fight against cybercrime. Nonetheless, Xi's anti-corruption campaign has failed to fundamentally promote the rule of law, thereby leaving most cases handled by opaque party disciplinary bodies, which relies on strong political leadership and supervision and makes cooperation with state executive and judiciary less meaningful (Lang 2017; Deng 2018).

In this respect, the effects and implications of Xi's ongoing anti-corruption campaigns are far from clear. Empirical research and analysis of official statistics between 2012 and 2016 show that Xi's high-profile anti-corruption campaign 'has fallen short of its stated goal and appears to be doing more harm than good to the image of China's Communist party'.[16] Viewed from the economic parameter, many of the micro effects of Xi's anti-corruption drive have already been well documented including the change of government officials' consumption behaviour and the ensuing slowdown in the restaurant trade, a big dip in sales of luxury goods, a decrease in land transaction and economic growth in the private sector (Chen and Zhong 2017; Lu 2017). It seems that fighting graft too hard just might destroy China's economy too.[17] From the perspective of social capital and public trust, though the campaign's stated aim is to hold all levels of Chinese officials accountable for abuses of power, a new study finds that 'the higher the number of reported graft cases in a prefecture, the more people in the area perceive Beijing as being more corrupt than their local government'.[18]

Reasons for the Chines people's persistent mistrust towards the ruling party might well dwell in the CCP's centralization of power which, in the eyes of the Chinese people, is mainly responsible for corrupt practices of local governments and the CCP's failure of tackling them. In the longer term, the campaign's scope and length may have lasting damaging effects upon the party leadership's image.[19] Ultimately, despite Xi's high-profile leadership, the CCP's remains trapped in a difficult fight resonating what the former party elder Chen Yun once said: 'Fight corruption too little and destroy the country; fight it too much and destroy the Party.'[20]

Concluding remarks and discussion

This chapter has adopted four parameters (economic, cultural and social capital, institutional and leadership ones) to explore the relationships between corruption, economic growth and anti-corruption in the Chinese context. Its findings are fourfold with economic, social, institutional and transnational implications, respectively.

First and foremost, corruption has played an important 'greasing-the-wheels' function in the reform China. The past periodic anti-corruption campaigns served to steer economic overheating and introduce symbolic clean-up action without being able to address the root causes of graft, which are linked to negative social capital with the emergence and building of strategic corrupt networks and promotion pattern led by the big tigers. Meanwhile, as the CCP's political legitimacy has been eroded by the spread of virulent corruption reflected in the high interaction between economics and politics, Xi's high-profile anti-corruption campaign turned out to be necessary in order to rescue the CCP from its (self-made) political crisis. However, despite its centralizing disciplinary power, Xi's anti-corruption crackdown proves to be detrimental for economic growth, particularly in the private sector and land transaction market. Coupled with the ongoing trade war launched by the US president Donald Trump,

China's economic slowdown and rising debts may prove to be decisive in shaping Xi's anti-corruption course in the near future.

Secondly, at the level of cultural and social capital, Xi's anti-corruption drive might have helped purge corrupt networks and change the consumption behaviour of state functionaries. Such top-down leading control system still falls short of addressing the issue of social trust and the perceptions of corruption in the Chinese context. As long as the CCP continues to rule *beyond* the law and the Chinese people remain deprived of obtaining legal education concerning the rule of law, the lack of institutional and social trust between the ruling party and the ruled continues to pose a fundamental challenge for the party-state regime (Hakhverdian and Mayne 2012). In this regard, the author suggests to introduce legal and civic education as first steps to help redefine the relationship of social trust and corruption in terms of *guanxi*-practices and to address increasing social mistrust triggered by Xi's move towards dictatorship.

Thirdly, at both institutional and leadership levels, Xi's centralization power can have both strategic advantages and damaging effects upon the CCP's rule. On the one hand, Xi has pushed for governance reform by centralizing the anti-corruption control system and promoted action-oriented reformers (see Chapter 2, section 'The Emergence and Consolidation of One-Man Leadership'), thereby signalling his intention to address China's social and economic needs. On the other hand, Xi's Mao-style, ideology-driven interventions into the activities of the SOEs and private economies have deviated from pragmatism embraced by his precedents. Some observers suggest that, in order to deter corruption effectively, the Chinese government will eventually have to embrace with more rule of law. Some practical reform steps would prove to be helpful, including 'creating a civil code to define acceptable commercial practices, basic property rights and the status of private companies.[21] In the longer term, China will need more sweeping – and more politically sensitive and courageous – reform steps 'to ensure that private actors have more access to major resources, like land and financing, without having to rely on personal connections to local officials'.[22]

Finally, China's interest in the global fight against transnational bribery can provide opportunities to engage China for gradually orienting towards OECD standards which may help create a facilitating domestic environment for the generation of institutional and social trust. Derived from a cross-national comparative context, Rothstein and Stolle (2008) detect a causal mechanism between societies with effective, impartial, and fair street-level bureaucracies and generalized trust. Though it will definitely be a long way for China to go in introducing any *independent* legal institutions for tackling corrupt practices, these institutional characteristics may well serve as a plausible reference for reform-minded elites in their search to re-design the social contract with their people, at least in a post-Xi era.

Notes

1   Noted by Minxin Pei in his talk with Robert Siegel. See Siegel (2017).
2   See Zhongguo Jijian Jiancha Bao (2018).

3 Commented respectively by Do Tien Sam, editor-in-chief of the China Research Journal based in Vietnam, Peter J. Li of University of Houston, and Macharia Munene at Kenya's US International University. See Xinhua (2017).
4 See The World Bank Group (2012); Transparency International (2009); OECD (2007).
5 'Chapter 1: Social trust and its origin', available at http://essedunet.nsd.uib.no/cms/top ics/2/1/ (accessed 20 June 2018).
6 See Overholt (2015).
7 Adapted from Transparency International's 'Internet CPI'. Cited in He (2000: 246).
8 Overholt (2015).
9 Huang (2018).
10 Ibid.
11 Cited in Strittmatter (2019: 24–31).
12 See www.spp.gov.cn/gzbg, cited in global legal insights, 'Bribery & Corruption 2018 / China' (2018).
13 Cited in Lockett (2016).
14 See Brown (2013).
15 See Deuber (20192019: 1).
16 See EN13.
17 Cited in Sudworth (2014).
18 Ni Xing and Li Zhen at the Institute of Governance and Public Affairs of Guangzhou's Sun Yat-sen University conducted this study. Their study surveyed 83,300 people nationwide by telephone and was published in the latest edition of China's Journal of Public Administration. Cited in Lockett (2016).
19 Ibid.
20 Cited in Osnos (2014).
21 Huang (2018).
22 Ibid.

Bibliography

Ahmad, Eatzaz, Muhammad A. Ullah and Muhammad I. Arfeen, 'Does Corruption Affect Economic Growth?' *Journal of Economics*, 49 (2) (2012), pp. 277–305.

Bai, Jie, Seema Jayachandran, Edmund J. Malesky and Benjamin A. Olken, *Does Economic Growth Reduce Corruption? Theory and Evidence from Vietnam*, 28 October (2014).

Baquero, Marcello, 'Corruption, Political Culture and Negative Social Capital in Brazil', *Revisita Debates*, 3 (3) (2015), pp. 139–57.

Bass, Bernard M., 'Does the Transactional-Transformational Leadership Paradigm Transcend Organizational and National Boundaries?' *American Psychologist*, 52 (2) (1997), pp. 130–9.

Bass, Bernard M., *Leadership and Performance beyond Expectations* (New York: Free Press, 1985).

Begovic, Boris, *Corruption: Concepts, Types, Causes, and Consequences.* Center for International Private Enterprise. Economic Reform, Feature Service, 21 March (2005).

Bjornskov, Christian, 'Combating Corruption: On the Interplay between Institutional Quality and Social Trust', *Journal of Law and Economics*, 54 (1) (February 2011), pp. 135–59.

Breit, Eric, Thomas T. Lennerfors, Lena Olaison, 'Critiquing Corruption: A Turn to Theory', *Ephemera: Theory & Politics in Organization*, 15 (2) (2015), pp. 319–36.

'Bribery & Corruption 2018 / China' (2018). Available at https://www.globallegalinsights.
    com/practice-areas/bribery-and-corruption-laws-and-regulations/china#chapterco
    ntent1 (accessed 27 June 2018).
Brown, Kerry, 'Will China's Leaders Regret BoXilai's Fall?' *BBC News*, 22 September
    (2013). Available at https://www.bbc.com/news/world-asia-china-24019450 (accessed
    28 February 2019).
Burt, R. S., *Structural Holes: The Social Structure of Competition* (Cambridge, MA: Harvard
    UP, 1992).
Caiden, G., 'Corruption and Governance', in G. Caiden, O. Dwivedi and J. Jabbra (eds.),
    Where Corruption Lives (Bloomfield: Kumarian Press, 2001), pp. 15–38.
Callahan, William, 'Social Capital and Corruption: Vote Buying and the Politics of Reform
    in Thailand', *Perspectives on Politics*, 3 (3) (2005), pp. 495–508.
Chen, Nan and Zemin Zhong, *The Economic Impact of China's Anti-Corruption
    Campaign* (Preliminary Draft) 16 September (2017). Available at tiny.cc/pcdi
    (accessed 15 December 2018).
Chr. Michelsen Institute (CMI) & Norwegian Institute of International Affairs (NUPI),
    Research on Corruption: A Policy Oriented Survey, authored by J. Chr. Andvig
    and Odd-Helge Fjeldstad, Inge Amundsen, Tonne Sissener and Tine Soreide,
    commissioned by NORAD, final report, December (2000).
Collier, Michael W., 'Explaining Corruption: An Institutional Choice Approach', *Crime,
    Law & Social Change*, 38 (2002), pp. 1–32.
D'Amica, Nicholas, 'Corruption and Economic Growth in China: An Empirical Analysis',
    Senior Honors Projects, 78 (2015). Available at http://collected.jcu,edu/honorspapers/78
    (accessed 23 June 2018).
Dang, Li and Ruilong Yang, 'Anti-Corruption, Marketisation and Firm Behaviour:
    Evidence from Firm Innovation in China', *Economic and Political Studies*, 4 (1) (2016),
    pp. 39–61.
Deng, Jinting, 'The National Supervision Commission: A New Anti-Corruption Model in
    China', *International Journal of Law, Crime and Justice*, 52 (2018), pp. 58–73.
Deuber, Lea, 'Chinas Schicksalsfrage (China's Destiny Question)', *SZ*, 2 March (2019).
Dong, Bin, *The Causes and Consequences of Corruption*. Doctoral thesis at the School of
    Economics and Finance, Queensland University of Technology, March (2011).
Dong, Bin and Benno Torgler, *The Causes of Corruption: Evidence from China*. Institutions
    and Market Series. Queensland University of Technology, Australia (2010).
Eek, Daniel and Bo Rotstein, *Political Corruption and Social Trust*. The Quality of
    Government (QOG) Institute, Göteborg University, QOG Working Paper Series 3 (2005).
Friedrich, Carl J., *The Pathology of Politics: Violence, Betrayal Corruption, Secrecy and
    Propaganda* (New York: Harper & Row, 1972).
Gintel, Samuel R., 'Fighting Transnational Bribery: China's Gradual Approach', *Wisconsin
    International Law Journal*, 31 (1) (2013), pp. 1–34.
Graaf, Gjalt de, 'Causes of Corruption: Towards a Contextual Theory of Corruption', *PAQ*
    Spring (2007), pp. 39–86.
Graeff, Peter, 'Why Should One Trust in Corruption? The Linkage between Corruption,
    Norms and Social Capital', in Johan G. Lambsdorff, Markus Taube and Matthias
    Schramm (eds.), *The New Institutional Economics of Corruption* (London and
    New York: Routledge, 2005), pp. 40–58.
Graeff, Peter and Gert Tinggaard Svendsen, 'Trust and Corruption: The Influence of
    Positive and Negative Social Capital on the Economic Development in the European
    Union', *Quality & Quantity*, 47 (5) (2013), pp. 2829–46.

Granovetter, Mark, 'Problems of Explanation in Economic Sociology', in N. Nehria and R. Eccles (eds.), *Networks and Organizations: Structure, Form and Action* (Boston: Harvard Business School Press, 1992), pp. 25–56.

Granovetter, Mark, 'The Impact of Social Structure on Economic Outcomes', *Journal of Economic Perspectives*, 19 (1) (2005), pp. 33–50.

Hakhverdian, Armen and Quinton Mayne, 'Institutional Trust, Education, and Corruption: A Micro-Macro Interactive Approach', *Journal of Politics*, 73 (3) (July 2012), pp. 739–50.

Hao, Yufan and Michael Johnston, 'Corruption and the Future of Economic Reform in China', in A. Heidenheimer and Michael Johnston (eds.), *Political Corruption: Concepts and Contexts*. 3rd ed. (New York: Routledge, 2017), pp. 583–604.

He, Zengke, 'Corruption and Anti-corruption in Reform China', *Communist and Post-Communist Studies*, 33 (2000), pp. 243–70.

Heidenheimer, Arnold, 'Perspectives on the Perception of Corruption', in A. Heidenheimer and Michael Johnston (eds.), *Political Corruption: Concepts and Contexts*. 3rd ed. (New York: Routledge, 2017), pp. 141–54.

Heiman, Fritz and Mark Pieth, *Confronting Corruption. Past Concerns, Present Challenges, and Future Strategies* (Oxford: Oxford UP, 2018).

Huang, Yukon, 'China's Economy Is Not Normal: It Doesn't Have to Be', Opinion', *New York Times*, 13 March (2018). Available at https://www.nytimes.com/2018/03/13/opini on/china-economy-corruption.html (accessed 28 June 2018).

Hutchcroft, Paul D. 'The Politics of Privilege: Rents and Corruption in Asia', in A. Heidenheimer and Michael Johnston (eds.), *Political Corruption: Concepts and Contexts*. 3rd ed. (New York: Routledge, 2017), pp. 489–512.

Jain, Arvind K., 'Corruption: A Review', *Journal of Economic Surveys*, 15 (1) (2001), pp. 71–121.

Khan, Mushtaq H. 'Patron-Client Networks and the Economic Effects of Corruption in Asia', in A. Heidenheimer and Michael Johnston (eds.), *Political Corruption: Concepts and Contexts*. 3rd ed. (New York: Routledge, 2017), pp. 467–88.

Ko, Kilkon and Cuifen Weng, 'Critical Review of Conceptual Definitions of Chinese Corruption: A Formal–legal Perspective', *Journal of Contemporary China*, 20 (70) (2011), pp. 359–78.

Kroeber, Arthur R., *China's Economy: What Everyone Needs to Know* (Oxford: Oxford UP, 2016).

Lambsdorff, Johan G., Markus Taube and Matthias Schramm, 'Corrupt Contracting: Exploring the Analytical Capacity of New Institutional Economics and New Economic Sociology', in Johan G. Lambsdorff, Markus Taube and Matthias Schramm (eds.), *The New Institutional Economics of Corruption* (London and New York: Routledge, 2005), pp. 1–15.

Lambsdorff, Johan G., *The Institutional Economics of Corruption and Reform: Theory, Evidence and Policy* (Cambridge: Cambridge UP, 2007).

Lang, Bertran, *Engaging China in the Fight against Transnational Bribery: 'Operation Skynet': The Need for a European Response*, OECD Global Anti-Corruption & Integrity Forum (2017).

Li, Hui, 'The "Clean-Up" Actions in Anti-Corruption Strategies of Contemporary China: A Case from H-City's Local DIC Institutions, 1981–2004', *Journal of Public Administration*, 2 (2010). Available at http://en.cnki.com.cn/Article_en/CJFDTOT AL-GGXZ201002008.htm (accessed 12 December 2018).

Li, Ling, 'Performing Bribery in China: quanxi-Practice, Corruption with a Human Face', *Journal of Contemporary China*, 20 (68) (2011), pp. 1–20.

Licht, Amir N., Chanan Goldschmidt and Shalom H. Schwartz, 'Culture Rules: The Foundations of the Rule of Law and Other Norms of Governance', *Journal of Comparative Economics*, 36 (4) (2007), pp. 659–88.

Lin, Chen, Randall Morck, Bernard Yeung and Xiaofeng Zhao, *Anti-Corruption Reforms and Shareholder Valuations: Event Study Evidence from China*, National Bureau of Economic Research (NBER) Working Papers Series, No. 22001, February 2016, revised May (2018). Available at https://www.nber.org/papers/w22001.pdf (accessed 29 January 2019).

Lockett, Hudson, 'China Anti-corruption Campaign Backfires', *Financial Times*, 9 October (2016). Available at https://www.ft.com/content/02f712b4-8ab8-11e6-8aa5-f79f5696c 731 (accessed 15 August 2018).

López, José A. P. and José Manuel Sánchez Santos, 'Does Corruption Have Social Roots? The Role of Culture and Social Capital', *Journal of Business Ethics*, 122 (4) (2014), pp. 1–12.

Lu, Xi, *Essays in China's Anti-Corruption Campaign*. Dissertation, Agricultural and Resource Economics, University of California, Berkeley (2017).

Mo, Pak Hung, 'Corruption and Economic Growth', *Journal of Comparative Economics*, 29 (2001), pp. 66–79.

Nahapiet, Janine and Sumantra Ghoshal, 'Social Capital, Intellectual Capital, and the Organizational Advantage', *Academy of Management Review*, 23 (2) (1998), pp. 242–66.

Nas, Tevfik F., Albert C. Price and Charles T. Weber, 'A Policy-Oriented Theory of Corruption', *The American Political Science Review*, 80 (1) (1986), pp. 107–19.

Newton, Kenneth, *Political Support: Social Capital, Civil Society, and Political and Economic Performance*. UC Irvine CSD Working Papers, 22 August (2006).

OECD, 'Defining Corruption', *OECD Observer*, No 260 March (2007). Available at http://oecdobserver.org/news/archivestory.php/aid/2163/Defining_corruption.html (11 January 2019).

Osburg, John, 'Making Business Persona: Corruption, Anti-Corruption, and Elite Networks in Post-Mao China', *Current Anthropology*, 59 (Supplement 18) (2018), pp. 149–59.

Osnos, Evan, 'China's Fifteen-Billion-Dollar Purge', *The New Yorker*, 2 April (2014). Available at https://www.newyorker.com/news/news-desk/chinas-fifteen-billion-dollar -purge (accessed 15 November 2018).

Overholt, William, 'The Politics of China's Anti-Corruption Campaign', *East Asia Forum* (2015). Available at http://www.eastasiaforum.org/2015/09/15/the-politics-of-chin as-anti-corruption-campaign/ (accessed 26 June 2018).

Pearce, Craig L., Charles C. Manz and Henry P. Sims Jr., 'The Roles of Vertical and Shared Leadership in the Enactment of Executive Corruption: Implications for Research and Practice', *The Leadership Quarterly*, 19 (2008), pp. 353–59.

Pena, López, Jose Atilano and Jose Manuel Sánchez Santos, 'Does Corruption Have Social Roots? The Role of Culture and Social Capital', *Journal of Business Ethics*, 122 (4) (2014), pp. 697–708.

Quade, Elizabeth A., 'The Logic of Anticorruption Enforcement Campaigns in Contemporary China,' *Journal of Contemporary China*, 16 (50) (2007), pp. 65–77.

Rose-Ackerman, Susan, *Corruption: A Study in Political Economy* (New York: Academic Press, 1978).

Rose-Ackerman, Susan, 'When Is Corruption Harmful? in A. Heidenheimer and Michael Johnston (eds.), *Political Corruption: Concepts and Contexts*. 3rd ed. (New York: Routledge, 2017), pp. 353–74.

Rothstein, Bo, 'Corruption and Social Trust: Why the Fish Rots from the Head Down', *Social Research*, 80 (4) (2013), pp. 1009–32.

Rothstein, Bo and Dietlind Stolle, 'The State and Social Capital: An Institutional Theory of Generalized Trust', *Comparative Politics*, 40 (4) (2008), pp. 441–59. Available at https://www.researchgate.net/publication/272213133/download (accessed 20 August 2018).

Sampson, Steven, 'The Anti-Corruption Package', *Ephemera: Theory & Politics in Organization*, 15 (2) (2015), pp. 435–43.

Sands, Barbara N., 'Market-Clearing by Corruption: The Political Economy of China's Recent Economic Reforms', *Journal of Institutional and Theoretical Economics (JITE)*, 145 (1989), pp. 116–26.

Siegel, Robert, 'A Look at How China's Anti-Corruption Campaign Has Affected Ordinary Citizens', www.npr.org, 24 October (2017). Available at https://www.npr.org/2017/10/24/559889548/a-look-at-how-chinas-anti-corruption-campaign-has-affected-ordinary-citizens (accessed 27 December 2018).

Soreide, T., *Drivers of Corruption* (World Bank: Washington, 2014).

Strittmatter, Kai, 'Sieben Sachen (Seven Things)', *Süddeutsche Zeitung Magazin*, Nr. 5, 1. February (2019).

Sudworth, John, 'The Real Costs of China's Anti-Corruption Crackdown', *BBC News*, 3 April (2014). Available at https://www.bbc.com/news/blogs-china-blog-26864134 (accessed 27 June 2018).

Tantardini, Michele and Jean-Claude Garcia-Zamor, 'Organizational Social Capital and Anticorruption Policies: An Exploratory Analysis', *Public Organization Review*, 15 (4) (2015), pp. 599–609.

Tavits, Margit, *Causes of Corruption: Testing Competing Hypotheses*, Nuffield College, Oxford University, 23 March (2005).

Taube, Markus and Matthias Schramm, 'Private Ordering of Corrupt Transactions: The Case of the Chinese *guanxi* Networks and Their Challenge by a Formal Legal System', in Johan G. Lambsdorff et al. (eds.), *The New Institutional Economics of Corruption* (London and New York: Routledge, 2005), pp. 181–97.

The World Bank Group, 'Combating Corruption' (2012). Available at http://www.worldbank.org/en/topic/governance/brief/anti-corruption (accessed 29 June 2018).

Thompson, Dennis F., 'Theories of Institutional Corruption', *Annual Review of Political Science*, 21 (2018), pp. 495–513.

Transparency International, *China: Overview of Corruption and Anti-Corruption*, Anti-Corruption Helpdesk, written by Nieves Zuniga and reviewed by Robert M. Kukutschka, 10 April (2018).

Transparency International, 'What Is Corruption?' (2009). Available at https://www.transparency.org/what-is-corruption#define (accessed 29 June 2018).

Trinh, Duy D., 'Corruption Driven Reform: China's Economic Reforms in the Post-Mao Period', *Inquiries Journal/Student Pulse*, 5(4) (2013), http://www.inquiriesjournal.com/a?id=734 (accessed 20 June 2018).

Uslaner, Eric M., 'Trust and Corruption', in Johan G. Lambsdorff et al. (eds.), *The New Institutional Economics of Corruption* (London and New York: Routledge, 2005), pp. 76–92.

Vannucci, Alberto, 'Three Paradigms for the Analysis of Corruption', *LaBoUR & Law Issues*, 1 (2) (2015), pp. 1–31.

Vian, Taryn, 'Review of Corruption in the Health Sector: Theory, Methods and Interventions', *Health Policy and Planning*, 23 (2008), pp. 83–94.

Wang, Luyao, 'The Impacts of Anti-Corruption on Economic Growth in China', *Modern Economy*, Published Online in Scientific Research Publishing (SciRes) (2016), pp. 109–17. Available at scrip.org/journal/me (accessed 15 August 2018).

Wang, Yuanyuan and Jing You, 'Corruption and Firm Growth: Evidence from China', *China Economic Review*, 23 (2) (2012), pp. 415–33.

Wedeman, A., 'Anticorruption Campaigns and the Intensification of Corruption in China', *Journal of Contemporary China*, 14 (42) (2006), pp. 93–116.

Wedeman, A., *Double Paradox: Rapid Growth and Rising Corruption in China*, 1st ed. (Cornell UP, 2012).

Wedeman, Andrew, 'Development and Corruption: The East Asian Paradox', in E. T. Gomez (ed.), *Political Business in East Asia* (London: Routledge, 2002), pp. 34–61.

White, Andrew, 'The Paradox of Corruption as Antithesis to Economic Development: Does Corruption Undermine Economic Development in Indonesia and China, and Why Are the Experiences Different in Each Country?' *Asian-Pacific Law and Policy Journal* 8 (1), Research Collection School of Law (2006), pp. 1–34.

Xinhua, 'China, World Stand to Benefit Big from Xi's Anti-corruption Campaign', 22 June (2017). Available at http://www.chinadaily.com.cn/china/2017-06/22/content_298451 12.htm (accessed 4 February 2019).

Yu, Olivia, 'Corruption in China's Economic Reform: A Review of Recent Observations and Explanations', *Crime Law Social Change*, 50 (2008), pp. 161–76.

Zhongguo Jijian Jiancha Bao, 'In the Pursuit of Efficiency, While Fighting against Corruption Surrounding the Mass', *The website of Ministry of Supervisor and Central Discipline Inspection Commission*, 24 December (2018). Available at http://www.ccdi. gov.cn/bbply/201812/t20181224_185629.html (accessed 19 January 2019).

6

Is it possible to harmonize universalism with localism? Deliberating human rights discourse in China

Yean-Sen Teng

Introduction

The idea of human rights is universal; therefore, the enjoyment of human rights for everyone is without a slightest doubt a necessity. However, the truth is that not everyone has the same protection and enjoyment of human rights. The situation is even conspicuous in China. Apparently, various factors, namely political, economic, social, cultural and historical, to name but a few, are attributable to the situation of human rights deficit therein. Seemingly, political factors, namely the undemocratic system and lack respect the rule of law, are the most critical reasons to that effect. Democracy[1] is the prerequisite and the fundamental infrastructure for the construction of human rights in any society; otherwise the discourse of human rights is nothing but lip service and nonsense. A society having the problem of human rights deficit usually will look for a methodology to the effect of justifying its deficit. The applied methodology in discoursing human rights in this case, in addition to the political purpose, may have the effect to conceptualize the idea of human rights in a particular way that could degenerate the value of human rights in global context. Localism is the case. Human rights are subsumed under constitutional law, and as a result, the universality of human rights is subject to constitutional authority and finds its legitimacy in localism. The idea of human rights is thus understood as the grace of legislation. Human rights as such are the child of law.[2] Since human rights are subject to constitutional legitimacy, the normativity of human rights is ipso facto to be trimmed for the ideological preference of the constitution. Consequently, states without making commitment to international human rights treaties are even not to be afraid of human rights deficit or their violation. A state, such as China, argues for collective human rights, especially the rights to development, and merits our deliberation whether the discourse of human rights as teleological and developmental could be justified with respect to accommodate between universalism and localism.

The purpose of this study intends to conduct a conceptual analysis on the methodological issues in human rights discourse and to examine their validity through normative observation. By examining the state of play with regard to human rights localism, looking into its justification and limits, the methodology applied to harmonize universalism with localism may be discoursed.

Other than the 'grand style' of human rights discoursed by universalism, to de-conceptualize human rights for the practical satisfaction of basic needs that encompass those social goods that are essential to human subsistence, such as, food, housing, medical care and security may mean a lot in the deliberation of the duty of government in discharging human rights obligation.[3] Conceptually, there is nothing wrong to treat human rights as 'minor style' of certain basic rights suitable for basic needs especially from the viewpoint of social justice. Human rights are better to serve the practical needs than to talk in vain. There is no point to elaborate the abstract norm of human rights when the basic needs are terribly deficit. Having said that, it will be legitimate for us to deliberate the issue whether it is possible to accommodate between universalism and localism when the latter is supportive of the uncompromising features of Asian perspective of human rights.

International human rights law and China's engagement

Since the establishment of the People's Republic of China in 1949, it has ratified twenty-seven international human rights conventions.[4] Some of its domestic laws are thereafter enacted to the effect of implementing international human rights norms.[5] In accordance with the treaty obligation, China has been proud of abiding by the treaty obligation in submitting their national human rights reports to the relevant treaty organs properly. International human rights norms, in this instance, have the prima facie influence on the development of human rights in China. In the ratification of these human rights conventions, China did not accept all the obligations and made reservations to certain provisions. For example, in the *Convention on the Elimination of All Forms of Discrimination against Women* a reservation was made to Article 29, paragraph 1. Similar reservation was made to Article 22 of the International Convention on the Elimination of All Forms of Racial Discrimination. The two reservations are concerning dispute settlement between contracting parties with respect to the interpretation or application of the Conventions. Other reservations made by it include the following: (1) Articles 20 and 30 (1) of the *Convention against Torture and Other Cruel, Inhuman or Degrading Treatment or Punishment*; (2) Article 6 of the *Convention on the Rights of the Child* and (3) Article 8(1) a of the *International Covenant on Economic, Social and Cultural Rights*.

In accordance with Article 19 of Vienna Convention on the Law of Treaties, States are entitled to make reservation to the treaty if the treaty does not prohibit the reservation, nor the reservation is incompatible with the object and purpose of the treaty. Accordingly, the reservations to those human rights treaties made by China are not illegitimate and lawful. However, it is worth noting that China seems not happy to allow other states to get involved in its 'human rights enterprise',[6] which it regards as very domestic issues and is subject to the principle of non-intervention under UN Charter. One Chinese law professor underlines the principle with a remark as such,

> The prevailing international human rights legal order is not built upon the compulsory basis, rather it is based on the nation states' voluntary accession [to the international human rights treaties] to respect human rights with the spirit of promoting international protection of human rights. That said, nation states' accession to international human rights treaties is an act of sovereignty, therefore, it never exists any institution to make human rights overrides sovereignty.[7]

China is determined to participate in the international arena and to get involved in international affairs; international human rights issues are of course no exception in that regard. However, China has strongly opposed the subordination of sovereignty to international human rights law. From the perspective of conventional paradigm of international law, sovereign states' voluntarism and consent are the normative basis of international law. It is so especially with reference to treaty rules, which are in nature contractual. Paradigmatically, China's position and standpoint are impeccable. For China, though the protection of human rights is the common goal of all humankind, its measures and methods of protection are not to be universalized, rather, they are to be localized following each nation's conditions and social context. Consequently, any criticism on the human rights deficit especially in the area of civil and political rights will be rejected as biased as based on double standards.[8] There is no need to be a relativist or localist; one may easily find that the insufficiency and deficiency in human rights protection in the state of play in international community are not exclusive to China only. Looking into the measure of anti-terrorism in some states, where personal freedom and integrity are seriously damaged and overlooked, the criticism on China's human rights policy and practice is seemingly an application of double standards.[9]

In fact, China is proud of promoting economic and social rights as it has improved the living standard of its populations. On 26 October 1979, the elite *Guangming Daily* posted an editorial, titled 'A Brief Discussion on the Questions of Human Rights'. This is the first time the term 'human rights' appeared in a major Chinese newspaper. Its mentioning of human rights suggested that the propaganda machine decided to confine the nature and scope of the human rights discourse. The editorial argued, since the communist revolution eliminated all types of exploitation and instituted substantive equality in China, it is no longer necessary to emphasize or even to mention the protection of human rights. Human rights as such were treated as remains of the obsolete bourgeois, a parochial conception of Western imperialism. Although human rights discourse may be mobilized instrumentally for China to counter the criticism from the Western states, the article seemed to set the tone and approach of Chinese government to the idea of universal human rights.

The mood swung into action when China issued its National Human Rights Action Plan for 2009–10; it was really an important step and signal in making concrete, public commitments to the protection of human rights. It would, in theory, make it possible to measure progress and hold the government accountable for any shortcomings in human rights. The Action Plan was the first official document as the state's programme aimed at human rights. In the press release issued by the National Congress on the assessment of the Plan, it said, 'This is a solemn commitment of Chinese government in human rights field. It is a significant measure to realize respect and protection of human rights as a constitutional principle, to advance positively scientific development and to promote social stability.'[10]

Going into details of the development in the various human rights topics, under the heading of 'the State of Play as regards Comprehensive Execution,'[11] the report refers to the impact and the threat to the enjoyment of human rights caused by the financial crisis in the year of 2009 to 2010. Then it says that more than ¥40,000 billion were invested into protective measures on housing, the infrastructure of agriculture, livelihood engineering for medical, sanitary and educational enterprises, facilitating railway, highway and airport construction and facilities, accelerating eco-environmental construction, improving the income of suburban residents especially those low-income populations. It leads the world with conspicuous improvement in macroeconomic recovery and the raising of living standards.

Furthermore, it remarks to the progress as insisting in respecting and protecting human rights and assisting scientific development, furthering social cohesion and effectively protecting the rights to equal participation and equal development by the whole memberships of the community. In addition, the report concludes to unite the respect and protection of human rights with the construction of democracy and rule of law, positively and steadily furthering the reform of political system and to protect civil and political rights in accordance with law.

In examining the development in human rights, special emphasis was placed on the aspect of economic rights and more on the collective perspective. It is sensible that the collective rights in terms of development are vital to the realization and enjoyment of human rights;[12] nevertheless, the core value of human rights as a free agent is not so evident in its emphasis on the protection and respect of human rights.

Further to that, the National Human Rights Action Plan for 2012 to 2015 was issued by State Council on 11 June 2012. It signalled the Chinese human rights enterprise has entered into a new phase of planned, continuous and comprehensive development, said the press release.[13] In 2004 the Chinese constitution inserted the provision that the state should respect and protect human rights, since then the respect and protection of human rights were regarded as the fundamental principle of good governance. For the purpose of realizing the constitutional principle, Chinese Government enacted and amended a series of legislation with the idea of constructing a human rights legal system based on socialism of Chinese features.

This period of Action Plan emphasized in the guiding ideology is to promote a more just and harmonious society, and strive to make every member of society to live more dignified and happier. Human rights protection refers not only to enable everyone to survive and develop, to promote socioeconomic development, but also to promote social justice and harmony. As to the most concerned issues in the community such as safety production; adjustment of income distribution pattern; compensation for expropriation of house and land; equalized the public health services; equitable allocation of the resources on food, drugs and safety drinking water; endemic disease control, and education, air quality and pollution control; prohibition of torture and illegal detention; protecting the rights of criminal accused including the right to access lawyer, transparency of government information and public opinion's supervision; preventing gender discrimination and domestic violence, etc. This demonstrates that the Chinese government has the courage to face all kinds of problems in the area of human rights protection and to take positive measures to cope with new challenges.

An important highlight of this Action Plan is its emphasis on dissemination of the concept of human rights in the whole society, knowledge of the universality of human rights. It highlights to integrate human rights education not only into the civil servants training programmes, but also in primary and secondary schools. It intends to create an educational environment that respects human rights.

In light of this, it is hopeful that the 'Action Plan' is really intending to establish the required infrastructure for the seeds of human rights to grow. Nevertheless, with respect to the underdevelopment in establishing the specific indicators and benchmarks to evaluate the progress of human rights, particularly concerning civil and political rights, one may wonder whether the plan could constitute a positive commitment to the prospect of full enjoyment of human rights in China. Further evidence of development is required for us to answer the question.

In fact, China has been accused for violating human rights mostly in several aspects, such as the freedom of speech, religious freedom, torture, discrimination against ethnic minorities. China continues to target activists and their family members with harassment, imprisonment and torture. Even under repeated urges from some Western countries for the release of the Nobel Peace Prize winner Liu Xiaobo from the imprisonment, the Government of China responds that it is for only the 1.3 billion Chinese people have a say on China's human rights.[14] To pardon a person who had a different vision of the idea of human rights and was dissatisfied with the progress of human rights when most people applauded the development of human rights, even in the design of its idiosyncratic mould, could be detrimental to its pride and self-confidence.

Methodological observations of human rights

What are human rights? In the discourse of human rights, the answer entails the issue of methodology inevitably. Any solution to the methodological problem in this concern will conceptualize the proposition, 'what are human rights?' which thereon allow legal officials and practitioners to apprehend, communicate and apply the 'concept' in a non-arbitrary manner in the discourse of the human rights issues internally and externally in international community. Looking into the pattern of social practices in the discourse of human rights, the methodology clearly dichotomizes into universalism and localism or cultural relativism.[15] Universalism, conceptually, refers to the idea of human rights as universalized valid and to be applied in international community with reference to a relevant concept of global governance to that effect. It urges for a universal standards of human rights that are recognizable all over the world. In this regard, the normative contents and the items of human rights as demonstrated in international conventions are to be applied uniformly. If human rights are the entitlements of being a human person, the argument for universalism is without a slightest doubt the necessary conclusion to that effect. The United Nations General Assembly proclaimed the idea of human rights as universally valid in the international community when the Universal Declaration of Human Rights was adopted on 10 December 1948. It has been hailed as an historic event of profound significance as one of the greatest achievements of human civilization and became the International Magna Carta of all mankind.

Human rights are the rights simply for being human, conceptually, they are universal by definition. The discourse of human rights under this method is focusing on the value setting and idea-construction. Accordingly, the concept of human rights is context independent; it is a matter of pure reason. Having said this, one may draw a clear line between universalism and relativism based on the conceptual engagement with the subject matter, whether it is the idea or the content that counts. The idea of human rights deals with the form of human rights and defines the value of human rights as such.

By contrast, while the contents of human rights look into the substantive aspects of human rights, the subject matter is thus context dependent. It refers to the threshold of standards as the ingredients of each right. That said, epistemologically, one who adopts formalism towards international human rights law might be deemed as universalists, properly so-called. The knowledge of human rights is that of 'non-inferentially justified belief'.[16] The idea and even the conceptions of human rights as moral rights are self-evident and should be common to all cultures on earth.[17] Any theorist who may intend to argue for a universally valid human rights regime is appealing to be a foundationalist. In that regard, there may have 'thick' and 'thin' approaches to the non-inferentially justified belief. The former deems that all human rights conceptions and normative contents are universally valid and cannot bear any exceptions in relations to spatial differentiations. By contrast, the latter is of the opinion that even though the idea and value of human rights are of non-inferential belief and valid for all, the normative contents are subject to spatial considerations and can be varied from the perspective of the nature of rights which are not so much of high intensity with the purpose and significance of the agents from the perspective of teleological viewpoint. These categories of rights based on the justified belief of 'common good' that human agents should have the rights in the context of the practical experience in order that something good may bring about.[18] The right to work, the right to education, the right to assembly and association, and the right to marriage life, right to free movement, right to belief and religion, right to cultural identity are the conspicuous examples that satisfy the institutional design and presumptive virtue of the 'grand style' of community life.[19] In this connection, some words that are so familiar to our experience in the management of the political matters and the environment, for example, public participation, free will, equality, are in reality presumptuous elements for those rights to claim their justification. These 'thin' human rights are in nature made up to cure inherent deficit of our practical reasonableness.

By way of contrast, relativism or localism connotes that human rights cannot be universal due to the reality of different social backgrounds and cultural context.[20] In other words, the Western idea of political liberalism should not be taken for granted to be the common concern and value pattern of differentiated communities in the world.[21] Viewing from the distinctive idea of human rights, the contents and standards of human rights are surely to be varied for practical possibilities. Methodologically, the approach to the theory of human rights can be termed as 'realism' or 'pragmatism'. They are not fond of the predetermined presumptions in the understanding of human rights value and standards. Therefore, they prefer the concept of human rights as practical reason to that of pure reason. One thing to be noted is that, without abandoning the value of human rights,[22] though the relativists believe that the concept of human rights is context dependent, it is still functioning as certain value to human society. However, instead of believing in metaphysical articulation of human rights, it urges that it should be elaborated and articulated in terms of national laws and be applied in the form of traditional and societal arrangements, rather than in abstract standards as understood in universalism. Accordingly, the value of human rights in the context of social varieties will be selective and empirical.

In addition, a new form of human rights discourse – human rights irrationalism – is emerging to the effect that urges human rights as nothing but a pennon for some interest-identical group of persons to march off claims sui generis. It is irrational because the rights they claim are strange to the normative theory of rights, which can be deemed as based on rationalism.[23] Naturally, those claims are radical or idiosyncratic to the normal pattern of behaviours and traditional way of life. In that connection, the claim originated from irrationalism includes but not limited to those rights sui generis, namely the right to die, same sex rights to family life, right to discriminate, right to work as a slave,[24] right to trade one's body[25] or organs, freedom to use personal body, for example prostitution.

The development of such claims rights entails our attention in the discourse of human rights even without this affecting our discussion of methodology.

Following from that, the different approach or discourse of human rights may change the appearance, contents and even the concept of human rights. Human rights, therefore, as a protean-faced concept is thus recognized.[26] The absence of a proper theory of human rights is of course a factor in that connection.[27] Recalling that the dignity of human beings appeared in the first Article of the Universal Declaration of Human might serve as the core value to that effect, the concept of dignity as applied in the constitutional interpretation in domestic legal systems is varied and carries with different contents.[28] Bearing that in mind, human rights perhaps agreed in words but not in reality is because we are still not fully equipped to answer the question, 'What are human rights?' Accordingly, the analysis of the above theories of human rights is, of course, not evaluative, rather, it is descriptive as a reflection of the state of play in the world community.[29]

Justification for localism and its limits

Cultural relativists view universal rights as insensitive to cultural differences and, if the cultural differences admitted, the criteria used to evaluate the difference with respect to the standard set forth by the universal human rights are biased.[30] As one pointed out, 'Human rights law is committed to setting universal standards using legal rationality, yet this stance impedes adapting those standards to the particulars of local context. ... Those who resist human rights often claim to defending culture.'[31] In this connection, the idea of universality of human rights is a tool for justificatory interference with other states' domestic affairs. Some Asian developing states therefore call the human rights doctrine a new form of Western imperialism. However, other than the methodological approach to the relativist of human rights, what is the focal point of the Asian argumentation for localism? Alternatively, are there practical reasons for developing states in Asia to claim for localism? Are there any justificatory grounds that localism could be accommodated with universalism, if the latter is the right thesis in deliberating human rights?

Practically, Asian states are eager to catch up the movement of modernization and the tide of globalization, in that connection, economic development becomes the most urgent target to aim at. Rephrasing economic development as purely the course of pursing economic profits and growth,[32] policy maker will exclude and wipe out those hurdles that have adverse effects or do not contribute positively to that effect. Right to development or economic development is not ipso facto contrary to the protection of human rights; on the contrary, it is the basis in the construction of human rights with respect to the basic needs of human persons.[33] Since economic development is understood as equivalent as to economic growth, it becomes pragmatist and consequentialist. From the perspective of economic growth/development, human rights will thus be arranged and classified vis-à-vis their relative weight and contribution to economic growth/development. As a result, the utilitarian formula 'the greatest happiness of the greatest number' constitutes the golden rule in the implementation of human rights. Apparently, the underlying philosophy for such an economic growth/development is much on realism and pragmatism, rather than on humanism and idealism.[34] When economic growth/development is processing in pragmatic terms as for the competitive power of growth of certain industries vis-à-vis the world economy, it could make the vulnerable groups less protected and treated even unfavourably. The core value of economic growth/development that aims at the constant improvement of the well-being of the entire population and of all individuals will thus be missing. The argumentation that human right violations are unavoidable in the process of development explains the case. Asian states, therefore, argue that the level of development should be taken into account in evaluating the scope of satisfaction of human rights.

The ASEAN Human Rights Declaration (AHRD) adopted at the 21st Summit of ASEAN in Phnom Penh in November 2012 by the ten member states was hailed by some as a landmark development, 'a legacy for our children', said the Philippine Foreign Secretary Albert del Rosario. It reaffirmed their commitment to the Universal Declaration of Human Rights (UDHR), the *Charter* of the United Nations, the Vienna Declaration and Programme of Action, and other international human rights instruments to which ASEAN Member States are parties. They state their view of the interdependence and indivisibility of human rights and stressed the need for universality, objectivity and non-selectivity of human rights. All human rights and fundamental freedoms in this Declaration must be treated in a fair and equal manner, on the same footing and with the same emphasis. However, they also emphasize that the realization of human rights must be considered in the regional and national context bearing in mind different political, economic, legal, social, cultural, historical and religious backgrounds. Localism and cultural relativism are thus reaffirmed.

Though not overlooking the value of human rights, it is trimmed for the purpose and object of Asian prospect. In this regard, human rights are not at the core of governance; rather, they tend to compromise with security and the so-called development. The value of human rights to that effect is practical and experimental and inferential from the perspective of domestic legal order. Principle 6 as such demonstrates the regionalism, rather than the universality, of human rights by stating, 'Tthe enjoyment of human rights and fundamental freedoms must be balanced with the performance of corresponding duties as every person has responsibilities to all other individuals, the community and the society where one lives.' Seemingly, only the 'good citizen' who have fulfilled their duty as per the community or state, they are endowed with the rights. Under the heading of Asian particularism, the validity of human rights is not non-inferential, and in the discourse of human rights, it is to be determined and recognized by the domestic legal system with respect to the 'internal point of view'.[35] As one correctly pointed out, 'Human-rights culture, even as normatively thin, remains a cultural particularism.'[36]

In practice, some difficulties inherent in the application of universal human rights norms in culturally diverse societies, such as China, are recognized in the Vienna Declaration, which, while affirming the ultimate goal of universal protection, makes clear that

> while the significance of national and regional particularities and various historical, cultural and religious backgrounds must be borne in mind, it is the duty of States, regardless of their political, economic and cultural systems, to promote and protect all human rights and fundamental freedoms.[37]

What does it mean that the significance of national and regional particularities and various historical, cultural and religious backgrounds must be borne in mind when all states are to discharge their duty to protect human rights and fundamental freedoms? Does the reminder imply that the substantive contents of human rights, rather than the concept of human rights should be the focal points in the construction of human rights protection? If it is referring to the substantive contents of human rights, then there is no any awkward situation for all states to discharge their duties to protect human rights with a protean face. There is no such thing as violation of human rights vis-à-vis their domestic legal regimes. The extent and scope of the protection and enjoyment of human rights are to be assessed with respect to domestic legal regimes rather than international human rights norms. This is the position of the orthodoxy of cultural relativism or localism. Human rights as culture denote the contents of rights, rather than the concept of rights.

Conversely, if the situation is in the conceptual analysis of human rights, the justification for localism is also at ease with no awkward problems. The discourse that human rights are rights to have simply as a human being and from this premises that the universality of human rights is valid in any legal systems. This is the traditional orthodoxy of human rights universalism. The features of the form of universalized human rights are cognizable as follows. Human rights are claim rights of individuals that all human persons possess 'independently of their sociopolitical affiliations'[38] and that entail transnational obligations addressed to all states. In this connection, one correctly pointed out, if human rights are considered to be universally valid, they must be systematically independent not only of particular ideals of sociopolitical institutions, but also of any form of special sociopolitical bonds or other reciprocal relations.[39] In other words, sociopolitical institutions as the primary sphere of practical significance for human rights are to be excluded from the interpretation of human rights; in other words, there is no conceptual link between the concept of human rights and institutional arrangements.[40] In this sense, 'human rights either protect pre-social and pre-conventional values that enable persons to enjoy further social and political rights, or they promote properties that are necessary for human agency or are essential characteristics of human agency.'[41]

Explained as such, human rights to be universally valid must be on the premises that the concept of human rights is pre-conventional and pre-social. That said, the statement that the universal validity of human rights is founded on international human rights agreements is thus dubious with respect to the normative analysis of the treaty obligation. Since treaty by itself is not law as such, the obligation originated from such an international treaty is not transnational or supranational in relation to its legal effect. The treaty may be an instrument in which the law is stated, but it is not itself the law.[42] Therefore, the general rule of treaty obligation is known by the maxim *pacta tertiis nec nocent prosunt*. The urge for transnational obligation upon states to protect human rights as a form of universalism is therefore groundless and doubtful, unless the relevant and specific obligation is originated from customary international law or peremptory norm, *jus cogens*, which is non-derogable. Some rules of international human rights law, for example torture, slavery and genocide are of the characteristic of *jus cogens* and generally recognized as such.[43]

Consequently, before we can all agree that international human rights law has the effect of general rules of international law and carries with it the legitimate authority universally;[44] conceptually, the argument of human rights localism can be justified.

As mentioned earlier, in China, human rights are internalized as constitutional rights subject to constitutional law. Hence, human rights are not different from other legal rights in terms of their statutory force. To constitutionalize human rights could make them more culture sensitive. 'Constitutional rights are rights that have been recorded in a constitution with the intention of transforming human rights into positive law – the intention, in other words, of positivizing human rights',[45] opined Alexey. In this connection, the underlying concept of human rights is positivistic, rather that idealistic, or naturalistic and the outcry for the positivistic approach to human rights is strongly on localism of human rights. Localizing the standards of human rights is taking a strong lead in human rights advocacy in Asian elites, especially from the perspective of materialism in an autocratic society such as China.[46]

In a sense, to institutionalize human rights with legal force is beneficial to the implementation of the rights. After all, states are the sole duty-bearer to fulfil their obligation to protect human rights. Therefore, to internalize human rights into domestic legal system is the warrant for the realization of enjoyment of human rights. However, in the incorporation of international human rights norm into domestic legal system and thus to localize human rights is not at odds with the concept of human rights obligation as mentioned above. In this connection, whether there is any limit on the justification of human rights localism? Alternatively, even if human rights localism can be justified due to the theoretical deficiency of international law in the normative analysis of treaty obligation, does it have the legitimacy to be sustained?

The case of China demonstrates that a deficit of legitimacy for localism can be detrimental to the realization of human rights. The Chinese government suppresses however local human rights deliberation efforts. During its preparatory work in drawing the National Human Rights Plan in 2008, it arrested several active dissidents led by Xiaobo Liu, who drafted 'The Charter 08' on the World Human Rights Day (10 December) and called for significant political reform in China. Liu was detained later and charged with a crime of inciting subversion. On 23 June 2009, he was officially arrested and sentenced to eleven years of imprisonment for infringing national security under Section 105(1) of the Criminal Code on 25 December 2009.

Based on the conviction that international human rights as conventional rights devoid of general application, they are subject to sovereign will and its commitment, in this sense, to curb the fundamental freedoms of conscience and expression of its citizens is not a surprise. For human rights localism, the contents and standard are inevitably varied vis-à-vis different situations and conditions of societies. That said, localism could be by default cynical to the full protection of human rights with respect to international human rights norms.

Considering the possible loss of legitimacy, constitutional interpretation of human rights, therefore, should resort to international human rights law lest human rights localism becomes too thick to accommodate to universalism. The constitution law of South Africa demonstrates the case.[47] In the interpretation of the rights in the Bill of Rights, Section 39(1) provides:

> When interpreting the Bill of Rights, a court, tribunal or forum – (a) must promote the values that underlie an open and democratic society based on human dignity, equality and freedom; (b) must consider international law; and (c) may consider foreign law.

The once debate between universalist and particularist was eventually phased out by the Constitution. The Constitution also secures and strengthens an influential role for international law by section 233, which gives constitutional effect to the interpretive presumption of compliance of national legislation with international law: 'When interpreting any legislation, every court must prefer any reasonable interpretation of the legislation that is consistent with international law over any alternative interpretation that is inconsistent with international law.'

The peremptory terms of the provision relating to international law provides a clear message to the courts that in interpreting the rights of the Bill of Rights the legitimate authority dwells in international human rights regime.

Localized human rights may have its reason from the internal point of view of a domestic legal order. From the perspective of outsiders, however, especially with a presupposed viewpoint of the universally valid concept of human rights, localized human rights is but an excuse for political purpose and could be used as a defence to the infringement of human rights.[48] The reasons for more culturally relative human right doctrine in order to promote and safeguard their cultural differences and characteristics are, in fact, doubtful and unjustified when in China and some Asian countries cultural relativism is not used to justify the cause, but rather to justify the suppression on those who are in defiant to the regimes.[49]

Conclusion: Possible (or impossible) harmonization

What are human rights? Why are the rights with an adjective 'human' so important as to be different from other rights? Arguments in favour of assigning a special legal status to human rights normally either base on the ground that human rights have some inherent values merit special protection, or advocate that human rights are valid universally, 'all-inclusive, systemic context: the world, global justice, and international law'.[50] They are rights that all persons have and that apply to all human beings. The statement that some individual claim rights can be qualified as human rights, one has to demonstrate the features which make human rights with the status of specificity as compared to other individual claim rights, or what makes them 'universal' or 'inalienable' as to be compatible with the meta-ethical constructivism.[51]

Or put it other way round, what are the values that deserve to justify the primacy of human rights over legal rights and social values? Are those values morally incontestable in the context of value pluralism?[52] To argue for moral values of human rights discourse could as a result invite the engagement of localism or relativism on the contestability of value monism. In arguing for the universality of human rights, one therefore correctly points out that they are not functioning as 'moral trumps' as opposed to other weighty moral concerns.[53]

As we have pointed out earlier, from the perspective of conceptual analysis of human rights and some related theory of international law, universalism fails to provide a satisfactory normative basis for universally valid human rights to be justiciable in domestic courts. To justify the priority of human rights over ordinary legal rights calls for normative justification. However, the truth is not so, as one pointed out correctly, 'contemporary human rights system and much of the thinking underlying them ultimately lack both a normative foundation as well as conceptual certainty'.[54] It seems that there exists an insurmountable gap between ideas and practices of human rights.[55] In other words, the orthodoxy of universalism is nothing but nominal, rather than real. By contrast, localism though downgrades the value of human rights; nevertheless, it generates the validity of human rights in the context of a legal regime.

Having said that, how can we accommodate localism to universalism or vice versa, if necessary? Universalism has conceptual flaw but is helpful in the discourse of human rights protection in a global context. One correctly pointed out, 'The acceptance of human rights in politics has provoked major changes in the political thinking and behaviour of both rulers and the ruled, and in so doing has left its imprint on human rights theory and practice.'[56] Localism, however, not only has semantic fallacy but also is inadequate for the full protection of human rights if the authority concerned disregards the substantive values that are supportive of democratic legitimacy.[57]

Since both approaches are devoid of a satisfactory construction of the concept of human rights, we are obliged to review which flaw is easier to amend so as to restore the normative legitimacy to human rights norms. Two possible prescriptions may be available to cure the conceptual disease: normative and structural.

If human rights are to be valid as claim rights, they are to live in a definite regime.[58] That said, 'validity' implies the justification of rules when individual claim rights are envisaged.[59] In this connection, human rights are valid only as conventional rights where an international human rights regime is established to validate the rights. So while civil and political rights can be enforced under the regime of the European Convention on Human rights by way of application to the European Court of Human Rights, the indivisible economic and cultural rights are without such effects.[60]

Following from that, conceptually, human rights to be universally valid are not to be deemed as claim rights that are valid only in a definite legal regime, but rather as moral rights, which 'belong exclusively to the ideal dimension of law'. Therefore, Alexey opined,

> 'The validity of human rights qua moral rights depends on their justifiability and on that alone. Thus, human rights exist if they are justifiable. Now, human rights are justifiable on the basis of discourse theory, for the practice of asserting, asking, and arguing presupposes freedom and equality, and the ideas of freedom and equality imply, together with further premises that can be well established, human rights. Human rights, therefore, are discursively necessary.'[61] For Alexey, the transformation of human rights into constitutional rights, namely into positive rights, 'represents the efforts to connect the ideal with the real dimension.'[62]

Human rights can have universal validity is on the ground that they are justified on their own. They are independent from political institutions and conventional arrangements, and, in this sense, they are universally valid. As one correctly pointed out, 'Human rights can be understood to refer not to the source of rights but to those who possess them, the basis of such universal (human) rights being left comfortably unclear. The important point is that all human beings possess the rights, so that the enquiry can cross national boundaries.'[63]

This is the case of universalism. Since they are not rights qua claim rights, they avoid being drawn into the controversy of validity with respect to their conceptual flaws.

Human rights qua moral rights, structurally, are thus construed as 'a standard of legitimacy for sociopolitical and legal institutions'.[64] To conceive human rights as standards is to allocate human rights in the position of secondary-order norms that justify the primary-order rules. In this sense, 'human rights' are conceived of as secondary norms, which articulate general standards of 'rightness'.[65] Human rights are 'discursive rationality' if and only if we are to live in a society in which a handful of postulates are posited. Human rights are thus the standards originated from those postulates. Having said that, the question, 'How can accommodation be made between universalism and localism?' is to be answered on the premises whether human development is developed into a more 'human' prospect. If the answer is positive, human rights localism should accommodate itself to universalism vis-à-vis the international standards and construe them as moral rights. If negative, human rights universalism with the inherent deficit of conceptual flaw is to lose their justification for human rights protection systematically and coherently. As a result, their normative legitimacy is losing simultaneously. In that case, to accommodate human rights universalism to localism is thus required lest the human rights protection worsens. In other words, to constitutionalize or localize human rights standards can serve as parameters to evaluate the scope and extent of bad governance and as justificatory tool to rectify the authority of the rulers. Perhaps, this is what the idea of human rights really counts.

Notes

1. Be careful the idea should not be easily assimilated with the institution of majoritarianism which implies the static and formalistic institution of democracy. Rather, democracy should have the substantive elements of mutual trust and dialogue between or among different interested groups. See also Dworkin (2008).
2. See Weston (1992) in Steiner, Alston and Goodman (2008: 478).
3. Claude and Weston (2006: 161–9).
4. Among the eight core human rights treaties of the UN, the PRC signed the International Covenant on Civil and Political Rights but yet ratified it. Among those core treaties, the PRC neither signed nor ratified the International Convention on the Protection of the Rights of All Migrant Workers and Members of Their Families.
5. One of the significant enactments is the Labor Contract Law, in which some labour standards and rights as comparable to that of international labour standards of ILO are promulgated in 2007 and operative from 1 January 2008.
6. The phrase 'human rights enterprise' appears in the assessment report on the National Human Rights Action Plan for 2009–10 that refers to all measures concerning the protection and enjoyment of human rights, for example, legislations, research, discourse.
7. Jihong (2005: 231). See also Yunlong (1998: 131, 191–5). (author's translation).
8. Inaugural speech given by Mr Lo Howtsi, director, Chinese Association for Human Rights Research at the Beijing Human Rights Forum 2008. (author's translation).
9. Peerenboom (2004).
10. Assessment Report on National Human Rights Action Plan for 2009–10, National Congress, press office, People's Republic of China. Available at http://big5.xinhuane t.com/gate/big5/news.xinhuanet.com/2011-07/14/c_121665648.htm
11. Ibid.
12. Claude and Weston (2006: 164–6).
13. Available at http://politics.people.com.cn/BIG5/70731/18145384.html
14. Ruz, Human rights: What is China accused of?
15. Particularism is sometimes used to identify the phenomenal characteristic of a culture as opposed to the mainstream of cultural pattern. See Gregg (2010).

16 James W. Nickel and David A. Reidy, Philosophy, collected in Moeckli, Shah and Sivakumaran (2010: 43).
17 Ibid. pp. 43–4.
18 The focal analysis of human dignity in international (human rights) law may demonstrate the case. See Capps (2010: 106–25).
19 Capps (2010: 80–2).
20 As the UN drafted a Universal Declaration of Human Rights in 1947, the American Anthropological Association (AAA), however, disputed the notion of rights valid across all cultural boundaries when the cultural differences are vital to the understanding of the value and contents of human rights. For the AAA, 'what is held to be a human right in one society may be regarded as anti-social by another people, or by the same people in a different period of their history'. Apparently, the statement is based on some a priori assumptions: that any rights-claim is necessarily a cultural claim; and that cultural 'validity' can only be local because no single cultural system is universally embraced. Accordingly, since all rights are cultural context, then no right is culture free. Interestingly, fifty years on, it changed its position. It now claims that every person, regardless of native culture or local community, does indeed possess universal rights simply as humans, regardless of differences among human cultures so intriguingly significant as to justify a discipline of cultural anthropology. American Anthropologist Association, Statement on Human Rights, 49 American Anthropologist 539 (1947), collected in Steiner, Alston and Goodman (2008: 528–30).
21 Donnelly (2003: 107–23), Hatch (1983: 8).
22 Realists may be sceptical, but they are definitely not radical or critically nihilistic. Realists may be sceptical but they are definitely not radical or critically nihilistic. Cf. McCoubrey and White (1999: 203).
23 The Statue of Council of Europe in its preamble reaffirms their devotion to the spiritual and moral values, which are construed as the cumulative influence of Greek philosophy, Roman law, the Western Christian Church, the humanism of the Renaissance and the French Revolution are the sources of the rationalism. See Robertson (1961: 2), in Steven Greer, Europe, collected in Moeckli, Shah and Sivakumaran (2010: 457). The Universal Declaration of Human Rights, Article 1, 'All human beings are born free and equal in dignity and rights. They are endowed with reason and conscience and should act towards one another in a spirit of brotherhood', also demonstrates the case.
24 Migrant workers, sometimes, 'voluntarily' waive their rights in order to seek a job in the workplace may have the impression to claim the right to be treated discriminately.
25 In a constitutional interpretation (No. 666) in Taiwan, a Grand Justice in her separate opinion arguing for the right to trade human body has the effect of relying the irrationalism of human rights. Based on the premises that sex freedom is part of personal liberty, hence, sex as an object, for example a commodity, for transaction, is not as having equivalent effect to trade for human person because the body used for transaction as sex object is still under the control of the human person's free will. The argument, it seems, wrongly ignored that the sex transaction, a form of contract, even invalid on the ground of public morality, entails the buyer to use and control the human body, in this regard, the human person's free will surely can refuse to offer sex to the buyer by means of breaching the contract. Consequently, to separate the human body from the human person for the purpose of sex transaction is not a valid argument for defending personal liberty and human dignity. Available at http://jirs.jud icial.gov.tw/ENG/CETransfer.asp?goto=c&datatype=c02&code=666

26 Teng (2011).

27 See Raz (2007).

28 McCrudden (2008).

29 The percentage of each approach in Taiwan is too early to tell without a proper survey in that regard; however, the composing member of the distinctive approaches demonstrates roughly as such, the academics inclined to adopt universalism, the politician prefers relativism or localism, and the NGO's or human rights advocates favour irrationalism.

30 Merry (2008: 524–7).

31 Merry (2008: 524–5).

32 Conceptually, economic development is a matter to be differentiated from economic growth and profits even they are closely related. Considering that economic development an indispensable component of the development of comprehensive prospect that may include social, cultural and political process, which aim at the constant improvement of the well-being of the entire population and of all individuals, economic development is surely for the full realization of human rights. See General Assembly resolution, Declaration on the Right to Development, A/RES/41/128 (4 December 1986)

33 Thomas Pogge, Recognized and Violated by International Law: The Human Rights of the Global Poor, available at http://www2.ohchr.org/english/issues/poverty/expert/docs/Thomas_Pogge_new.pdf

34 Philosophically, Confucianism is a genuine philosophy of humanism. The teaching and doctrine are all devoted to the full grown of human persons within the community. In this sense, it is teleological in that each normative agent will live by the natural law to the full development of his personality. Alternatively, it is relational rather than egoistic as regards the perfection of being can only be accomplished in the state of harmonious relationship, whether mutually or collectively. China strongly advocates human rights as collective rights, instead of individual rights, may be inspired by the chronically error of Confucianism instead of the true grit of Confucius.

35 Hart (1997: 89).

36 Gregg (2010: 289, 297).

37 Vienna Declaration and Programme of Action, United Nations General Assembly, UN Doc. A/CONF.157/23 (12 July 1993) paragraph 5.

38 Griffin (2008: 50).

39 Griffin (2008: 50).

40 Griffin (2008: 50)

41 Griffin (2008: 51).

42 Fitzmaurice, Some Problems Regarding the Formal Sources of International Law (1958) collected in Harris (2010: 35).

43 *Filartiga v. Pena-Irala*, 630 F. 2d. 876 (1980); (1980) 19 I.L.M. 966; Case of *Al-Adsani v. The United Kingdom*, Application no. 35763/97, Judgment, 21 November 2001.

44 The concept of legitimate authority based on service conception clarified and defended by Joseph Raz can be found in his article, 'The Problem of Authority: Revisiting the Service Conception', available at http://ssrn.com/abstract=999849

45 Alexey (2010: 167, 178).

46 However, it may be incorrect to conclude that positivistic approach in the discourse of human rights must be based on materialism. Nevertheless, positivistic approach to human rights will lead to relativistic discourse of human rights necessarily.

47 Grant (2006).

48 Charlesworth and Chinkin (2000: 222).

49 Asian Human Rights Charter, formally declared on 17 May 1998 in the city of Kwangju in South Korea on 14 to 18 May, clearly stated that the claim of 'Asian Values' is but a smokescreen for their authoritarianism. 'Authoritarianism has in many states been raised to the level of national ideology, with the deprivation of the rights and freedoms of their citizens, which are denounced as foreign ideas inappropriate to the religious and cultural traditions of Asia. Instead there is the exhortation of spurious theories of "Asian Values" which are a thin disguise for their authoritarianism'. See Background to the Charter, recital 1.5.

50 Chwaszcza (2010).

51 Chwaszcza (2010: 340).

52 Beck (2008: 312; 316–25).

53 James W. Nickel and David A. Reidy, Philosophy, collected in Moeckli, Shah and Sivakumaran (2010: 55). Nevertheless, human rights without moral convictions or concerns might eventually slip into the camp of realist or even that of irrationalism. For Feinberg, moral rights seem to be less valuable than legal rights, since they are validly claim them as effectively as legal rights. Chwaszcza (2010: 337).

54 Beck (2008: 313).

55 The question, 'why is there such a gap?' may invoke two different approaches of criticisms on the concept of human rights, practical and conceptual critiques. Critiques as such are an either to show that human rights fail to live up to the theory, as they are not true to their words or to despise them as constructed on false or flawed premises. See Marie-Benedicte Dembour, Critiques, collected in Moeckli, Shah and Sivakumaran (2010: 65).

56 Julie Mertus, politics, collected in Moeckli, Shah and Sivakumaran (2010: 88).

57 It is not our concern here to discuss the issue whether democracy should have with it some substantive values as opined by Pope John Paul II addressed to the Polish Parliament ('Sejm'). He argued that 'as history demonstrates a democracy without values easily turns into open or thinly disguised totalitarianism'. Paul II, (1999), part 5, cited by Sadurski (2006: 377; 392).

58 Normally, this is an issue concerning the theory of the sources of law, whether national or international. When a legal rule can be identified in a legal regime, then it is valid to that effect. Strictly, only the formal sources of law have the justificatory power to justify a legal rule as valid. Other than the formal source, material or substantive sources, namely public morality, ethical convictions, custom, are working as supportive evidence to identify a legal rule its validity. Moral rights thus differ from legal rights primarily with respect to the type of source. Chwaszcza (2010: 337). See also Hart (1997: 98–110).

59 Chwaszcza (2010: 337).

60 Campbell, Ewing and Tomkins (2011: 2).

61 Alexey (2010: 172). The discourse theory explained by him as 'discourse theory is a procedural theory of practical rationality. According to discourse theory, a practical or normative proposition is correct (or true) if and only if it can be the result of a rational practical discourse. The conditions of discursive rationality can be made explicit by means of a system of principles, rules, and forms of general practical discourse. This system comprises rules that demand non-contradiction, clarity of language, reliability of empirical premises, and sincerity, as well as rules and forms that speak to the consequences, and to balancing, universalizability, and the genesis of

normative convictions. The procedural core consists of rules that guarantee freedom and equality in discourse by granting to everyone the right to participate in discourse and the right to question as well as to defend any and all assertions.' (footnotes omitted) Alexey (2010: 172).

62   Alexy (2010: 178).
63   Weinreb (1992: 279–80), cited in Chwaszcza (2010: 335).
64   Chwaszcza (2010).
65   Chwaszcza (2010: 335).

Bibliography

Alexey, Robert, 'The Dual Nature of Law', *Ratio Juris*, 23 (2) (2010).

Beck, Gunnar, 'The Mythology of Human Rights', *Ratio Juris*, 21 (3) (2008), pp. 312–47.

Campbell, Tom, K. D. Ewing and Adam Tomkins (ed.), *The Legal Protection of Human Rights: Sceptical Essays* (Oxford: Oxford UP, 2011).

Capps, Patrick, *Human Dignity and the Foundations of International Law* (Portland: Hart Publishing, 2010).

Charlesworth, H. and C. Chinkin, *The Boundaries of International Law: A Feminist Analysis* (Manchester: Juris Publishing, Inc., 2000).

Chwaszcza, Christine, 'The Concept of Rights in Contemporary Human Rights Discourse', *Ratio Juris*, 23(3) (2010), pp. 333-364.

Claude, Richard Pierre and Burns H. Weston (ed.), *Human Rights in the World Community: Issues and Action*, 3rd ed. (Philadelphia: University of Pennsylvania Press, 2006).

Donnelly, Jack, *Universal Human Rights in Theory and Practice* (Ithaca: Cornell UP, 2003).

Dworkin, Ronald, *Is Democracy Possible Here? Principles for a New Political Debate*, Ch. 5, 'Is Democracy Possible' (Princeton: Princeton UP, 2008).

Grant, Evadné, 'Human Rights, Cultural Diversity and Customary Law in South Africa', *Journal of African Law* 50 (2006), pp. 2–23.

Gregg, Benjamin, 'Anti-Imperialism: Generating Universal Human Rights out of Local Norms', *Ratio Juris*, 23 (3) (September 2010), pp. 289–310.

Griffin, James, *On Human Rights* (Oxford: Oxford UP, 2008).

Harris, David, *Cases and Materials on International Law*, 7th ed. (London: Sweet & Maxwell, 2010).

Hart, H. L. A., *The Concept of Law*, 2nd ed. (Oxford: Oxford UP, 1997).

Hatch, Elvin, *Culture and Morality: The Relativity of Values in Anthropology* (New York: Columbia UP, 1983).

Jihong, Mo, *International Conventions on Human Rights and China* (Beijing: International Issues Books Publisher, 2005).

McCoubrey, H. and Nigel D. White, *Textbook on Jurisprudence* (Oxford: Oxford UP, 1999).

McCrudden, Christopher, 'Human Dignity and Judicial Interpretation of Human Rights', *EJIL* 19 (2008), pp. 655–724.

Merry, Sally Engle, 'Human Rights and Gender Violence, Ch. 1, Culture and Transnationalism', collected in Henry J. Steiner, Philip Alston and Ryan Goodman, *International Human Rights in Context: Law, Politics, Morals*. 3rd ed. (2008), pp. 524–27.

Moeckli, Daniel, Sangeeta Shah and Sandesh Sivakumaran, *International Human Rights Law* (Oxford: Oxford UP, 2010).

Paul II, John, 'Address to the Polish Parliament', 11 June (1999). Available at http://www.vatican.va/holy_father/ john_paul_ii/travels/documents/hf_jp-ii_spe_11061999_warsaw-parliament_en.html.

Peerenboom, Randall P., *Assessing Human Rights in China: Why the Double Standard?* The Berkeley Electronic Press (bepress), Legal Series (2004) Working Paper 336. Available at http://law.bepress.com/expresso/eps/336

Raz, Joseph, *Human Rights Without Foundations*, University of Oxford Faculty of Law Legal Studies Research Paper Series, Working Paper No. 14/2007.

Robertson, A. H., *The Council of Europe: Its Structure, Functions and Achievements* (London: Stevens & Sons, 1961).

Ruz, Camila, 'Human Rights: What Is China accused of?' *BBC News Magazine*. Available at www.bbc.com/news/magazine-34592336.

Teng, Yean-Sen, 'A Protean-Face of Human Rights in Taiwan', *International Law Association Asia-Pacific Regional Conference*, Taipei, 31 May (2011).

Sadurski, Wojcieech, 'Law's Legitimacy and "Democracy-Plus"', *OJLS*, 26 (2) (2006).

Steiner, Henry J., Philip Alston and Ryan Goodman, *International Human Rights in Context: Law, Politics, Morals*. 3rd ed. (Oxford: Oxford UP, 2008).

Weinreb, Lloyd, *Natural Law and Rights, in Natural Law Theory: Contemporary Essays*, Robert P. George (ed.) (Oxford: Oxford UP, 1992).

Weston, Burns, *Human Rights, 20 New Encyclopedia Britannica*. 15th ed. (Chicago: Britannica Group, 1992).

Yunlong, Li, *Nutshell on Human Rights Issues* (Chengdu: Suchun Renming Publisher, 1998).

7

Realizing the Chinese Dream beyond China

A prospect connecting the domestic dimension with the international one

Miao-ling Lin Hasenkamp

Part 1 has highlighted that China's governance reforms at home and the allure of autocracy beyond the region have a twilight character. China's authoritarian capitalism has been unique in transforming an autarchic agricultural society into an important buffer for the global economy, albeit serious problems of corruption (see Chapter 5). But it is not a normal economy with open markets, free individual choices and social mobility. Instead, the CCP party-state regime has been successful in controlling the economic and social life of its people with skilful propaganda tools, thereby justifying and reinforcing its legitimacy of political reign. During the reform era, China experienced several phases of allowing concurring voices for the discussion of possible reform models while tackling economic and financial malaise and social unrest (see Chapter 2). The changing understanding of rule of law at the CCP elite level has further facilitated the emergence of an environment of individual legal action through such channels as Administrative Litigation courts (see Chapter 4). At the same time, the transformation of collective elite rule towards one-man rule under Xi's leadership has revealed the instability of the Chinese political system which has been constantly subject to fierce power struggle between different factions. Ultimately, Xi's move towards a one-man leadership paradoxically proves to be both a necessary survival strategy in saving a corrupt regime and a destabilizing force for the CCP while enhancing its repressive rule throughout the country (Chapter 2).

With the spread of Xi-ism found in the absolute loyalty of state media, local governments and business to follow Xi's leadership, the Chinese people see no other choice than consume what the government wants them to read, to watch, and to believe (Chapter 3). The study of career mobility of the provincial chiefs shows that by controlling the propagandists' careers and their work, the CCP has installed powerful mechanisms for social control. Furthermore, the comprehensive double-edged anti-corruption campaign in the midst of vigorous governance reforms as well as the localization discourse of human rights have marked CCP's tactic political efforts in tackling social discontent towards corruption and deterring the diffusion power of international norms (i.e. the rule of law, anti-corruption and human rights norms, see Chapters 4–6). If the Chinese model tells unambiguously a successful story of countering Western influence and presenting an alternative development model with its autocracy, several questions inevitably come to the foreground: What motivates China to become great? Has China already begun to engage the world? If yes, what are its strategies and tools? Is China in the zenith of its long march towards political and technological supremacy?

China Dream between aspiration and reality

From 2013 onward, international politics has seen some new propaganda storm and several important events in re-shaping geopolitical and economic relations in the international system: notably President Xi's inaugural presidential speech in referring to 'the China Dream' in March 2013 and the launching of the offensive (One) Belt and (One) Road Initiative (OBOR or BRI) in linking Eurasia and African regions (discussions about BRI see also Chapter 2 'The prospect of democracy in China'; Chapter 9 'India and China: Overcoming the great wall of mistrust'; Chapter 11 'China in sub-Saharan Africa: Implications for democracy promotion'; and section 'China's Autocracy and Its Political Influence: Is the Deepening of Authoritarianism Inevitable?' in Chapter 12); the damaging US–China trade disputes and tensions since 2018; and China's ambition to lead in advanced industries ranging from 5G technology, artificial intelligence (AI), to biotechnology and quantum computing.

In his first address to the nation as head of state on 12 March 2013, Xi mentioned the term 'the China Dream' several times which is regarded as a guideline for the realization of the Chinese road:

> We must make persistent efforts, press ahead with indomitable will, continue to push forward the great cause of socialism with Chinese characteristics, and strive to achieve the Chinese dream of great rejuvenation of the Chinese nation. … To realise the Chinese road, we must spread the Chinese spirit, which combines the spirit of the nation with patriotism as the core and the spirit of the time with reform and innovation as the core.[1]

While Xi did not explicitly explain what 'the China Dream' means, observers share the opinion that Xi's vision of 'the China Dream' is to liberate China from the past humiliation and to make China a strong nation again with a strong military and technology. The Chinese Dream pursues objectives with a twin set of goals: 'to create a well-off society by 2020 and to achieve rejuvenation of the Chinese nation by 2050 via national rejuvenation and socialist modernization'.[2] Xi's ambition to make China great again is not new in the CCP's leadership legacy. As noted by Julian Gewirtz, in the midst of China's long march towards technological supremacy, Xi builds up the framework defined by his predecessors which sees technological progress both as a means to economic and military prowess as well as 'an ideological end in itself – offering final proof of China's restoration as a great power' after decades of humiliation.[3]

Later, BRI was introduced to serve as a roadmap in realizing the Chinese Dream. BRI proves to be a powerful economic and foreign policy strategy. It consists of two major routes – one overland and one maritime involving the building of six major economic cooperation corridors and several key maritime pivot points across Eurasia, the Indian Ocean, Africa and Oceania. In March 2015, China issued a BRI action plan which has been coordinated by the National Development and Reform Commission in close cooperation with the Ministries of Foreign Affairs and Commerce. In funding the initiative, besides China's policy banks which have provided massive funds for Chinese enterprises to operate along the axes, the Asian Infrastructure Investment Bank (AIIB) was established for the initiative, funded by countries globally. Through BRI, China obviously intends to create a facilitating environment for exercising its political and economic influences, globally and regionally, in the following respects: (1) Renminbi is expected to become the main trading and investment currency in new OBOR markets for facilitating the expansion of the Chinese banks that shall serve the globalization of the Chinese economy, including online retailing and the collection and use of big data; (2) OBOR should help expand China-controlled telecommunication networks and service globally; (3) OBOR is deemed to address China's domestic energy needs through generating and transmitting mining and energy projects; (4) OBOR shall also help expand China's Beidou satellite navigation system in the coming years. In spite of China's ambitious claims that OBOR will include sixty-five countries, 4.4 billion people and about 40 per cent of global GDP, the current realities remain pedestrian: in February 2016, China has reportedly established seventy-five overseas economic and trade cooperation zones in thirty-five countries.[4] Greece and Italy's recent engagement with BRI in 2019 has prompted the West's serious concern over China's growing strength as illustrated by BRI. Guy Verhofstadt, the EU's lead Brexit negotiator, criticized Italy's decision to join BRI being 'antithetical' to European interests.[5]

Furthermore, the trade tensions and negotiations between the United States and China since 2018 have considerably strained the world economy, leaving the world's two largest economies further apart with deteriorating economic effects on both sides. It also has put President Xi under intense internal pressure. On the part of the United States, President Trump's combative approach is supposed to secure a historic trade deal with China that would ensure the import of billions of dollars' worth of American farm products into China and stop Beijing from 'stealing' technology from US companies.[6] On the part of China, Xi's leadership has been challenged by his rivals and opponents with the accusations that Xi has exposed the 'core interests' of the ruling system to American interference. However, Xi's authoritarian rule to mobilize internal resources – even at the cost of realizing his 'Chinese Dream' – might well provide advantages for China to survive from the damaging US–China trade war in the longer term. As put by Junhua Zhang, regardless of the high pressure from the United States, China will *hardly* alter its decade-long development strategy through the adoption of *asymmetric* nonmarket economy approaches, which will enable China to continue to catch up with and even surpass the leading industrial nations.[7] This is the essence of Xi's grandiose '*Made in China 2025*' Plan, which is related directly to the question how Beijing pursues its dream through upgrading its technologies.

China's ambition to take the lead in advanced technologies like AI, autonomous vehicles, robotics and 5G is no longer a secret. Its receipt for success dwells in China's adherence to a state-led industrial policy which, as US intelligence sources say, relies mainly 'on intellectual property theft, forced technology transfers, cyberespionage and discriminatory treatment of foreign investment'.[8] These concerns over unfair trade practices have led to the introduction of Trump's tariffs on the import of Chinese goods and the blocking of Huawei and other Chinese tech giants from access to US market. As there is no clear way out to strike a trade deal between the United States and China, the changed environment of global trade in blocking Huawei's deployment of 5G technology in the Western sphere has already had deterring effects upon Xi's pursuit of his China Dream through unflinchingly supporting Huawei and the domestic semiconductor industry.

In light of the beginning fervent rivalry between the West and China surrounding 5G technology which ensures a promise of more economic growth and more power for whichever lead country in the future, Part 2 closely looks at how China has been exercising its political influence, globally and regionally. At the global stage, in many ways, China has been profiting from the geopolitical consequences of the US decline in abandoning its commitment to a liberal democratic world order, thereby facilitating China's pursuit of interests abroad with an authoritarian appeal and mercantilist spearhead, as found in Huawei's successful expansion in world markets. The studies of the US foreign policy construction of China, bilateral relationship between China and India, and China's engagements in Latin American and Africa have indicated the upcoming of concurring regional powers, in which identity construction and alliance building are undergoing a volatile change (see Chapters 8–11). The enemy of yesterday could become a potentially attractive partner today as the United States has lost its moral leadership in dictating regional and international cooperation. That said, China's one-man leadership is not immune to any crises and incidents. Like democracy's erosion whose causes often have a home-made character (e.g. Russia's oligarchic economy in support of Putin's rule), China's march towards a dictatorship spotlights the essential instability of its political system and may prepare for the beginning of the end of its economic miracle which has been dictated by a strong collective elite leadership prescribed by Deng Xiaoping. Hence, the challenges posed by China's rise may turn out to be less pressing as one has assumed in the beginning. Instead, attentions are needed to look at not only the effects of Xi's power concentration but also at the inherent drawbacks and recession democracy faces today. On the part of the democratic world, at stake is the reinvention of democratic participation through innovative institutional designs that should encourage citizens and non-citizens alike to reinvigorate deliberation processes while tackling highly complex intertwined problems and searching for compromises and solutions. In so doing, the spread of autocracy and exclusive nationalist discourses may be timely contained in an age of ambiguity and uncertainty.

Notes

1   Cited in BBC News (2013).
2   Jash (2016).

3 Gewirtz (2019).
4 For more details about the reactions towards BRI see Wade (2016), Wilson (2016).
5 TeleSur (2019).
6 Swanson (2019).
7 Zhang (2019).
8 McBride and Chatzky (2019).

Bibliography

BBC News, 'What Does Xi Jinping's China Dream Mean?' 6 June (2013). Available at https://www.bbc.com/news/world-asia-china-22726375 (accessed 31 August 2019).

Gewirtz, Julian B., 'China's Long March towards Technological Supremacy: The Roots of Xi Jinping's Ambition to "Catch Up and Surpass"', *Foreign Policy*, 27 August (2019). Available at https://www.foreignaffairs.com/articles/china/2019-08-27/chinas-long-march-technological-supremacy (accessed 2 September 2019).

Jash, Amrita, 'China's "One Belt, One Road": A Roadmap to "Chinese Dream"?' *IndraStra Global*, No. 2, 10 February (2016). Available at SSRN: https://ssrn.com/abstract=2771079 (accessed 4 September 2019).

McBride, James and Andrew Chatzky, 'Is "Made in China 2025" a Threat to Global Trade? *Council on Foreign Relations*, 13 May (2019). Availabel at https://www.cfr.org/backgrounder/made-china-2025-threat-global-trade (accessed 2 September 2019).

Swanson, Ana, 'As Trump Escalates Trade War, U.S. and China Move Further Apart with No End in Sight', *The New York Times*, 1 September (2019).

TeleSur, 'Greece "Appreciates" Joining China's Belt and Road Initiative', 15 May (2019). Available at https://www.telesurenglish.net/news/Greece-Appreciates-Joining-Chinas-Belt-and-Road-Initiative-20190515-0022.html (accessed 4 September 2019).

Wade, Geoff, 'China's "One Belt, One Road" Initiative', *Parliament of Australia* (2016). Available at https://www.aph.gov.au/About_Parliament/Parliamentary_Departments/Parliamentary_Library/pubs/BriefingBook45p/ChinasRoad (accessed 3 September 2019).

Wilson, W. T., 'China's Huge "One Belt, One Road" Initiative Is Sweeping Central Asia', *The National Enquirer*, 27 July (2016).

Zhang, Junhua, 'Huawei and the Damaging U.S.-China Trade War', *Australian Economics Center*, June (2019). Available at https://www.austriancenter.com/huawei-trade-war/ (accessed 31 August 2019).

Part 2

The international dimensions: China's rise as a leading global actor

8

China and the 'adversary' dynamic in US foreign policy discourses in the twenty-first century

Dirk Nabers and Robert G. Patman

Introduction

Alongside the Islamic world, China plays a prominent role as an 'Other' that helps differentiate 'Western' identity in an increasingly 'globalized world'. In media representations all around the world, China is often depicted in a simultaneous and contradictory fashion as a great polluter on the earth, the global production platform flooding the world with cheap products, the world's most significant human rights violator, the practitioner of 'unfair trade' and – given extensive defence spending and the largest army on the planet – the only real competitor to the United States in international terms. The US-based *Time* magazine had already in the mid-1990s anticipated this development in an article called 'Waking Up to the Next Superpower',[12] while the German weekly *Der Spiegel* marked what it called the 'Birth of a New Global Power'[3]. In China's neighbouring countries in East Asia, it is the former's growing demand of resources on the world market, its escalating share in intra-regional imports and increasing attraction of foreign direct investment (FDI) that have habitually been emphasized since the turn of the millennium. Not surprisingly, high domestic economic growth rates in China over more than three and a half decades have led many observers to the conclusion that China will be the next superpower in the Asia-Pacific region and beyond).[4] This conviction has fuelled the concern that other states might serve their own purposes well by changing their policies from balancing to bandwagoning China.[5]

The construction of China as the significant 'Other' of Western cultures is particularly visible in the field of foreign policy, since foreign policy serves to continually redefine the position and, hence, the identity of a nation within the international system. Quite prominently, David Campbell has emphasized that

> states are never finished as entities; the tension between the demands of identity and
> the practices that constitute it can never be fully resolved, because the performative

nature of identity can never be fully revealed. This paradox inherent to their being renders states in permanent need of reproduction: with no ontological status apart from the many and varied practices that constitute their reality, states are (and have to be) always in a process of becoming.[6]

It follows, therefore, that there is no objective essence of a state or nation; rather, the ontological referent becomes the meaning that is produced by particular foreign policy practices. The very being of a state or nation is what is at stake in the conduct of foreign policy. In the following analysis, we will thus argue that the identity of a nation is to a significant degree instituted by changing foreign policy practices. The notion of a country's identity is shaped through the process of political articulation, and this is where the prospect for change is incorporated: On the one hand, no foreign policy discourse is closed or total, which leaves potential room for further development; on the other hand, the possibility of its transformation rests in its continuous contacts with competing, alternative discourses. This leads to the important argument that an identity can never be fixed; it remains a function of foreign policy practices.

Taking the argument of the continuous transformation of national identity through foreign policy as a theoretical starting point, the aim of the following analysis is twofold: first, we will trace foreign policy changes of the United States towards China by looking at China as an adversary or antagonist of American foreign policy. The notion of antagonism derives its meaning from the theoretical argument that difference constitutes the essential defining criterion for any notion of society, be it a local community, a nation-state, a supranational group of states or a transnationally operating network. It works invisibly in a dyadic relationship as well as in complex, global social linkages. Difference defines the borders of social groups and therefore the limits of their identity. Without difference, there would be no borders, no politics of inclusion and exclusion, no conflict, no peace. In essence, difference can be positively and negatively connoted, as 'constitutive Other' in the former and 'antagonist' or 'adversary' in the latter meaning. In any case, both 'constitutive Others' and 'antagonists' are 'significant Others' of an actor whose actions gain meaning through their position in a web of differential relations. Antagonists as significant Others play a fundamental role not only in shaping foreign policies but also in limiting the options for national identity formation of a particular country.

Secondly, by focusing on antagonism, an alternative approach to foreign policy change can be introduced, which endogenizes corporate identities and departs from constructivist approaches that see foreign policy as shaped by rules, norms and identities. In the next section, we will first delineate the nexus between antagonism and foreign policy change. On that basis, we will trace US foreign policy towards China from 2001 to 2018. After a brief outline of general trends in US–China relations, we will analyse two cases: the currency dispute and the dialogue about nuclear non-proliferation. The conclusion will summarize the most important theoretical findings.

Conceptualizing antagonism

Every society is constituted as a web of differential relations between its members. The limit of a society is one of exclusion: it is not just one more element in a structure of differences, but one in an antagonistic relationship to the inside. As political theorist Ernesto Laclau summarizes in one of his later works:

> The only possibility of having a true outside would be that the outside is not simply one more, neutral element but an excluded one, something that the totality expels from itself in order to constitute itself.[7]

Antagonism implies the contamination of an inside by the outside, making the full constitution of the inside as a sutured totality impossible. In taking the continuous movement of differential relations for granted, identity cannot gain objective, positive content, in the empirical sense of the term. It can neither be understood as real opposition, where two poles clash according to the laws of physics; nor can it be seen as a contradiction of two mutually excluding concepts. Antagonism implies the openness of one identity to be infected by other.

The simplicity of this approach is exemplified by the verdict 'to be something is always not to be something else',[8] from which two consequences follow: first, exclusion has a moral dimension; it is never neutral, but often takes the form of subordination. Relations between in-group and out-group – in other words – are power relations. Secondly, equivalence is not synonymous with identity: equivalence presupposes difference but can eventually lead to the formation of tentative collective identities. Thus, identity needs an external force for its very existence; without this 'Other', identity would be different. Hence, annihilation or destruction of this excluded 'Other' would lead to a radical identity change, and a negative assertion of the excluded becomes the prevalent mode of representation. The 'Other' continuously feeds back on the identity of the Self.

In order to assemble huge social groups, such as nations, under the umbrella of a single collective identity, politics has to employ the so-called empty or floating signifiers. Empty signifiers are characterized by an indistinct or non-existent signified, that is terms that can have different meanings and can thereby serve to unite disparate social movements. They have no fixed content and can embrace an open series of demands. Empty signifiers signify the universal. Their purpose 'is to give a particular demand a function of universal representation – that is to give it the value of a horizon providing coherence to the chain of equivalence and, at the same time, keeping it indefinitely open'[9]. To assume the role of an empty signifier, any particularity must void itself of its very particularity. An empty signifier is never completely empty; the idea of universality never completely universal – quite the contrary is true: universality, as materialized in the form of an empty signifier, 'is the symbol of a missing fullness' (Laclau 1996: 28). Examples for empty signifiers are 'order' or 'democracy', but also universal terms that political action is oriented around, such as human rights or justice; in these cases, the empty signifier signifies a logically unattainable universality. On the other hand, floating signifiers can assume different meanings for different social groups depending on the nature or topic of the discourse; examples are expressions like 'freedom' and 'equality'. In the time of German Nazi fascism, for example, left-wing signifiers like 'the people' or even 'socialism' were hegemonized by a radical right-wing discourse.

In the War on Terror, for instance, empty signifiers like 'the people', 'freedom', 'liberty' and 'order' functioned as horizons, as a 'surface of inscription' for a number of specific political articulations. Textual analysis unveils a bifurcation of the world into protagonists and antagonists in President Bush's speeches, representing the latter as malign and evil[10]. Within the logic of equivalence, each demand in an emerging hegemonic discourse is physically linked with a chain of other demands; each one of them invokes a series of other signifiers. Relations of equivalence are textured between the American people, freedom and civilization on the one hand and tyranny and barbarism on the other. It is the American people that 'loves freedom' and 'defends freedom'. In contrast, President Bush undyingly uses Manichean discourse to construct the 'evil Other', at the same time stressing the goodness of the United States. The identity of the United States as a community of the good is contingent on reference to a constitutive Other, or outside. In that context, the term 'terror' or 'terrorist' represents fear and is increasingly exploited as an antonym of American identity. Hegemonic politics to a great part consists in the management of political representation, while any single signifier represents both the logic of equivalence and the logic of difference.

In the following, we will trace the role of China as an adversary in US foreign policy discourses between the years 2000 and 2018. In the two selected areas, we will specifically focus on two interrelated questions: (1) How do foreign policy practices construct identity by relying on binary constructions between Self and Other? (2) Given the incomplete nature of any identity, how can foreign policy change be understood as an ongoing, constant phenomenon? The two questions are related to the nexus between identity and foreign policy change.

US representations of China: From Bush to Trump

From Bush to Trump

Until the advent of the Trump administration in January 2017, American foreign policy towards China had been remarkably stable since the late 1970s. In the past, it was almost natural that a new administration reconsidered the overall US foreign policy strategy towards China once in office. After President George W. Bush took office in January 2001, there was a clear attempt to rebrand US foreign policy. At that time, the domestic discourse in the United States was already characterized by dislocation, hesitation and insecurity, triggered by an unprecedented aggrandizement of the capabilities of People's Republic. Two weeks before the 11 September terrorist attacks, Deputy Defence Secretary Paul Wolfowitz predicted that China is 'almost certain' to become a superpower this century and could emerge as a threat to the United States. It has been argued widely in poststructuralist literatures that the construction of an

'Other', which presents an integral part of processes of threat creation, is the very essence of foreign policy.[11] The extent of threat creation is directly related to the shape of foreign policy, and Wolfowitz was clear about the direction US foreign policy was to take under the Bush administration: 'I would say overall we're concerned about the direction of Chinese policy, and the developments we see there. … I don't think China has to be a threat, but I think if we're complacent, then we could actually contribute to the opposite effect.'[12] By representing China this way, it becomes clear that the eventuality of a hegemonic discourse depends on the construction of a threatening, excluded outside: 'a radical exclusion is the ground and condition of all differences';[13] it is the unifying ground of any system. What follows from this is that there are relations of equivalence between in-group actors, which create antagonisms to other social groups – in this case China as an adversary in US foreign policy.

A conspicuous feature of the Bush administration's policy towards China since 2001 has been an increasing concern about the continually growing defence budget of People's Republic. At a Singapore Conference in June 2005, for instance, Secretary of Defense Donald Rumsfeld openly asked for the true motivations behind China's escalating military budget and hinted at a congressionally mandated DOD report published in 2005 that emphasizes Beijing's policy of understatement in defence affairs. He contended that China not only pursues a policy of quantitative expansion, but also aims at a qualitative restructuring of its army that includes long-distance missile forces. Concluding that 'no nation threatens China', Rumsfeld ends with a number of questions: 'Why this growing investment? Why these continuing large and expanding arms purchases? Why these continuing robust deployments?'[14]

On that background, it comes without surprise that Bush's experienced foreign policy team had been extremely critical of President Clinton's foreign policy. They rejected Clinton's embrace of strategic partnership with China, endorsed the traditional view that security was fundamentally determined by the military means of sovereign states, and advocated 'a distinctly American internationalism'.[15] Before 11 September 2001, President Bush repeatedly represented China as inferior and responsive to American pressure. After being convicted of espionage, two Americans scholars were finally released in July 2001, 'because of the pressure our Government has put on China'.[16]

Antagonisms are logically located external to society, and by depicting China as a human rights violator, Bush implicitly constructs the United States as the opposite, as a member of the civilized Western hemisphere. As Bush continues: 'Perhaps China is beginning to realize that, as she begins to deal with Western nations, she's going to have to make better decisions on human rights.'[17] Already at this stage, the focus on freedom that became a major characteristic of Bush's rhetoric after 11 September 2001 was a noticeable feature of the discourse about China. As Bush himself put it: 'There was a big debate – I'm sure you heard about it – as to whether or not China ought to be allowed into what's called the World Trade Organization. I argued vociferously that they should be, because I believe a country that trades with the rest of the world is a country more likely to embrace freedom.'[18]

In this context, the concept of 'freedom' serves as a nodal point of American identity articulations. From the very origins of the idea of American exceptionalism, it has been coupled with the imperative to export freedom and liberty into the world, as the fourth president of the United States, James Madison, has legendarily pronounced in 1829, it amounts to 'the hope of Liberty throughout the world'.[19] The trauma of antagonism and the lack that identity embodies are linked here, for the subject has to identify with a privileged signifier in order to establish itself temporarily. The privileged signifier fulfils the role of integrating the subject into the social sphere. To perform this task of integration, a signifier has to assume the role of an empty or a floating signifier. 'Freedom' represents such a signifier. It continued to dominate US foreign policy discourses especially after 11 September 2001.

After the terrorist attacks on the World Trade Centre in New York and the Pentagon in Washington, the Bush administration articulated its relationship with China in a different manner. China became a conspicuous subject of US identity constructions after 2001. In the immediate aftermath of 11 September, China was prominent in the groundswell of international support for a shocked America. The Bush administration declared an all-out war against global terrorism, and Beijing quickly expressed its diplomatic solidarity with America's 'new war'. On 10 October 2001, Bush emphasized that he 'had a great conversation with Jiang Zemin of China about his desire to join us in fighting terrorist activities'.[20] The statement is typical for far reaching dislocations of societal structures (such as after wars or terrorist attacks like the one on 11 September 2001). The negativity of the discourse, characterized by the construction of antagonistic frontiers with enemies, is increasingly receding in this process and is gradually replaced by positive identification with new positions. The 'lack' that was triggered by the crisis can potentially be resolved and old adversaries become temporary allies. As Bush put it in his State of the Union Address in January 2002: 'In this moment of opportunity, a common danger is erasing old rivalries. America is working with Russia and China and India, in ways we have never before, to achieve peace and prosperity'.[21]

However, the impression by many observers that US unilateralism quickly emerged as the dominant strain in the Bush administration's approach to the war on terror seemed to limit the political scope of rapprochement between America and China. As a permanent member of the UN Security Council, China successfully helped oppose the efforts of the Bush administration to secure UN authorization for use of force against Iraq in early 2003 for failing to meet its disarmament obligations, although Bush had pressurized President Jian Zemin on that issue when they met in October 2002. As Bush stated: 'I urged President Jiang to support a new Security Council resolution demanding Iraq fully disarm itself of weapons of mass destruction'.[22] When the Bush administration responded by bypassing the UN and leading an invasion of Iraq in March 2003, Beijing made it clear that it opposed the invasion, but it did not use harsh language in doing so. At the same time, the two countries continued military-to-military relations, cooperated on anti-terror initiatives and worked together on an international effort to restrain North Korea's nuclear weapons activities.[23]

In the years that followed, it was also evident that the discourse about China's increasing stake in the global economy, and its burgeoning links with the largest economy in the world, namely, that of the United States, affected bilateral ties. During the Bush years, Chinese exports to the United States continued to grow strongly and Beijing became a major investor in the American economy buying up American debt and US Treasury Bonds with its vast accumulation of surplus dollars.[24] By 2008,

China held more than \$870 billion in US government Treasury Bonds. But if China's economic transformation reinforced cooperation with the United States, it also had competitive implications for the relationship between the two countries. In repeated State of the Union Addresses delivered by Bush, China was not even mentioned,[25] before mentioning China as a rival in 2006: 'The American economy is preeminent, but we cannot afford to be complacent. In a dynamic world economy, we are seeing new competitors like China and India. And this creates uncertainty, which makes it easier to feed people's fears'.[26]

The renewed focus on China came as no surprise. In 2004, for example, China had signed a landmark trade agreement with ten South-East Asian countries which could eventually unite 25 per cent of the world's population in a free-trade zone. In 2006, Beijing hosted the China–Africa summit which resulted in the signing of business deals worth nearly \$2 billion, and Chinese promises of billions of dollars in loans and credits.[27] Meanwhile, the dramatic improvement in the Chinese economy has facilitated a steady improvement in China's military capabilities. In 2007, it was reported that China had carried out a missile test in space, shooting down an old weather satellite. Such developments, moreover, came at a time when there was widespread suspicion or even hostility to the Bush's administration 'war against terrorism'. By 2007, the fall in the global reputation of the United States had reached catastrophic proportions. A British Broadcasting Corporation (BBC) World Service survey of more than 26,000 people across twenty-five countries found that only 29 per cent believed that the United States was having a positive influence internationally.[28]

Barack Obama had campaigned against George W. Bush's ideas and approach to foreign policy, and his election victory in November 2008 seemed to mark the revival of multilateralism in US international thinking. According to Obama, the 'simple truth' of twenty-first century is that 'the boundaries between people are overwhelmed by our connections'.[29] The Obama administration said that the US faced an 'extraordinary array of global challenges' in the post-Bush era. These challenges included 'poorly guarded nuclear weapons and material, a global financial meltdown, conflicts in Afghanistan and Iraq, Iran and North Korea building their nuclear weapons capabilities … pandemics and a climate that is warming by the day'. Further, as Susan Rice put it – at that time US Ambassador to the UN – 'these are transnational security threats that cross national boundaries as freely as a storm. By definition, they cannot be tackled by any one country alone'.[30] To renew American leadership in the world, President Obama pledged 'to rebuild the alliances, partnerships, and institutions necessary to confront common threats and enhance common security. … America cannot meet the threats of this century alone, and the world cannot meet them without America'.[31]

With respect to China, President Obama said that the relationship between the United States and China would largely shape the history of the twenty-first century. During his first visit to China after winning the presidency, Obama outlined his vision of greater engagement between the United States and China. He said that the United States does 'not seek to contain China's rise. On the contrary, we welcome China as a strong and prosperous and successful member of the community of nations'.[32] But President Obama seemed to imply that China must be prepared to take on more global responsibilities as its economic and military power increases. He emphasized that

Washington and Beijing needed to forge closer ties to address a host of international challenges whether it be lifting the global economy out of a deep recession, combating climate change or countering nuclear proliferation. Building on a 2006 Sino-American initiative, Obama and Chinese Premier Hu Jintao established the US–China Strategic and Economic Dialogue in 2009 as an annual platform for bilateral high-level discussions to institutionalize, in Secretary of State Clinton's words, 'a new pattern of cooperation between our governments and a forum for discussion'.[33] All this suggests that the Obama administration had refashioned the idea of US global primacy, so favoured by his predecessor, to accommodate China as a possible partner in leadership.

This all changed when President Trump took office in January 2017, giving 'America First' priority and calling into question previous bilateral and multilateral relationships. The most important pillars of American exceptionalism were visible in Trump's first year in office: antagonism, leadership and transcendental legitimization, centring on the fundamental notion of 'freedom'. Strength was articulated by Trump as the basis for any negotiations. The forty-fifth president seemed predisposed with an alleged loss of respect by allies and rivals alike, which had to be restored through power. As we will see, the discussion of China is illustrative here. During his foreign policy speech in April 2016 Trump claimed that 'China respects strength and by letting them take advantage of us economically, which they are doing like never before, we have lost all of their respect. … A strong and smart America is an America that will find a better friend in China, better than we have right now'.[34]

On the basis of this general overview, we can now ask for the role of China as an adversary in US foreign policy practices. Do signifiers like 'freedom', 'democracy', 'human rights' and 'justice' play a dominant role in the relations with China? And do binary constructions between the American Self and the Chinese Other serve to stabilize the identity of the United States in times of a continued increase of China's importance in world affairs?

The currency dispute

In contrast to the discourse about world security after 11 September, China has increasingly assumed the role of the most significant Other in US foreign policy in the economic realm. While many observers still questioned China's future as a 'superpower' at the turn of the millennium, the question mark slowly faded away in global media reports over the first decade of the new century, being replaced by assessments of 'China's next stage of growth'.[35] The new question for foreign policy actors in the United States was how to deal with a rapidly developing China, and the answers were usually coupled with anxiety, ambiguity and doubt. Such a situation of uncertainty is what we have labelled dislocation in the theoretical part of this chapter, and we will illustrate in this section that the economic discourse in the United States has increasingly been dislocated between 2000 and 2010.

In the last two decades, the sensitive question of the exchange rate between the US dollar and the Chinese renminbi (RMB) has been described as the 'lightning rod' for US–China trade relations.[36] Already since 1994, the Chinese government pursued a policy of intervening in currency markets to regulate the appreciation of the renminbi against the US dollar and other currencies. It has been criticized over a decade and a half that this policy has made Chinese exports to the United States considerably low priced, and, conversely, US exports to China much costlier. Moreover, it has been maintained for a long time that these actions would lead to deteriorating economic imbalances – a trend that would have the potential to undermine the world trading system in the medium term.[37]

Interestingly however, throughout the first George W. Bush administration, Washington's stance towards Beijing has shown little signs of radical change and has widely been characterized as constant and smooth.[38] As already indicated in the previous section, China's role of an antagonist receded in the first phase of the American-led war against terrorism. It was in the autumn of 2005 when the State Department unveiled a new policy framework for the relationship with China. At the end of the first and the beginning of the second Bush administration, a number of prominent US politicians started to espouse a harsher stance on economic and currency issues. It is hence maintained here that a visible change has taken place in Washington's relations with China. Since 2005, the exchange rate of the Chinese renminbi against the US dollar has taken the limelight, and during the 110th Congress in 2007, the three most prominent bills strongly advocated the view that the Chinese currency is 'misaligned' and 'manipulated'. Although no strict measures were eventually taken, the second Bush administration openly warned that eventually it would have to opt for uni- and multilateral trade remedies if the renminbi is not revalued.[39] It goes without saying that asserting the identity of a particular Other in negative ways always implies asserting one's own identity in positive ways. While China is represented as the manipulator, America articulates its role as the protector of free exchange rates. The United States and its allies protect the rules of international trade and finance; in contrast, 'competitors, such as China and other countries, … don't abide by any rule'[40].

To reiterate the central argument of this chapter, we have maintained in the theoretical outline of this chapter that antagonism goes hand in hand with discursive dislocation. A discourse is dislocated when it cannot integrate or explain certain events. Those 'events' remain incomprehensible; they are characterized by uncertainty over what they signify and imply. They cannot be incorporated within existing frameworks of intelligibility. Dislocation can thus be seen as an important prerequisite for social change in general and foreign policy change in particular. It usually results in new institutional practices, very well visible in the institutionalization of the 'war on terror'.

In the specific case of the currency dispute, what are the sources of dislocation that the discourse draws on? And what are the institutional measures taken between 2005 and 2010? First of all, three reasons for the intensification of the debate over the Chinese currency are easily identified within the wider foreign policy discourse in the United States: a significant expansion of China's account surplus, an enormous build-up of foreign exchange reserves and a rapidly growing amount of FDI.[41] These tendencies are deliberately constructed within the domestic political discourse in the United States to legitimate a particular policy vis-à-vis China. Nicola Nymalm thus argues 'that the issue is not a purely economic and financial one, but a reflection of how the rise of China on the global scene – especially viable though in economic and financial figures – is affecting the US conception and understanding of liberal trade policy'.[42]

At this stage, numerous members of Congress started to push for a more insistent stance of the Obama administration in the controversy, including the designation of the People's Republic as a 'currency manipulator' under US trade law. In the first decade of the dispute, China had not been cited as such a manipulator.[43] The global financial crisis, which broke out in 2008, did not visibly intensify the discourse within the United States. In fact, China even stopped the rise of the renminbi. In April 2010, Beijing again indicated it would allow the renminbi to strengthen through a gradual loosening of currency bands in the near future. Between 2008 and 2010, several measures to reform the renminbi exchange rate regime were undertaken. Amid this new development, a number of currency-related bills were brought into Congress, but different majorities in the House and the Senate led to a stalemate, and no strict measures were taken against Beijing under the Obama administration.

One may therefore state that US foreign policy has changed; yet, it is difficult to analyse Washington's stance towards China solely on the basis of substantial acts. It is helpful to look at how representations of China within the Congressional Record changed. In that context, the classification of China as a 'Communist dictatorship', 'Communist country', 'Communist system' or 'regime' in the period analysed in this chapter is a conspicuous feature of the foreign policy discourse in the United States. While China is at times also constructed as an adversary or even 'threat' and 'evil empire', the United States is represented as 'no greater advocate for free markets', 'a great promise' and 'the only hope in the world' on the one hand, and 'second only to the Japanese in unpopularity in China' on the other hand.[44]

The analysis of the proliferation of binary predications and nominations between 2000 and 2018 takes us back to the main argument of this chapter: identity needs an external force for its very existence; without this 'other', identity would be different. The People's Republic was not only seen as an economic competitor but as a 'deadly' one, which 'is openly hostile to the basic values which make us Americans'. This representation of China as 'a currency cheat'[45] continued when Trump became president. Trump had already announced he would designate China a 'currency manipulator' during the 2016 election campaign trail. But in office Trump seemed to initially backtrack on this commitment. Then in April 2018, President Trump once again accused China of currency manipulation – a behaviour which he said was 'not acceptable'[46]. Trump's renewed allegations were not supported by the US Treasury, which declined to describe any major US major trade partners in such terms.[47] Empty signifiers like democracy, freedom and human rights structure the discourse and constitute China as the antagonistic Other of US foreign policy. Moreover, the particular constructions of China institute a 'cognitive framework' that determines what reaction is appropriate and what reaction is inappropriate to react to the 'China challenge'. Finally, by constructing China as the future superpower, the discourse in the United States is constantly dislocated, opening up possibilities for foreign policy change.

Countering nuclear proliferation

Textual analysis unveils a bifurcation of the world into protagonists and antagonists in Bush's speeches especially after 11 September, representing the latter as malign and evil. In the field of countering nuclear proliferation, however, China had already been portrayed as a possible hindrance before the terror attacks. On the eve of 9/11, Australian prime minister John Howard and President Bush 'reaffirmed the importance of China's observance of its non-proliferation undertakings and underlined their close interest in China's respect for human rights'.[48] Later, in 2002, President Bush welcomed the prospect of China's support in preventing North Korea from acquiring nuclear weapons, stating: 'I thought it was a very interesting statement that Jiang Zemin made in Crawford, where he declared very clearly that he wants a nuclear-weapons-free Korean Peninsula. That was, in my judgment, an important clarification of Chinese policy that I hope the North Koreans listen to.'[49]

The Bush administration linked counter-proliferation efforts with its 'war on terror'. Convinced that 'rogue states and terrorists … are seeking weapons of mass destruction', President Bush noted that the United States and China had overlapping interests in 'the current war on terrorism and in promoting stability on the Korean peninsula'[50]. It was reported in 2003 that the Bush administration was urging Beijing to put pressure on China to exert influence on North Korea to abandon its nuclear programme.[51] But there was domestic criticism in the United States that the Bush administration was not doing enough to counter nuclear proliferation. The 2004 Democratic presidential contender, Senator John Kerry, said: 'We've got to lead the world now to crack down on proliferation as a whole. But the President has been slow to do that.'[52]

Barack Obama had campaigned against George W. Bush's ideas and approach to national security, and his election victory in November 2008 brought a tilt towards multilateralism in the counter-proliferation strategy of United States. This approach envisaged active engagement with 'partners' like China. Together with free trade and coordinated efforts against climate change, Barack Obama identified non-proliferation as one of the top priorities in bilateral relations, at the opening session of the first US–China Strategic and Economic Dialogue in July 2009 issuing a warning to the Chinese government: 'Make no mistake: The more nations acquire these weapons, the more likely it is that they will be used.'[53] Among other things, the Obama administration maintained publicly that a 'pragmatic and effective relationship between the United States and China is essential to address the major challenges of the 21st century',[54] such as non-proliferation of nuclear weapons. On 24 September 2009, the Obama administration won the support of China at the United Nations Security Council approval for the objective of a world free of nuclear weapons.[55] At the same time, the Obama team emphasized the need to 'pursue the denuclearization of the Korean peninsula and work to prevent Iran from developing a nuclear weapon.'[56] It was interesting to see that China's role as an adversary receded into the background in this context and a chain of equivalence was established against North Korea. Confronting Iran, Obama said in 2010: 'But what's clear is, is that they have not said yes to an agreement that Russia, China, Germany, France, Great Britain, and the United States all said was a good deal and that the Director of the IAEA said was the right thing to do and that Iran should accept.'[57] The logic of equivalence constitutes the fullness of a community by linking together a plurality of unfulfilled demands, difference contradicts this logic. Different identities are grouped together in opposition to another camp to form a chain of equivalence.

However, North Korea generally showed a limited interest in engagement.[58] Tension on the Korean peninsula spiked to some of its highest levels since the 1950–3 Korean War after the sinking of a South Korean ship in 2010 which killed forty-six sailors, an exchange of artillery fire between the two sides, nuclear sabre-rattling from the North Korean government, and threats of war from both North and South Korea.[59] While China seemed to share with Washington the goal of de-nuclearizing North Korea, it was apparently reluctant to do anything that would destabilize the regime in Pyongyang.[60] Policy approaches between the US and China with regard to the goal of North Korean denuclearization often lacked effective coordination.[61]

Meanwhile, there remained a concern in the United States that China was providing a gap in fully enforcing UN sanctions against Iran, which the government in Beijing supported. During a visit to Beijing in September 2010, Robert Einhorn, the US State Department's special adviser for non-proliferation and arms control, expressed the US concern that certain Chinese companies were violating UN sanctions against Iran, perhaps without the knowledge of the Chinese government.[62]

Nevertheless, at that time, the Obama administration and EU officials argued they believed that the sanctions had hindered Iran's efforts to acquire carbon fibre and to manage steel, an alloy that can be used to make centrifuges that enrich uranium to fuel a nuclear bomb. The fact that Hassan Rouhani defeated Mahmoud Ahmadinejad in the Iranian presidential elections of August 2013 may be seen as some form of vindication for the two-track approach of the Obama administration towards Iran since 2010. And that political change seemed to lend impetus to US and Chinese efforts to curb the possible development of nuclear weapons in Iran.

In November 2013, Beijing apparently played the role of broker in a 'historic deal' that Iran struck in principle with six world powers aimed at curbing Tehran's nuclear programme in exchange for initial sanctions relief.[63] It was reported that 'China pulled off a delicate balancing act in the negotiations between Iran, seen by Beijing as a long-term partner, and the US'. Rapidly increasing economic and military cooperation between Iran and China may have played a part in this diplomatic breakthrough. Two years later, on 14 July 2015, the P5+1 group, that included China, signed a Joint Comprehensive Plan of Action with Iran. This agreement prescribed limits on Iran's nuclear programme by eliminating pathways to a nuclear weapons programme in exchange for the gradual removal of international economic sanctions against Teheran.

In light of this, it is tempting to interpret America's changing representation of China under the Obama administration as simply a reflection of the changing distribution of political, economic and military power between the two most prominent actors in the international system. On this view, the Obama administration's willingness to work closely with China on global problems was directly linked to the conviction that America, like other great powers before it, had entered a period of long-term decline and was being increasingly challenged by China as the world's number one power. In short, the more accommodating and inclusive rhetoric of the Obama government towards China had essentially been a function of declining American power. It is true, for example, a report by a US government agency predicted with 'relative certainty' the emergence of a global multipolar system within the next fifteen to twenty years, and that 'few countries are poised to have more impact on the world … than China'.[64]

In his 2016 presidential campaign for the White House, the Republican candidate, Donald J. Trump, subscribed to the view that the 'weakness' of the Obama administration led to the signing of what he repeatedly described as an 'insane' and 'terrible deal' for the United States. Among other things, Trump argued that the lifting of international sanctions against Iran helped to finance what he described as Teheran's policy of 'meddling' and 'terror' in the Middle East, a view that was strongly supported by the Netanyahu government in Israel. In May 2018, President Trump withdrew the United States from the Iran nuclear agreement despite the widely held view there was no better alternative arrangement for curbing nuclear proliferation in Iran. To date, the other signatories to the 2015 agreement have continued to uphold this deal.

A second possible explanation for Obama's counter-proliferation efforts towards Iran related to President Obama's distinctive understanding of US exceptionalism.[65] According to this view, the Obama leadership simply did not accept the US political system was long-term decline as Trump and other critics alleged. It was conceded that other players in the international system such as China and India had certainly experienced a dramatic improvement in their economic and political fortunes but such changes did not necessarily threaten the superpower status of United States. Indeed, the Obama leadership said it was very confident about the vitality and sustainability of the US political system. In Obama's words, 'History offers a clear verdict. Governments that respect the will of their own people, that govern by consent and not coercion, are more prosperous, they are more stable, and more successful than governments that do not.'[66] Moreover, the Obama leadership seemed to be convinced that globalization had fundamentally reshaped the context of global politics to the point where the idea of a single global hegemon in a deeply interconnected world had become structurally problematic. That is to say, many of the major economic, security and environmental challenges facing sovereign states in the twenty-first century can now only be resolved on an international basis. Thus, Obama's opening to China to cooperate in countering nuclear proliferation in Iran reflected the belief that unilateral options are largely ineffective in today's world, and that the US democratic political system – characterized by elite competition through regular elections – had little to fear from expanded cooperation with a rising authoritarian superpower although the reverse, of course, may not true for its authoritarian partner. Trump fundamentally reversed this stance, which sheds light on the indeterminacy of identities and the contingency of foreign policy.

Conclusion

In this chapter, we have put forward the argument that the identity of a nation is to a significant degree instituted by antagonistic relations to significant Others. It was shown that the Obama administration had to come to terms with a foreign policy discourse that constructed China as a significant Other of the United States, thereby implicitly representing China as an integral part of the United States' foreign policy identity. As identity remains partial, it can never be full or complete. The same holds true for foreign policy, which is constantly changing, even if the broader picture remains unaltered. As

David Shambaugh observes, 'US grand strategy toward China – since Richard Nixon opened talks with Beijing in the early 1970s – has shown remarkable continuity.'[67] Even after the Tiananmen massacre of 1989, the Bush senior administration wished to maintain peaceful relations with China and placed only limited sanctions on the regime in Beijing. In the period under scrutiny in this chapter – 2000 to 2010 – the first half (2000 to 2005) is best characterized by stability and exerted cooperation. During the first George W. Bush administration, Washington and Beijing resumed regular high-level visits and mutual exchanges of working level officials, recommended military-to-military relations, started to develop anti-terror schemes, and collaborated for a peaceful settlement of the lingering conflict on the Korean peninsula. FDI soared in both directions, and the overall cooperation climate seemed constructive. However, suspicion and resentment seemed to play their role in the background. As Suettinger and Talbot put it: 'Amid all the change – the forgetting, if you will, of Tiananmen – the relationship between the United States of America and the People's Republic of China has remained one of wary distrust that occasionally deteriorates into enmity.'[68] It is against this psychological background that a more active foreign policy stance was adopted in the second half of the decade. This modest change cannot be attributed to external developments, such as the world financial crisis, which was barely anticipated in 2005. Rather, foreign policy changes occurred after new representations of China became prominent in the United States.

One of these conspicuous changes can be seen in the establishment of chains of equivalence against new adversaries, such as Iran and North Korea. However, it also illustrates well the contingency of relations, as things changed quite dramatically under Trump. Equivalence highlights the community effect of a perceived common 'negative' or 'enemy'; the demands of different social groups are articulated into a larger common movement. Equivalence subverts all positive difference by it to a fundamental sameness. Yet, this sameness is illusionary. Due to the prominence of China in US foreign policy discourses, it can be expected that the representation of China as an adversary in different policy fields will continue.

Notes

1 Laclau (1985: 128); see also Laclau (1996) and Laclau (2005).
2 Prager (1996).
3 Spiegel (2004).
4 Bernstein and Munro (1997); Goldstein (1997/8).
5 Drifte (2003).
6 Campbell (1998: 12).
7 Laclau (2005: 70).
8 Laclau and Mouffe (1985: 128); see also Laclau (1996) and Laclau (2005).
9 Laclau (1996: 57f).
10 Nabers and Patman (2009); Nabers (2009).
11 See for example Nabers (2009).
12 NewsMax.com Wires, 29 August 2001.

13 Laclau (1996: 39, 52).
14 Rumsfeld (2005).
15 Bush (2001a).
16 Bush (2001b).
17 Ibid., p. 914.
18 Bush (2001c).
19 Madison (1900).
20 Government Printing Office (2001b).
21 The White House (2002a). When George W. Bush was asked for a comment on his expectations about a meeting with President Jiang Zemin in October 2001, Bush stated: 'I will tell him how important it is for the United States and China to have good relations.' (Government Printing Office 2001c).
22 Bush (2001d).
23 Dumbaugh (2003: 1f.); Dumbaugh (2006: p. 1f).
24 Cox (2008: 281).
25 Bush (2004), Bush (2005).
26 Bush (2006).
27 Cox (2008: 282).
28 British Broadcasting Corporation World Service (2007).
29 Obama (2009a).
30 Rice (2009).
31 Obama (2007).
32 Obama (2009b).
33 Clinton (2009).
34 Trump (2016).
35 Steinbock (2010).
36 Hufbauer, Wong and Sheth (2006: 10).
37 Morrison and Labonte (2013: 54 pages).
38 Dumbaugh (2006).
39 Hufbauer, Wong and Sheth (2006: 2f).
40 Bush (2006).
41 Morrison and Labonte (2013).
42 Nymalm (2015: 4).
43 Morrison and Labonte (2013: 8); Barfield (2010).
44 All quotes in this paragraph stem from Nymalm (2015).
45 Also Nymalm (2015).
46 Aleem (2018).
47 South China Morning Post (2018).
48 Government Printing Office (2001a).
49 Bush (2002b).
50 The White House (2002b).
51 Pomfret (2003).
52 Kerry and Bush (2004).
53 The White House (2009).
54 The White House (2010: 43).
55 United Nations Security Council (2009).
56 The White House (2010: 23–4).
57 Obama (2010).
58 Haggard and Noland (2010).

59 Branigan (2010).
60 Hill (2013).
61 O'Caroll (2003).
62 Garver (2011); Downs and Maloney (2011).
63 Chunshan (2013)
64 Mahubani (2008).
65 Patman and Southgate (2016).
66 The White House (2009a).
67 Shambaugh (2010).
68 Suettinger and Strobe (2003: 2).

Bibliography

Aleem, Zeeshan, 'Trump called China a Currency Cheat: Then He Changed His Mind. Now He's Changed It Again', *Vox*, 16 April (2018). Available at https://www.vox.com/ world/2018/4/16/17242946/trump-twitter-china-currency-devaluation-manipulation (accessed 6 July 2018).

Barfield, Claude, 'Congress and Chinese Currency Legislation', *VOX CEPR Policy Portal*, 16 April (2010). Available at https://voxeu.org/article/congress-and-chinese-currency-legislation (accessed 6 July 2018).

Bernstein, Richard and Ross H., Munro, *The Coming Conflict with China* (New York: Vintage, 1997).

Branigan, Tania, 'North Korea Threatens South over Report on Sinking of Warship', *The Guardian*, 20 May (2010). Available at https://www.theguardian.com/world/2010/m ay/20/north-korea-naval-ship-report (accessed 6 July 2018).

British Broadcasting Corporation World Service, 'World View of US Role Goes from Bad to Worse', 23 January (2007). Available at news.bbc.co.uk/2/shared/bsp/hi/pdfs/23_ 01_07_us_poll.pdf (accessed 6 July 2018).

Bush, George W., 'Text of George W. Bush's 2001 Address to Congress, Feb. 27, 2001', *The Washington Post*, 27 February (2001a).

Bush, George W., 'Remarks Prior to a Meeting With Virginia Gubernatorial Candidate Mark Earley and an Exchange With Reporters, National Archives and Records Administration', in Office of the Federal Register (ed.), *Public Papers of the Presidents of the United States* (Washington: Office of the Federal Register, National Archives and Records Administration (NARA), 2001b), pp. 913–16.

Bush, George W., 'Remarks to the National Future Farmers of America Organization', in Office of the Federal Register (ed.), *Public Papers of the Presidents of the United States* (Washington: NARA, 2001c), pp. 919–29.

Bush, George W., 'The President's News Conference with President Jian Zemin of China in Crawford, Texas', in Office of the Federal Register (ed.), *Public Papers of the Presidents of the United States*, Book 1 (Washington: NARA, 2001d), pp. 1897–900.

Bush, George W., 'Bush Talks to Press', *CNN*, 7 November 2002 (2002b). Available at http://transcripts.cnn.com/TRANSCRIPTS/0211/07/se.02.html (accessed 6 July 2018).

Bush, George W., 'Text of President Bush's 2004 State of the Union Adress', Washington *Post*, 20 January (2004). Available at http://www.washingtonpost.com/wp-srv/politics/ transcripts/bushtext_012004.html (accessed 6 July 2018).

Bush, George W., 'Text of President Bush's 2005 State of the Union Adress', *Washington Post*, 2 February (2005). Available at http://www.washingtonpost.com/wp-srv/politics/transcripts/bushtext_020205.html (accessed 6 July 2018).

Bush, George W., 'Text of President Bush's 2006 State of the Union Adress', *Washington Post*, 31 January (2006a). Available at http://www.washingtonpost.com/wp-dyn/content/article/2006/01/31/AR2006013101468.html (accessed 6 July 2018).

Bush, George W., 'Bush, German Chancellor Discusses Iran, United States European Command', 17 January (2006b). Available at http://www.eucom.mil/article/21374/Bush-German-chancellor-discuss-Iran (accessed 6 July 2018).

Campbell, David, *Writing Security: United States Foreign Policy and the Politics of Identity* (Minneapolis: University of Minnesota Press, 1998), p. 12.

Chunshan, Mu, 'The Iranian Nuclear Question: China's Perspective', *The Diplomat*, 27 November (2013). Available at https://thediplomat.com/2013/11/the-iranian-nuclear-question-chinas-perspective/ (accessed 6 July 2018).

Clinton, Hillary Rodham, 'Closing Remarks for U.S.-China Strategic and Economic Dialogue', *U.S. Department of State*, 28 July (2009). Available at https://2009-2017.state.gov/secretary/20092013clinton/rm/2009a/july/126599.htm (accessed 6 July 2018).

Cox, Michael, 'The USA and Asia-Pacific', in M. Cox and D. Stokes (eds.), *US Foreign Policy* (Oxford: Oxford UP, 2008).

Der Spiegel, 'China. Geburt einer Weltmacht', 11 October (2004).

Downs, Erica and Suzanne Maloney, 'Getting China to Sanction Iran', Foreign Affairs, 90/1 (2011), pp. 15–22.

Drifte, Reinhard, *Japan's Security Relations with China since 1989: From Balancing to Bandwaggoning?* (London: CRC Press, 2003).

Dumbaugh, Kerry, 'China-U.S. Relations', *US Department of State* (2003). Available at http://fpc.state.gov/documents/organizations/17320.pdf (accessed 6 July 2018).

Dumbaugh, Kerry, 'China-U.S. Relations: Current Issues and Implications for U.S. Policy', *CRS Report for Congress* (2006). Available at www.dtic.mil/get-tr-doc/pdf?AD=ADA462514 (accessed 6 July 2018).

Garver, John, 'Is China Playing a Dual Game in Iran?', *The Washington Quarterly*, 34/1 (2011), pp. 75–88

Goldstein, Avery 'Great Expectations: Interpreting China's Arrival', *International Security*, 22/3 (1997/8), pp. 689–711.

Government Printing Office, 'Joint Statement Between the United States of America and Australia, 10 September (2001a). Available at http://www.gpo.gov/fdsys/pkg/WCPD-2001-09-17/html/WCPD-2001-09-17-Pg1295-2.htm (accessed 6 July 2018).

Government Printing Office, 'Remarks Following Discussions With Secretary General Lord Robertson of the North Atlantic Treaty Organization', (2001b). Available at http://www.gpo.gov/fdsys/pkg/WCPD-2001-10-15/html/WCPD-2001-10-15-Pg1449.htm (accessed 10 March 2014).

Government Printing Office, 'Interview with Asian Editors', 16 October (2001c). Available at http://www.gpo.gov/fdsys/pkg/PPP-2001-book2/html/PPP-2001-book2-doc-pg1246.htm (accessed 10 March 2014).

Haggard, Stephen and Marcus Noland, 'Sanctioning North Korea: The Political Economy of Denuclearisation and Proliferation', *Asian Survey*, 50/3 (2010), pp. 539–68.

Hill, Christopher, 'The Elusive Vision of a Non-Nuclear North Korea', *The Washington Quarterly*, 36/2 (2013), pp. 7–19.

Hufbauer, Gary C., Yee Wong, Ketki Sheth, *US-China Trade Disputes: Rising Tide, Rising Stakes* (NY/Washington: Columbia UP, 2006), p. 10.

Kerry, John and George W. Bush, 'Transcript: Second Presidential Debate', *Washington Post*, 8 October (2004). Available at http://www.washingtonpost.com/wp-srv/politics/debatereferee/debate_1008.html (accessed 6 July 2018).

Laclau, Ernesto and Chantal Mouffe, *Hegemony and Socialist Strategy* (London: Verso, 1985).

Laclau, Ernesto, *Emancipation(s)* (London: Verso, 1996).

Laclau, Ernesto, *On Populist Reason* (London: Verso, 2005).

Madison, James, '"Outline" notes. Sept. 1829, Writings 9: 351-357', in G. Hunt (ed.), *The Writings of James Madison* (New York: G.P.Putnam's Sons, 1900).

Mahubani, Kishore, *The New Asian Hemisphere: The Irresistible Shift of Global Power to the East* (New York: PublicAffairs , 2008).

Morrisson, Wayne M. and Marc Labonte, 'China's Currency Policy: An Analysis of the Economic Issues', *Congressional Research Service*, 22 July (2013), 54 pages. Available at https://fas.org/sgp/crs/row/RS21625.pdf (accessed 6 July 2018).

Nabers, Dirk, 'Filling the Void of Meaning: Identity Construction in U.S. Foreign Policy after September 11, 2001', *Foreign Policy Analysis*, 5/2 (2009), pp. 191–214.

Nabers, Dirk and Robert Patman, '9/11 and the Rise of Political Fundamentalism in the Bush Administration: Domestic Legitimisation versus International Estrangement?', *Global Change, Peace and Security*, 20/2 (2009), pp. 169–83.

Nymalm, Nicola, *The China Discourse in the US Congress: Debates on the Chinese Currency 2003–2010*. PhD Dissertation (Kiel: Kiel University, 2015).

Obama, Barack, 'Renewing American Leadership', *Foreign Affairs*, 86/4 (2007), pp. 2–16.

Obama, Barack, 'Remarks by the President to the Ghanaian Parliament', (2009a), Available at http://www.america.gov/st/texttrans-english/2009/July/20090711110050abretnuh0.1079783.html (accessed 2 December 2010).

Obama, Barack, 'Obama Answers Questions from Fudan University and the Internet, 16 November 2009', (2009b) Available at http://www.america.gov/st/texttrans-english/2009/November/20091116095135eaifas0.900326.html (accessed 6 July 2018).

Obama, Barack, 'The President's News Conference', 9 February (2010), in Office of the Federal Register (ed.), *Public Papers of the Presidents of the United States* (Washington, 2010), pp. 187–94.

O'Caroll, Chad, 'N. Korea Wants Denuclearization Talks "Without Pre-Conditions"', *NK News*, 18 September (2003). Available at https://www.nknews.org/2013/09/n-korea-wants-to-resume-denuclearization-talks-without-conditions/ (accessed 6 July 2018).

Patman, Robert G. and Laura Southgate, 'Globalization, the Obama Administration and the Refashioning of US Exceptionalism', *International Politics*, 53/1 (2016), pp. 220–38.

Pomfret, John, 'Powell Pushing China to Lean on North Korea', *Washington Post*, 24 February (2003), p. A14.

Prager, Kirsten, 'China: Waking Up to the Next Superpower', *TIME*, 26 March (1996).

Rice, Susan, 'United Nations Is Vital to U.S. Efforts to Craft Better, Safer World', *New York University for Global Affairs*, 12 August (2009). Available at http://www.america.gov/st/texttrans-english/2009/August/20090813164826eaifas0.287945.html&distid=ucs (accessed 5 March 2011).

Rumsfeld, Donald, 'U.S. Secretary Donald Rumsfeld's Remarks to the International Institute for Strategic Studies', (2005). Available at http://singapore.usembassy.gov/060405.html (accessed 5 March 2011).

Shambaugh, David, 'A New China Requires a New US Strategy', *Current History*, 109/728 (2010), p. 219.

South China Morning Post, 'Donald Trump Slams China and Russia as Currency Manipulators, Contradicting His Own Treasury Report', 17 April (2018). Available at https://www.scmp.com/news/china/article/2142008/donald-trump-slams-china-and-russia-currency-manipulators-contradicting (accessed 6 July 2018).

Steinbock, Dan, 'China's Next Stage of Growth: Reassessing U.S. Policy toward China', *American Foreign Policy Interests*, 32/6 (2010), pp. 347–62.

Suettinger, Robert L. and Talbott Strobe, *Beyond Tiananmen: The Politcs of US China Relations, 1989–2000* (Washington: Hopkins, 2003), p. 2.

The White House, 'President Delivers State of the Union Adress', 29 January (2002a). Available at http://www.whitehouse.gov/news/releases/2002/01/20020129-11.html (accessed 20 December 2003).

The White House, 'The National Security Strategy of the United States of America', (2002b). Available at https://www.state.gov/documents/organization/63562.pdf (accessed 6 July 2018).

The White House, 'President Obama attends the U.S. China Strategic and Economic Dialogue', 28 July (2009). Available at http://www.whitehouse.gov/video/President-Obama-Attends-the-US-China-Strategic-and-Economic-Dialogue (accessed 6 July 2018).

The White House, *National Security Strategy of the United States of America* (Washington, 2010).

Trump, Donald J., 'Donald Trump's Foreign Policy Speech', *The New York Times*, 27 April (2016). Available at https://www.nytimes.com/2016/04/28/us/politics/transcript-trump-foreign-policy.html (accessed 6 July 2018).

United Nations Security Council, 'Resolution 1887' (New York, 2009). Available at http://unscr.com/en/resolutions/doc/1887 (accessed 6 July 2018).

9

India and China

Overcoming the great wall of mistrust

Rupakjyoti Borah

Introduction

The economic and military rise of China is one of the seminal features of our times. India is China's immediate neighbour and has historic ties with China stretching back into centuries. India and China represent two old civilizations, which have lived together in peace for millennia, except for a short border war in 1962. It was in the sixth century BC, that the birth of Confucius and Sakyamuni opened a new era of interaction between the Indian and the Chinese civilizations. Thereafter, Emperor Ashoka's propagation of Buddhism after his conversion in 256 BC brought China and India even closer.[1] Both countries came under colonial yoke; however, after shedding off the same, both have emerged as two of the fastest growing economies in the world. These two neighbours, which are also the two most populous countries in the world, have similar views on many issues and conflicting interests on many others. It does not help that India and China have completely different systems of governance. This article analyses the major areas of conflict and cooperation between the two Asian behemoths and elucidates the absolute imperative for peace between the two countries.

Various other Buddhist priests from India visited China in the aftermath of the spread of Buddhism and renowned Chinese scholars like Hiuen Tsang and Fa-hien came to ancient Indian universities like Nalanda. In spite of a long and rich history, both India and China were colonized by European powers and managed to shake off the colonial yoke after a long period of struggle and tremendous sacrifices. It is interesting to note that both India and China have a long history of strategic thinkers – while India has Kautilya (or Chanakya), China on the other hand has Sun-Tzu.

Indian doctor Dwarkanath Kotnis was part of a 1938 team of five Indian doctors who were sent to China to treat wounded soldiers during the Sino-Japanese war. Dr Kotnis lost his life in the course of duty and his mortal remains lie in the North China Martyrs' Memorial Cemetery in Hebei Province. Before his death, he was appointed as Director of the Dr. Bethune International Peace Hospital built by the Eighth Route Army.[2] The Chinese people still affectionately remember Dr Kotnis.

Meanwhile, the famous Indian poet, author, philosopher, artist and educator Rabindranath Tagore visited China in 1924 and again in 1929. Tagore, the first non-European to win the Nobel Prize for literature, was already a famous figure in China, with Chen Du Xiu, who was one of the founding fathers of the Communist Party of China (CPC), translating Tagore's prize-winning anthology, 'Gitanjali', way back in 1915. A famous Chinese writer, Guo Moruo was deeply influenced by Tagore while another renowned Chinese scholar Liang Qichao gave Tagore the Chinese name, 'Zhu Zhendan' (thunder of the oriental dawn) during his visit to China in 1924.[3]

India's first prime minister Jawaharlal Nehru believed in the concept of Afro-Asian unity and towards the same end, favoured close ties with China. In fact, Prime Minister Nehru supported China at all international fora and even relinquished India's claim to a seat in the UN Security Council (UNSC) in favour of China. Nehru was of the view that the Western powers had offered India a seat in the UNSC in order to break India–China friendship.[4] India was also the first non-communist country to establish an embassy in China. In 1954, India and China signed the Panchsheel (five principles of peaceful co-existence) agreement.[5]

However, India and, especially, Nehru were to be jolted out of their stupor when China attacked India in a 1962 border war. Though it did not break out into an all-out war, it was seen as a huge breach of trust by India, a blow from which the bilateral relationship has never recovered. After the 1962 war, relations remained frozen for a long time until the visit of the then Indian prime minister Rajiv Gandhi to China in December 1988, which was the first visit by an Indian prime minister to China since Jawaharlal Nehru's visit way back in 1954.

It was during Prime Minister Rajiv Gandhi's visit to China that the two countries agreed to establish a joint working group (JWG) to resolve the contentious border issue. In 1992, the then Indian president R. Venkataraman undertook a state visit to China, which was incidentally the first head of state-level visit from India to China.

Areas of divergence

However, the positives vibes generated by the many high-level official visits between the two countries cannot gloss over the huge trust deficit in many areas. There are many areas and issues where the two countries are not on the same page. The boundary dispute is one of the most important points of dispute between the two countries, with several rounds of talks being held to resolve the same. Though, during the then Indian prime minister Narasimha Rao's visit to China in September 1993, an Agreement on the Maintenance of Peace and Tranquillity along the Line of Actual Control (LAC) in the India–China Border Area was signed, the two sides have not been able to settle the border dispute. In fact, the Sino-Indian border is one among the only two of China's border disputes that has not been settled as yet.[6] Indian strategists see this as a deliberate ploy by the Chinese to keep India on the back foot on other issues.

China disputes the 1914 McMahon line which serves as the border between the two Asian giants and has also disputed the total length of the border. It claims the entire Indian province of Arunachal Pradesh and has raised objections when senior Indian politicians and officials have visited the province; in fact, China's claims over Arunachal Pradesh have grown shriller in the last few years.[7] This has raised many an eyebrow in the Indian establishment and in response to the Chinese moves, India has raised two mountain divisions and an artillery brigade to the deployed in Arunachal Pradesh.[8]

Another contentious topic is the issue of stapled visas to the citizens of the Indian province of Jammu and Kashmir by China, thereby questioning the status of the province within India. Indian officials have raised this issue with China many times at the highest political levels and China has agreed in principle to discontinue the same. It may be mentioned here that in the aftermath of the 1962 war, China seized 38,000 square kilometres of Indian territory in Jammu and Kashmir while Pakistan ceded another 5,120 square kilometres territory of Indian territory it had occupied in 1947–8 to China in 1963.[9]

India's second round of nuclear tests in 1998 dealt a big blow to the bilateral ties especially after the then Indian defence minister George Fernandes, publicly referred to China as India's 'enemy number one', though tempers cooled down later when the then Indian external affairs minister Jaswant Singh paid an official visit to China in June 1999 and both sides reiterated that 'neither country is a threat to the other'.[10] Indian observers and strategists have also been worried by Chinese attempts to encircle India in its immediate neighbourhood as a part of its so-called string of pearls strategy. China has funded ports and refuelling stations in Pakistan (Gwadar), Sri Lanka (Hambantota), Bangladesh (Chittagong) and Myanmar (Kyaukpyu).

India and China have been fighting it out in various parts of the world for energy resources, especially in Africa for oil. China has not openly supported India's quest to become a permanent member of the UNSC (United Nations Security Council) and has chosen to be ambiguous on this issue. Sharing of river waters is likely to emerge as one of the biggest areas of concern in the absence of a water-sharing agreement between India and China. Though there have been reports that China intends to divert the Yarlung Tsangpo river in its Tibet province, which enters the Indian state of Arunachal Pradesh as the Siang. However, China has stated that they are only building 'run of the river' dams.[11]

China also has raised objections over India hosting the Dalai Lama, but India has brushed aside these objections. India has time and again expressed support for the 'One-China' principle and has reiterated that the Dalai Lama would not be allowed to indulge in political activities. However, the issue of Tibet and Tibetan refugees in India has been an irritant in the ties between the two countries.

China and India have gone for massive arms purchases and defence modernization. India is now one of the world's biggest arms importers. As mentioned earlier, China claims the entire Indian state of Arunachal Pradesh and has in the past denied Chinese visas to Indian citizens from there.

In particular, the lifting of the 'technical hold' by China on the blacklisting of Pakistan-based terror outfit Jaish-e-Mohammed (JeM)leader Masood Azhar by the 1267 Committee of the UNSC signals not only a shift in China's position on the issue, but also a shift in Sino-Indian ties. It was the Pakistan-based Jaish-e-Mohammed that claimed responsibility for the deadly bombing in the Indian state of Jammu and Kashmir which killed forty paramilitary troops and brought India and Pakistan dangerously close to a war.[12]

After Beijing's repeated blocking of earlier proposals to enlist Masood Azhar as a global terrorist at the 1267 Committee, the United States, United Kingdom and France moved a draft resolution in the UNSC for the same purpose. This put China in a difficult spot since it would have to place on record its objections (in the Security Council), which would put it on a tight spot diplomatically.

Areas of convergence

Fortunately, differences in some major areas have not precluded India and China from cooperating in other areas, especially in trade. China has the world's second largest economy while India also has one of the fastest growing economies in the world. The economic potential of China and India is aptly illustrated by a Carnegie Endowment report 'The G-20 in 2050' which says 'by 2050, the United States and Europe will be joined in economic size by emerging markets in Asia and Latin America. China will become the world's largest economy in 2032, and grow to be 20 per cent larger than the United States by 2050'.[13] The Trump administration has been ratcheting up the pressure on Beijing on many fronts, especially on the trade front. This may explain Beijing's reach out to countries like Japan and India in the recent times. Hence, Beijing may have thought it prudent to yield some space to Washington on the Masood Azhar issue, which may help Beijing mend fences with Washington on other issues. In other words, 'sacrificing' Masood Azhar would not cost Beijing much.

On the issue of climate change, China and India have taken common positions as exemplified in the 2009 Copenhagen Climate Change Summit. In fact, the camaraderie witnessed between India and China at the Copenhagen Summit has been dubbed as the Copenhagen spirit.

India and China have also been cooperating in BRICS, an organization that is seen by many as an alternate model to the Western dominance of the global order. Meanwhile India, China and Russia have been trying to forge a consensus on many key issues, not to hedge against the West, but to ensure that their national interests are not compromised in the international arena. As part of this, the foreign ministers of Russia, India and China meet annually to discuss issues of mutual concern.

Beijing and New Delhi are also cooperating in the Asian Infrastructure Investment Bank (AIIB), where India is the second biggest shareholder after China. It is also worth mentioning here that China and India have a shared interest in fighting Islamist terrorism, particularly emanating from Pakistan. China has been fighting separatists in its restive Xinjiang province, who have close links with Pakistan-based Islamist terrorists. India, for long, has suffered from terrorist attacks staged by Pakistan-based outfits, the ghastly Mumbai attacks of November 2008 being a prime example.

The United States as a factor in Sino-Indian relations

The development of close ties between India and the United States is one of the most remarkable features of the period after the end of the Cold War. Although India's nuclear tests of 1998 temporarily jolted the fledgling relationship, it was soon back on track when the then US president Bill Clinton visited India in March 2000. India's geopolitical importance, strong economy and huge pool of highly qualified technical manpower make it very important for America's national interests. The signing of the Indo-US Agreement for Cooperation in the Peaceful Uses of Nuclear Energy on 10 October 2008 marked the end of India's nuclear isolation, though China was not too happy with the same and tried to block it at the Nuclear Suppliers' Group (NSG).[14]

India's improving ties with the United States have seen many Chinese observers expressing doubts that the United States is using India in order to counter China. Some quarters in India have also raised the same question, but the Indian government has been careful enough to allay any such apprehensions. India's former prime minister Dr Manmohan Singh repeatedly said that there is enough room for both India and China to grow.[15]

Former US president Barack Obama came to India on an official visit in November 2010 and in a major policy shift announced America's support for India's candidature as a permanent member of the UNSC. India and the United States now hold joint military exercises, something which was unthinkable during the Cold War era. Earlier, Russia was the supplier of choice for the Indian armed forces, which has changed in the period after the end of the Cold War. Many American defence firms have now entered the lucrative Indian defence market. The Indian Air Force (IAF) has already inducted into service the American-made Lockheed Martin C-130J Super Hercules aircraft.

At the same time, the US Navy and the Coast Guard in the recent times have been carrying out a string of Freedom of Navigation Operations (FONOPs) in the South China Sea and also in the Taiwan Strait. The Trump administration has been placing a lot of emphasis on India in its Indo-Pacific strategy. In the aftermath of the Pulwama terror attack of 14 February, the US NSA (National Security Advisor) John Bolton publicly announced that the United States supported 'India's right to self-defence' while Secretary Pompeo tweeted 'we stand with India as it confronts terrorism. Pakistan must not provide safe haven for terrorists to threaten international security'.

New Delhi and Washington are already coming closer than ever more and this is certainly not what Beijing would want. India has drastically increased its purchase of US-made weaponry, the induction of the US-made heavy lift CH-47F (I) Chinook helicopters by the IAF being a recent example. Meanwhile, American defence sales to India are expected to reach an estimated $18 billion this year, while American civilian manufacturers are also eyeing the Indian domestic aviation market.

China and India in Asia

China and India have also been trying to carve out their own areas of influence in Asia. It was in the early 1990s that India embarked on its 'Look East Policy', which was designed to reach out to the countries of Southeast Asia and East Asia with which India has had historical links but had lost out in the period after its independence. Since then, India's ties with the Southeast Asian and East Asian nations have improved tremendously. This policy has now been renamed as the 'Act-East Policy', after the Modi government took office in India. New Delhi became a sectoral dialogue partner of the ASEAN in 1992, while in 1996, it became a full dialogue partner. India conducts joint naval exercises with countries like Singapore, Indonesia and Thailand and became a member of the East Asia Summit in 2005, in spite of stiff Chinese opposition.

There cannot be any doubt that China has been a factor in the emerging ties between India and many of the countries in Southeast and East Asia. With Myanmar doing an about-turn in its ties with China, India stands to gain a lot from the same. China had already made deep inroads into Myanmar. Incidentally, in the past there have been reports of China setting up listening posts in Myanmar's Coco Islands which are very close to India's Andaman and Nicobar chain of islands.[16] China has also built a pipeline from the Myanmarese port city of Kyaukpyu to take crude oil from the oil-rich Gulf region to its southern city of Kunming. This will allow China to bypass the Straits of Malacca, which is a choke point. This will also be a game changer in Asian geopolitics since the Straits of Malacca is seen as China's Achilles' heel.

Meanwhile, India has been ramping up its ties with countries like Vietnam. In addition, India's relations with Japan also have seen a remarkable improvement in the period after the end of the Cold War. India's economic liberalization made it appealing to Japanese business interests. Though Japan reacted strongly to India's nuclear tests in 1998, the visit to India by the then Japanese prime minister Yoshiro Mori in August 2000 helped to put the relations back on track. Japan and India signed a Strategic and Global Partnership agreement in December 2006, while a Joint Declaration on Security Cooperation was issued in October 2008. Japan and India now have an annual summit at the prime ministerial level. One of the factors that has drawn Japan and India closer, of late, has been the increasingly belligerent attitude of China. Interestingly, India, Japan and the United States held their first-ever trilateral dialogue in December 2011 in Washington, D.C., which signals the increasing levels of cooperation between these three countries.

China, on the other hand, has tried to use Pakistan to balance India's growing reach. China has proliferated missile technology to Pakistan. The massive Gwadar port in Pakistan has been built with Chinese expertise. It is through the territory that Pakistan had illegally ceded to China in 1963 that the Karakoram highway, which connects China's Xinjiang region with the Gilgit–Baltistan region in Pakistan-occupied Kashmir (PoK), was constructed.[17] This is designed to give China direct access to the warm water Gwadar port in Pakistan's Balochistan province, which will help to bring in oil supplies to China from the Gulf region.

China is also helping to build a dam in Pakistani-occupied Kashmir at Bunji which is designed to generate 7000 MW of electricity.[18] Besides, the Chinese state-owned China National Nuclear Corporation will be building two additional nuclear reactors at the Chashma nuclear site – Chashma III and Chashma IV – in addition to the two that already exist.

China has also been rapidly courting Sri Lanka, supporting it militarily and diplomatically at the international fora, unlike India which has domestic compulsions in not openly backing Sri Lanka. China is financing the development of the Hambantota Development Zone in Sri Lanka, which includes, among others, a container port and an oil refinery.[19]

The next few years are going to see an increase in the conflict of interest between the two neighbours. The maritime arena may well become the next theatre of conflict. Meanwhile, a policy document produced by India's leading strategists notes 'the retention of strong U.S. maritime deployments in the Asia-Pacific theatre, a more proactive and assertive Japanese naval force projection, and a build-up of the naval capabilities of such key littoral states as Indonesia, Australia and Vietnam: all may help delay, if not deter, the projection of Chinese naval power in the Indian Ocean'.[20] China is increasingly flexing its muscles in the Indian Ocean region, which has been traditionally seen as India's backyard. As noted by Robert Kaplan, 'Competition between India and China, caused by their spreading and overlapping layers of commercial and political influence, will play out less on land, than in the naval realm.'[21]

The Wuhan spirit

However, in a positive step, Indian prime minister Narendra Modi met his Chinese counterpart, President Xi Jinping, in the Chinese city of Wuhan for an informal summit without a fixed agenda on 27 and 28 April 2018, catching many observers in both the countries and those in the wider world by surprise. This was primarily due to the fact the two neighbours had been involved in a series of spats both on the bilateral and the multilateral fronts.

This meeting in Wuhan is significant for a number of reasons.

First, New Delhi has refused to join the China-led One Belt One Road (OBOR) initiative (also known the Belt and Road Initiative (BRI)). The OBOR is, in many ways, a reinvention of the ancient Chinese Silk Road which ran from China to Europe and branched off to various countries, including India. Apart from the Maritime Silk Road, the other element of the OBOR is the Silk Road Economic Belt, through which China is trying to build land connectivity through the Central Asian countries to Europe.

One of Beijing's key reasons for the OBOR push is its gargantuan appetite for energy, which has seen it import energy resources from various parts of the world, especially the Middle East and Africa. Beijing has been slowly, but steadily trying to assert its presence in the Indian Ocean and beyond. It has also stepped up its cooperation with Pakistan with projects like the $46 billion ($61.8 billion) China–Pakistan Economic Corridor, which aims to connect Gwadar in Pakistan's Arabian Sea coast to Kashgar in Xinjiang province of Western China.

Secondly, the two countries have been locked in a stalemate since last year when Chinese forces began constructing a road in the Doklam region in Bhutan (in territory claimed by China), to which India objected, leading to a stand-off between the forces of the two countries. Fortunately, the two sides pulled back their troops just before Modi travelled to China for the BRICS (Brazil, Russia, India, China and South Africa) Summit in Xiamen in early September last year.

Thirdly, New Delhi has concerns regarding China's growing profile in the Indian Ocean region. Meanwhile, it is worthwhile to note that, once again (as in the past), Australia, India, Japan and the United States have revived the Quadrilateral Initiative (also known as the Quad). In the last instance in 2007, the Quad idea had to be rescinded in the light of protestations from Beijing. In addition, for the first time, China has set up a military base in Djibouti, which will help it establish a foothold in a very strategic location. At this point, it does not seem as if India has a clear strategy to deal with China's growing maritime presence in the Indian Ocean region.

India has always been the resident power in the Indian Ocean region with the sole exception of the United States. Its navy has had a commanding presence in the region between the Strait of Hormuz and the Strait of Malacca while its Andaman and Nicobar chain of islands lies at the entrance of the Strait of Malacca. The setting up of a tri-services command by India in the Andaman and Nicobar Islands gives it an unmatched reach in the region.

Fourthly, China's 'all-weather friendship' with Pakistan is worrisome for India, especially given the fact that Beijing has been alleged to supply nuclear and missile know-how to Pakistan. New Delhi has now become a member of other forums like the Australia Group and the MTCR (Missile Technology Control Regime), and the NSG is the last remaining hurdle.

Fifthly, India reels under a huge trade deficit when it comes to bilateral trade with China, which shows no signs of being narrowed. In 2017, though the total trade between India and China reached a historic high of $84.44 billion, the trade deficit has also ballooned to $51.75 billion in China's favour.

The statement issued by the Indian Ministry of External Affairs during the Wuhan summit noted that the two leaders 'issued strategic guidance to their respective militaries to strengthen communication in order to build trust and mutual understanding and enhance predictability and effectiveness in the management of border affairs'.[22] This could be very significant after what happened in Doklam last year.

After the Wuhan informal summit, Beijing also announced it would be slashing tariffs on twenty-eight medicines, including cancer drugs from India, though it received a lukewarm response from Indian pharmaceutical companies, as it takes a long time for such Indian companies to enter the Chinese market after prolonged field trials and approvals.

It will be premature to expect India–China relations to improve overnight following the Wuhan summit. There are still issues where the two sides do not necessarily see eye-to-see like the border issue and India's NSG-inclusion bid among others. However, the summit seems to have provided a much-needed safety valve following a period of tense relations between the two Asian neighbours. The summit has also offered the opportunity tor the two countries to reset their relationship.

China–India Relations on the upswing

Meanwhile, Beijing had much to gain to lifting its technical hold. In the aftermath of the US decision to end waivers for countries buying Iranian oil, it would be in China's interests to join ranks with India on this issue.

In addition, Beijing has realized that Pakistan is on a sticky wicket when it comes to terrorism. China has already invested a lot of money in the China–Pakistan Economic Corridor (CPEC) and would be wary of its investments going up in smoke if India–Pakistan skirmishes continue. The fact that India upped the ante with air strikes deep inside Pakistan after the Pulwama attack has made China sit up and take notice. It is worth noting here that China did not overtly criticize New Delhi after the air strikes.

Conclusion

The challenge for policy makers in both the countries will be not to let their differences get out of hand. How can India and China manage the same?

First, the two countries need to improve the people-to-people relations. While the two countries are neighbours, it is unfortunate that very few Indians travel to China and vice versa. The number of Indians visiting China is much less than Indians going to other countries of the world and the same is true with Chinese tourists visiting India. Tourism could be a major revenue earner for both the countries. Chinese tourists would be interested in Buddhist pilgrimage sites in India while Indians could visit Hindu religious sites like Mount Kailash and Lake Mansarovar. The Indian community in China is not too big, though there is an interesting trend of Indian students going to China to study medicine.

Secondly, on the boundary issue, both the countries will have to do some give and take, particularly in the uninhabited areas along the border. However, domestically this will be very difficult for both New Delhi and Beijing as there is bound to be stiff opposition to any such move.

Thirdly, the two countries need to work out a mechanism to share river waters since there is every likelihood that this issue could snowball into a major irritant in the ties between the two nations.

Fourthly, the two countries can go for joint patrolling activities in the Indian Ocean and the South China Sea in order to dispel fears of any conflict in the maritime arena between the two neighbours.

Fifthly, the two countries should think of developing new road links and opening more trading points to increase trade. It is worth noting that a Second World War-era road, the Stilwell Road, exists between India's Northeast to Kunming in China through Myanmar, though this has been lying unused. This road, if reopened, could spur the development of India's remote Northeast, though there are genuine concerns about illegal weapons and narcotics entering India from China through this route.

Sixthly, the two countries can think of increasing air connectivity between the two countries which will allow more people to travel between India and China for business or leisure. The Chinese and the Indian movie industries could think of some joint ventures. Indian Bollywood movies are very popular across the world and dubbed versions of Bollywood movies are now being screened in China, with Indian movies like *Dangal* and *Baahubali* going on to become big hits in China. The same could be done with Chinese movies in India.

India and China have lived together in peace for millennia apart from during the short border war of 1962. The growing attention being paid to each other can be seen in the increasing number of ministerial visits, bilateral agreements and cooperation in diverse fields between the two countries. What is remarkable is that while both the countries have agreed to disagree on certain issues, they have still decided to move on with their bilateral ties.

India's former National Security Advisor (and former foreign secretary), Shiv Sankar Menon is quoted as saying that 'the basic task of India's foreign policy is to enable the domestic transformation of India. This requires us to work for a supportive external environment that is peaceful, thus permitting us to concentrate on our domestic tasks. At the broadest level our foreign policy seeks security and support as we build and change our society and economy.'[23] The same is true for China and hence there is very remote possibility of an all-out war between the two, but the potential for border skirmishes do exist.

India has what can be best described as a *zhengyou* relationship with China rather than a '*pengyou*' relationship. A *pengyou* means a superficial friend while a *zhengyou* is a real friend who admits to problems in the friendship, but at the same time works hard to overcome them.[24] What is, however, certain is that if the twenty-first century is to be an Asian century, as many observers have predicted, peace between India and China is absolutely sine qua non. As Indian prime minister Narendra Modi noted in his keynote address at the Shangri-la Dialogue earlier in June this year in Singapore, 'I firmly believe that, Asia and the world will have a better future when India and China work together in trust and confidence, sensitive to each other's interests.'[25]

Notes

1 Ministry of External Affairs (MEA), Government of India, *India-China Bilateral Relations* (2012). Available , at http://meaindia.nic.in/meaxpsite/foreignrelation/china.pdf (accessed on April 23, 2012).

2 Ibid.

3 Rao (2011).

4 Roy (2011).

5 These five principles include (i) mutual respect for each other's territorial integrity and sovereignty; (ii) mutual non-aggression; (iii) Mutual non-interference in each other's internal affairs; (iv) equality and mutual benefit; and (v) peaceful co-existence.

6 See 'China Has Settled All Land Border Disputes Except with India and Bhutan' (2009).

7 Goswami (2012).

8 Pant (2011).

9 'India Wary of Sino-Pak strategic Link-up in Occupied Kashmir' (2009).

10 Ministry of External Affairs (MEA), n.1.

11 Goswami (2012: n.7).

12 Zheng (2019).

13 Uri (2009).

14 Pant (2011: n.8).

15 'India Wants "Best of Relations" with China: PM' (2011).

16 Shashikumar (2010).

17 Kan (2011).

18 'China's presence in PoK worries India'.

19 Pant (2011: n.13).
20 'Nonalignment 2.0 – A Foreign and Strategic Policy for India in the Twenty-First Century'.
21 Kaplan (2010).
22 Ministry of External Affairs (India).
23 Address by Foreign Secretary at the Bureau of Parliamentary Studies and Training on 'Indian Foreign Policy: Opportunities and Challenges' (2009).
24 Subrahmaniam (2010).
25 Ministry of External Affairs (India) (2018).

Bibliography

Ali, Ahmed, 'A Consideration of Sino-Indian Conflict', *Institute for Defence Studies and Analyses (IDSA), Issue Brief*, 24 October (2011). Available at http://www.idsa.in/system/files/IB_AConsiderationofSino-IndianConflict.pdf (accessed 20 April 2012).

Bertsch, Gary K., Seema Gahlaut and Anupam Srivastava (eds.), *Engaging India: U.S. Strategic Relations with the World's Largest Democracy* (New York: Routledge, 1999).

Chan, S., *East Asian Dynamism: Growth, Order and Security in the Pacific Region* (Boulder, CO: Westview Press, 1990).

Chellaney, Brahma, *Asian Juggernaut: The Rise of China, India and Japan* (New York: Harper Collins Publishers, 2010).

Chellaney, Brahma, *Water: Asia's New Battleground* (Washington D.C., Georgetown UP, 2011).

'China Has Settled All Land Border Disputes Except with India and Bhutan', 13 October (2009). Available at http://news.rediff.com/slide-show/2009/oct/13/slide-show-1-china-has-settled-all-land-border-disputes-except-with-india-and-bhutan.htm (accessed 20 April 2018).

'China's Presence in PoK Worries India', *Deccan Herald*,). Available at http://www.deccanherald.com/content/108151/chinas-presence-pok-worries-india.html (accessed 23 April 2018).

Doran, C. F., 'The Power Cycle and Peaceful Change', in J. A. Vasquez et al. (eds.), *Beyond Confrontation* (Ann Arbor: University of Michigan Press, 1995), pp. 179–98.

Garver, John W. L., *Protracted Contest: Sino-Indian Rivalry in the 20th Century* (Seattle: University of Washington Press, 2001).

Ghoshal, Baladas, 'India and China: Towards a Competitive-Cooperative Relationship?' *IPCS Issue Brief*, No. 153 (2010).

Goswami, Namrata, 'China's Territorial Claim on the Indian State of Arunachal Pradesh: Crafting an Indian Response', *IDSA Issue Brief*, 25 October (2011). Available at http://www.idsa.in/ system/files/IB_Chinasterrorialclaim.pdf (accessed 20 December 2011).

Goswami, Namrata, 'China's Territorial Claim on India's Eastern Sector: Tibet as Core', *New Delhi, IDSA Issue Brief*, 19 April (2012). Available at http://www.idsa.in/system/files/IB_ChinasTerritorialClaimon_Namrata_0.pdf (accessed 22 April 2018).

Hoffmann, S. A., *India and the China Crisis* (Berkeley and Los Angeles: University of California Press, 1990).

'India Wants "Best of Relations" with China: PM', *The Hindu Business Line*, 18 November (2011). Available at http://www.thehindubusinessline.com/industry-and-economy/economy/article2638590.ece?ref=wl_government-and-policy_art (accessed 13 March 2018).

'India Wary of Sino-Pak Strategic Link-up in Occupied Kashmir', *Indian Express*, 12 July (2009). Available at http://www.indianexpress.com/news/india-wary-of-sinopak-stra tegic-linkup-in/488346/ (accessed 15 January 2018).

'Indian Foreign Policy: Opportunities and Challenges', 21 July (2009). Available at http://164.100.24.207/inputprogram/lecturefiles/Shiv_Shankar.pdf (accessed 23 March 2018).

Kan, Shirley A., 'China and Proliferation of Weapons of Mass Destruction and Missiles: Policy Issues', *Congressional Research Service*, (2011). Available at http://fpc.state.gov/documents/organization/156523.pdf (accessed 17 February 2018).

Kaplan, Robert D., *Monsoon: The Indian Ocean and the Future of American Power* (New York: Random House, 2010).

Malik, J. M., 'Security Council Reform: China Signals Its Veto', *World Policy Journal*, 22 (1) (2005), pp. 19–29.

Mehta, Admiral Sureesh, 'India's National Security Challenges – An Armed Forces Overview', *Address At India Habitat Centre*, 10 August (2009). Available at http://mar itimeindia.org/sites/all/files/pdf/CNS_Lec_at_Habitat.pdf (accessed 20 June 2011).

Ministry of External Affairs (India), 'Prime Minister's Keynote Address at Shangri La Dialogue', 1 June (2018). Available at https://mea.gov.in/Speeches-Statements.htm?dt l/29943/Prime_Ministers_Keynote_Address_at_Shangri_La_Dialogue_June_01_2018 (accessed 28 June 2018).

Ministry of External Affairs (India), 'India-China Informal Summit at Wuhan'. Available at http://www.mea.gov.in/press-releases.htm?dtl/29853/IndiaChina+Informal+Summ it+at+Wuhan (accessed 27 June 2018).

Ministry of External Affairs (MEA), Government of India, 'India-China Bilateral Relations'. Available at http://meaindia.nic.in/meaxpsite/foreignrelation/china.pdf (accessed 21 June 2018).

'Nonalignment 2.0- A Foreign And Strategic Policy for India in the Twenty First Century'. Available at http://www.cprindia.org/workingpapers/3844-nonalignment-20-foreig n-and-strategic-policy-india-twenty-first-century p.13 (accessed 20 April 2018).

Pant, Harsh, 'China And India: A Rivalry Takes Shape', *Foreign Policy Research Institute*, Philadelphia (2011). Available at http://www.fpri.org/enotes/201106.pant.china_india .pdf (accessed 20 June 2018).

Pillsbury, M., *China Debates the Future Security Environment* (Washington DC: National Defense UP, 2000).

Raghavan, Srinath, *War and Peace in Modern India* (New Delhi: Permanent Black, 2010).

Rao, Nirupama, 'Lecture at Singapore Consortium for China-India Dialogue', (2011). Available at http://www.thehindu.com/news/resources/article1092783.ece (accessed 20 June 2018).

Roy, Bhaskar, 'Managing India – China Relations', (2011). Available at http://www.sout hasiaanalysis.org/%5Cpapers49%5Cpaper4834.html (accessed 20 June 2018).

Shashikumar, V. K., 'No War, No Peace', *Tehelka*, (2010). Available at http://www.tehelka. com/story_main47.asp?filename=Ne271110Coverstory.asp (accessed 10 May 2018).

Singh, Swaran, 'Indian Debate on Limited War', *Strategic Analysis*, XXIII (12) (2000), pp. 2179–83.

Subrahmaniam, Vidya(2010), 'A "zhengyou" Relationship with China', *The Hindu*, 10 June (2010). Available at http://www.hindu.com/2010/06/10/stories/2010061062390800.htm (accessed 30 January 2018).

Uri, Dadush, 'The G-20 in 2050', *Carnegie Endowment for International Peace*, (2009). Available at http://www.carnegieendowment.org/ieb/2009/11/19/g20-in-2050/lp4 (accessed 10 June 2018).

Zheng, Sarah, 'Why China Dropped Its Opposition to UN Blacklisting of Pakistan-based Chief Terror Masood Azhar', *South China Morning Post (SCMP)*, 2 May (2019). Available at https://www.scmp.com/news/china/diplomacy/article/3008614/why-chi na-dropped-its-opposition-un-blacklisting-pakistan (accessed 18 August 2019).

10

China in Latin America

Wolfgang Muno, Alexander Brand and Susan McEwen-Fial

Introduction: China's rise

China's rise in world politics is often seen as a harbinger of a new era in world politics (Ikenberry 2008; Lindsay 2011; Breslin 2013; Stuenkel 2016; Pei 2018). Alongside, Chinese activities throughout Latin America have developed at a remarkable pace. In recent years, Latin America has been deemed of strategic importance by China. Relations skyrocket after Hu Jintao's visit in Brazil, Argentina and Cuba in 2004. Since then, Latin America has changed from a blip on the Chinese economic horizon to a steady supplier of natural resources and increasingly of energy supplies. But economy is not the only realm of activity. China's 2008 White Paper on Latin America targeted growth in military ties as one of its objectives for the region. In the institutional arena, China has increased its diplomatic presence in the multilateral organizations of the region. Additionally, China is trying to build up its image through a 'soft power' strategy, establishing Confucius institutes in the region, offering scholarships, broadcasting CCTV in Spanish and charming Latin American governments through frequent visits. The new 2016 Policy Paper on Latin America and the Caribbean published on behalf of the Chinese government announced even bolder policy and investment plans as well as new soft power initiatives (Cardenal 2017).

This leads to another idea which links such power transition thinking with rather specific assumptions regarding foreign policy and international cooperation of authoritarian regimes (Kagan 2006; Erdmann et al. 2013; Mattes and Rodriguez 2014; Diamond, Plattner and Walker 2016; Walker and Ludwig 2017; Pei 2018). Authoritarian regimes are assumed to have special foreign policy motivations, ambitions as well as activities. One certain aspect of an alleged specific authoritarian foreign policy is embodied in the growing interest in whether China acts as an outside stabilizer for other authoritarian regimes in fact helping autocratic structures to survive and thus limiting global democracy (Bader 2014, 2015; Burnell 2010a,b; Walker and Ludwig 2017). Academic research has so far tended to reach rather ambivalent conclusions, if any at all, regarding any manifest and systematic interest on behalf of China to prop up and unite all authoritarian regimes across the globe. Some authors have indeed suggested that 'authoritarian solidarity' is an important ingredient in Chinese foreign policy (e.g. Kleine-Ahlbrandt and Small 2008; Burnell 2010b: 11; Walker and Ludwig

2017; Pei 2018). In contrast, Vanderhill excludes China *expressis verbis* in her recent study on autocracy promotion, but without giving evidence why (Vanderhill 2013: 6).

China has been considering Latin America as a region of heightened strategic importance in recent years, which has become a focus field of Chinese foreign policy activity (Gallagher and Porzecanski 2010; ECLAC 2011; Ellis 2011a,b, 2017; Cardenal 2017). Hence, Latin America provides a good testing ground for the aforementioned assumption. The central guiding question is: Can we identify patterns of an 'authoritarian nexus' vis-à-vis autocratic states on behalf of China?

Methodologically, we have chosen the technique of structured focused comparisons between different real types of relations in order to identify whether a relation is special vis-à-vis others or not (on the method itself see George 1979; George and Bennett 2004: 67–72). Consequently, we are looking for a specific intensity or specific patterns of exchange between China and autocracies in the Western hemisphere as compared to China's relations with comparable, non-autocratic states in the region. Following the logic of paired comparisons (Tarrow 2010), we compare each of the two obvious cases of relations to autocracies in the target region, namely Chinese-Cuban and Chinese-Venezuelan relations, to structurally similar cases (Chinese relations with Costa Rica and Chile, respectively).

In analysing whether Chinese activities throughout Latin America are intentionally seeking to nurture especially good relations with autocratic/authoritarian states, we define as a threshold for such an authoritarian nexus the following. First, we focus on internal features/state structures which allow a country to be categorized as 'autocratic'. China definitely has become one of the most important autocratic states today. In Latin America, Cuba is without doubt not only autocratic, but even a socialist autocracy, which makes Cuba the most likely case for special relations with China. The counterpart for Cuba is Costa Rica, structurally similar in size, population and importance, but notably different in the crucial variable 'regime type'. Costa Rica has been a stable democracy since 1949. Thus, if the logic of an authoritarian nexus holds, Costa Rica should constitute an unlikely case for a special relationship with China. Venezuela can be identified as a second obvious case in the region. An authoritarian, pro-socialist regime, Venezuela is a likely case, too, against the background of the idea of an authoritarian nexus. A suitable case of comparison for Venezuela is Chile, a structurally similar country with a resource-based economy, depending not on oil like Venezuela but on copper. Again, the notable difference is in the variable 'regime type': Chile has matured to a stable and successful democracy since re-democratization in 1989, which, in the logic of the alleged relation makes Chile an unlikely case, too.

A second, necessary qualification for an 'authoritarian nexus' is the existence of specific bilateral foreign policy schemes which indicate a preference for specifically intense cooperation and collaboration with autocratic regimes in the context of Chinese activities throughout the whole region.

In the following, first, we reflect on foreign policy analysis, IR theories and regime type, developing theoretically derived hypotheses on an 'authoritarian nexus'. Secondly, in order to test the hypotheses, we analyse Chinese activities in Latin America in the realms of (military) security, economic cooperation, institutional and soft power/ public diplomacy, attempting to find patterns of specific favouritism in Chinese relations with Cuba and Venezuela in contrast to China's activities in Costa Rica and Chile respectively.

Foreign policy analysis, IR theories and regime type

What role does regime type play in foreign policy analysis and IR theories? A surprisingly little one!

The first IR theory to be considered is realism. Realist thinking is a conglomerate of many ideas and assumptions about politics, especially international politics, a world view with several variants, but at the same time a central core.

Thucydides, Machiavelli, Hobbes and Morgenthau stand for the classical realist thinking. A crucial advancement has been made with structural realism or neorealism by Kenneth Waltz. Waltz criticized the anthropological perspective of realism as not convincing and invented a structural, systemic approach (Waltz 1959, 1979; see also Mearsheimer 2016).

Core of structural realism is the anarchical structure of the international system, resulting out of the absence of a higher authority. This anarchy leads to a permanent security dilemma for the most important actors in the international system, the states. Rules or treaties cannot be enforced like in a nation-state by an authority with monopoly of violence; therefore, no state can trust any other state.

This structure of the international system leads to a self-help system in which every states tries to be autonomous, not having to rely on the help of other states; therefore, cooperation is not very probable or rather limited to certain security alliances. While Waltz explicitly does not state a genuine foreign policy, we can derive realist foreign policy assumptions. Colin Elman emphasizes the possibility and necessity to formulate a neorealist foreign policy (Elman 1996).

States tend to secure their survival, they aim at security. In order to achieve security, they need power. So states increase their power. At the same time, states are rational actors, so they only act when they are threatened and as far as necessary because of cost-benefit-analyses.

However, every state is similar in this respect since every state wants to survive and has to survive, otherwise the state will disappear like Burgundy, the Austrian Empire or the Osman Empire. Therefore, regime type does not matter. Whether democratic or authoritarian, states pursue their national interest, which is securing their survival (and in order to achieve this, accumulating as much power as necessary).

Hence, a structural realist hypothesis would expect China to follow a strict pragmatic foreign policy in pursuing national interest and not favouring any other country on the grounds of regime type. In other words, China would not be selecting likely interaction partners for short- or mid-term economic cooperation or tactical alliance building according to the respective domestic structures of rule of such a partner country.

Hypothesis 1 (realist hypothesis): China is pursuing a purely pragmatic foreign policy towards Latin America and is not seeking especially strong bonds to authoritarian partners, that is not promoting autocracy.

The second IR theory to be considered is liberalism. Having several variants as well, regime type plays a central role in liberal theory (Panke and Risse 2016; see also Moravcsik 2003). The democratic peace theory, leaning on Kant's essay 'On Perpetual Peace', assumes that democracies are more peaceful than autocratic systems (see Doyle 1983). In the Kantian perspective, in a democracy the people can decide their own fate and assuming that they are rational actors, they won't opt for war because they can lose their property or even their lives. On the other hand, in autocracies, only the prince decides about war or peace, it's a 'prince's game'. Autocracies also use military adventures to detract from internal problems. In Andrew Moravcsik's rational liberal variant, the regime elites cooperate with like-minded elites in other countries having similar preferences, democratic elites with other democrats, autocratic elites with other autocrats (Moravcsik 1997).

According to liberalism, we would expect China to pursue a more active foreign policy towards Latin America, with a consistent preference for cooperation with other, seemingly like-minded autocracies in case of non-rivalling preferences.

Hypothesis 2 (liberal hypothesis): China is cooperating more intensely with other autocracies like Cuba and Venezuela because of a perceived like-mindedness and mutual interests/common preferences.

A third theory contender in IR is constructivism (Fierke 2016). The starting point of some prominent wing of IR constructivism is again the anarchy of the international system, a common assumption with neorealism and at the same time a fundamental difference. The difference lies in the forces which shape politics (Wendt 1999). While neorealism relies exclusively on material structures, constructivism emphasizes immaterial structures like ideas, norms and values. These can vary, so the anarchical system is not necessarily the Hobbesian state of nature, the state of war. This is just one possibility. 'Anarchy is what states make of it', as Alexander Wendt stated (Wendt 1992). In a Lockean world, states can live next to each other as respected rivals, and in a Kantian world, they may even become friends. It all depends on how states see other states, if they perceive them as friends, foes or rivals, as the material situation surrounding them is interpreted through the lens of certain ideas, norms and values. These ideas, norms and values are not individualistic but on a societal level. Resulting from this societal level are identities, that is perceptions of the self, but also perceptions of other states. Now the logic of state action rather resembles a logic of appropriateness, which means that states act according to their self-image, their identity (Wendt 1999).

We can therefore derive a constructivist foreign policy hypothesis. States act more aggressively against enemies, while, at the same time, they look for more intense cooperation especially with states they perceive as friends. The basis of such characterization is established through common values, norms and ideas. States with similar identities cooperate and look for friendship. We would hence assume that China would especially cooperate with states having similar norms, values and ideas, hence with other states like Cuba and Venezuela, being autocratic (in the case of Cuba) or at least semi-authoritarian (Venezuela) and alluding to some supposedly left-wing, socialist ideology.

Hypothesis 3 (constructivist hypothesis): China will see Cuba and Venezuela as friends and hence will seek to nurture closer bonds to them in particular due to perceived shared norms and orientations.

Conceptually then, IR realism would deny any autocracy promotion, while IR liberalism and constructivism would expect autocracy promotion, albeit for different reasons.

In order to discuss these hypotheses, we will analyse China's activities in Latin America in the following chapter, with a specific focus on comparing the Sino-Cuban and Sino-Venezuelan relations with the ones China entertains to Costa Rica and Chile, respectively.

China in Latin America

Military activities

For Latin America as a whole, China has increased its military exchanges with Latin American countries, including traditional US allies such as Colombia and Mexico as well as its own traditional ally Cuba, and Venezuela, Bolivia and Ecuador as new allies (Ellis 2011a: 14; Ellis 2017). Quite similar patterns of partnering can be found with regard to joint exercises and military dialogues: there is hardly any favouritism towards either Venezuela or Cuba. The People's Liberation Army also held joint exercises with Brazil and Peru, and, moreover, China also conducted arms sales to Argentina, Colombia and Peru. In total, military sales to Latin America comprised only approximately 9 per cent of China's total military weapons sales in 2010 and approximately 4 per cent in 2011. To sum up, China's military activity in Latin America has been relatively limited, although relations have expanded in recent years.

Despite their close rhetorical relationship, it does not appear that China treats Cuba as a special military partner. It has no confirmed physical military presence in Latin America, although some America security specialists suspect that the Chinese might have established at least one listening post in Cuba (Horta 2008; Ellis 2011a). In addition, Cuba has merely been one of several countries which has participated in forums such the first China-Latin America Defense Forum, held in China in November 2012, with six countries participating, including Colombia, Cuba, Bolivia and Uruguay (FMPRC 2012). Thus, there is little evidence of a preference for military ties with Cuba.

China's military relationship with Costa Rica represents China's tendency to mix security cooperation with commercial interests. Costa Rica is the only country in the world with no army, leaving China without an institutional outlet to deepen military ties. However, China has pledged recently to donate $25 million to the reconstruction of the National Police Academy as part of a scheme to foster commercial ties (Arias 2013). This blending of security and commercial interests is indicative of China's actions throughout the region and shows no discrimination between autocratic and non-autocratic regimes.

China's military relationship with Venezuela looks at first to be the strongest in the region because of the higher sales of military equipment. But this is due less to

Chinese strategic cooperation than to an arms embargo imposed in 2006 by the United States on Venezuela, which forced the Venezuelan military to diversify its arms acquisition. Venezuela, for decades a very good customer of US military products, especially aircraft (Venezuela was one of the first customers of F-16 in the world), was consequently forced to resort to arms sellers like Russia, Belarus and China. Venezuela has recently become the most important customer for Chinese arms sales in the region; the country purchased about two dozen K-aircraft so far, as well as a Chinese air surveillance system and L-15 fighters (Marcella 2012; Ellis 2017). However, apart from the very vivid arms trade, there are no exclusive military exchanges or military alliances between China and Venezuela which would indicate a special relationship.

Chile has maintained military relations with China since it recognized the PRC in 1970. China and Chile's navies have held exchanges with China's ships visiting Chile and Chile's training ship the Esmeralda having visited China several times Chile has also benefitted from China's increased military exchanges throughout Latin America. In regards to student exchanges in the military realm, it is remarkable that studies refer to the fact that it was students from non-autocratic countries (Colombia, Chile, Mexico, Peru and Uruguay) who went to the China's Defense Studies Institute, the Army Command College, the Navy Command School and the Naval Research Institute (Marcella 2012). Thus, it appears that China favours good military relations with a democratic country like Chile over a special relationship with autocratic regimes.

To sum up, it appears that China does not discriminate according to regime type while deepening these ties. Especially military cooperation with Cuba seems to be on a very low level. Although there are rumours about secret cooperation schemes and arms sales, due to a lack of data it is not possible to verify them at this juncture. Experts attribute this apparent restraint to the fact that China does not want to offend the United States openly in its own backyard. Increased arms sales to Venezuela resemble a strategy of the exploitation of commercial opportunities rather than a closing of the ranks among autocracies. There are no exclusive alliances or forms of cooperation with Cuba or Venezuela. Instead, Chinese cooperation in the realm of security includes Chile and even with Costa Rica, a country without an army, as well as a host of other democratic states in the Western hemisphere. This pattern disputes the idea of a special authoritarian nexus in the realms of military and security cooperation.

Economic activities

With its abundant natural resources, Latin America fits perfectly in with China's goal of strengthening its comprehensive national strength (*zōnghé guólì*) in order to become a great power. China's 'go out' policy (*zǒuchūqū zhànlüè*), promulgated by Jiang Zemin, supports this endeavour as it officially sanctions state support for Chinese firms to invest abroad to secure natural resources and know-how as well as to open new markets.

Trade and investment are the two main economic activities under scrutiny. Trade relations show the asymmetrical relationship: 72 per cent of Latin American exports to China are primary goods, while 90 per cent of Chinese exports to the region are manufactured goods (CEPAL 2018). Between 2001 and 2013, trade increased twenty-twofold and reached a 268 billion high, in 2017, the value of trade was $266 billion, after a four-year long contraction in the wake of the world financial crisis. In 2018, trade value reached $306 billion (Carvalho 2019). The most important trade partners are Brazil and Mexico, followed by Chile and Venezuela. While Brazil, Venezuela and Chile are having a trade surplus with China, all other countries of the region have a deficit in trade relations with it; Mexico's deficit amounts to $65 million in 2017, more than all others combined (CEPAL 2018).

Investments have mainly concentrated on petroleum and mining activities; hence Brazil, Peru and China are the main recipients of Chinese Foreign Direct Investment (FDI) in the region (see Table 10.1).

A case in point is Chinese long-term mining projects in the region. A recent study by Gonzalez-Vicente which explicitly considered the suggestion that 'market rules are not fundamental but secondary to political and geostrategic concerns' (and hence analyses a question that is similar to ours) has, however, demonstrated that there are no specifically intense economic activities in autocratic regions, even if opportunities exist in principle (Gonzalez-Vicente 2012). Chinese companies have so far rather avoided Venezuela despite its mineral wealth; the top Chinese mining projects in Latin America are all located in democratic countries, such as Peru, Chile and Ecuador.

In addition to FDI, loans represent another important Chinese economic activity in Latin America. China's principal banks, led by the China Development Bank, have lent more than $140 billion to the region in the last decade. Most important recipients here are Venezuela and Brazil (see Table 10.2).

While Venezuela is an important outlier, receiving alone more than 40 per cent of loans, overall, the picture is mixed. Cuba does not receive any loans, while democratic states receive loans. If we include foreign aid, Cuba enters the frame again. Pei mentions four countries in the region receiving important amounts of foreign aid, Venezuela, Ecuador, Brazil and Cuba (see Table 10.3).

Like its relationship with the rest of Latin America, China's economic relationship with Cuba has strengthened over the years, although the size of trade in no way compares to China's trade with partners like Brazil. Cuban-China bilateral trade reached nearly $2 billion in 2012, making China the second largest single country trading partner for Cuba. In 2016, 13.4 per cent of Cuba's exports went to China, dominated by nickel and sugar (WTO 2018). Cuba is looking to increase economic cooperation with China and

Table 10.1 Chinese FDI in Latin America 2005–17, in US Dollars (in billion)

Country	FDI	Country	FDI
Brazil	65.5	Peru	20.1
Argentina	11.0	Mexico	6.7
Venezuela	*2.0*	Ecuador	1.9
Cuba	*1.4*	Colombia	1.1
Panama	0.7	*Costa Rica*	*0.7*
Bolivia	0.5	*Chile*	*0.4*
Nicaragua	0.3	Paraguay	0.2
Uruguay	0.2		

Source: CEPAL 2018.

Table 10.2 Chinese Loans in Latin America 2015–16, in US Dollar (in billion)

Loans Country	Loans
Venezuela	62.2
Brazil	36.8
Ecuador	17.4
Argentina	15.3
Bolivia	3.5
Mexico	1.0
Costa Rica	0.395
Chile	0.15

Source: CEPAL 2018.

Table 10.3 Chinese Foreign Aid in Latin America 2000–14, in US Dollars (in billion)

Country	Aid Country	Aid
	Venezuela	10.8
	Ecuador	9.7
	Brazil	8.5
	Cuba	6.7

Source: Pei 2018.

has become China's largest trading partner in the Caribbean. In 2011, China National Petroleum Corporation signed a $4.5 billion deal to upgrade Cuba's Cienfuego refinery (WSJ 2012). However, disappointing drilling results led to the departure of a Chinese-built rig from the region (Krauss and Crave 2012). Recent Chinese activities in Cuba seem to have intensified, in particular, Premier Le Keqiang's visit to Havana in September 2016 aroused attention not least given the flurry of agreements signed and the alleged plan to turn Cuba into China's new regional 'investment hub'. On the other hand, one could not but miss the timing of such recently increased activity towards Cuba. Not only did it seem that the recent rapprochement between the United States and Cuba had an impact on strategic calculations of China vis-à-vis Cuba as reliable minor cooperation partner in what is supposedly an amicable relationship. It was also the first visit ever of a Japanese prime minister to Cuba in early September 2016 which arguably did not go unnoticed in Beijing. In that sense, the fanfare with which Le Keqiang's visit has been hailed and the new sense of importance of Chinese-Cuban relations owe more to circumstances and a shifting strategic calculus than to any preference for bolstering autocratic rule abroad. In sum, relations are quite asymmetrical and limited compared to other Latin American states, which is not surprising, keeping in mind the limited economic incentives Cuba offers. Cuba is, after all, a very poor country with limited resources.

In contrast to its weak economic ties with Cuba, China has been steadily increasing its relations with Costa Rica since 2007, when Costa Rica controversially switched recognition to the PRC away from Taiwan (Haro Navejas 2013). Trade has taken off since a Free Trade Agreement between the two countries came into force in 2011, particularly in the amount of Chinese imports. By 2016 China was the second main source of imports for Costa Rica at 13.6 per cent and ranked seventh in Costa Rica's exports for the first half of 2013 (MOFCOM 2013; WTO 2018). Costa Rica maintains a large trade deficit with China due to the high tech nature of Chinese imports to Costa Rica, primarily cellular equipment, computers and microprocessors. Costa Rica's exports to China include processors, electrical equipment, orange juice pulp and copper scrap. During Xi Jinping's visit to Costa Rica in June 2013, agreements worth nearly $2 billion were reached (Arias 2013). The Export-Import Bank of China lent Costa Rica nearly $400 million, $296 million for the upgrading of the highway between San Jose and Puerto Limón, and $101 million for public transportation vehicles (Cota 2013). The biggest agreement was the $1.3 billion project to modernize the oil factory in Limón, largely through a $900 billion loan from the China Development Bank (Arias 2013; Williams 2013). Thus China continued to deepen its economic relationship with its only Central American partner. But 2016 has marked a year of disappointment for Costa Rica. While the cancellation of a joint venture oil refinery project – sold before as the landmark symbol of Chinese-Costa Rican cooperation – made the headlines in early 2016, later on it became apparent that the Chinese also refused to buy $1 bio in Costa Rican bonds offered by the government.

In Venezuela, China has mainly focused on oil (see Giacalone and Briceño Ruiz 2013; Ríos 2013). Venezuela has reserves larger than Saudi Arabia, and Chinese oil companies are involved in that business, mainly via joint ventures with Venezuela's state-owned oil company PDVSA. But China had already started in the oil business in Venezuela in 1997, before Chávez became president (Ellis 2010; Ríos 2013). Additionally, China has given several large loans to Venezuela, which will be repaid in oil deliveries, in total worth more than $62.2 billion. However, not only oil is interesting for China. Chavista economic policy has almost completely destroyed Venezuela's manufacturing base, which has created opportunities for Chinese companies and products. Haier, Huawei and ZTE have successfully entered the Venezuelan market – Huawei and ZTE in telecommunications in a joint venture with the Venezuelan government, producing cell phones. Haier has delivered more than 300,000 consumer appliances since 2010 to be sold in state-owned supermarkets. Beyond these enterprises, China Railway is constructing more than 1000 kilometres of railroad and Huawei more than 2,000 kilometres of new fibre optic lines (on China in Venezuela, see Ellis 2013; Agustín 2016). All these economic operations have made Venezuela one of the five Chinese 'strategic partners' in Latin America, with more than 300 bilateral agreements and more than 80 major projects. Trade has risen significantly, from $200 million in 1999 to $10 billion in 2011. Venezuela is the fifth most important investment country for Chinese FDI, after Brazil, Peru, Argentina and Mexico, and the fourth most important trade partner in Latin America. In August 2015, a Venezuela–China Commission met in Caracas in order to strengthen further cooperation and sign new agreements. These operations arguably resemble good economic opportunities for China. In turn, through its economic cooperation with China, the Venezuelan government is able to deliver some consumer goods and infrastructure to its demanding population; in this sense, Chinese-Venezuelan economic cooperation might stabilize the autocratic structures in Venezuela, but rather by default. This impression is fostered by recent reports that Russia is 'beating China to Venezuela's oil fields' (O'Donnell 2016). Continued problems of Venezuela's oil company PDVSA to fulfil its obligations to ship certain quantities of oil to China in order to repay large parts of the roughly $62 bio in loans Venezuela had obtained until 2018 might become crucial in the future relations. In case China accepts to substantially re-negotiate the terms of the deal, issues new loans in light of upcoming economic collapse or otherwise provides a more than symbolic lifeline to the Maduro government, one could speak of favouritism towards an autocratically ruled country. In recent years, China seemed to be more cautious in the wake of the severe Venezuelan crisis, but just recently, in July 2018, the Development Bank of China has announced a new $5 billion loan for PDVSA (Venezuelanalysis 2018). This move has to be seen in the light of further and tighter sanctions the United States imposed in 2018 after the presidential elections in Venezuela. Whether this fosters an authoritarian-nexus-argument or is just a move to secure the oil flow and repayments has to be seen. At all, China continues to support the Maduro regime at least to a certain extent.

Similar patterns of economic transactions can be identified with respect to Chinese activities in democratic Chile. Chile, the first Latin American country to sign a free trade agreement with China, is of heightened economic interest for China because of its mineral resources (Gachúz 2012). Although Chile is a rather small country, and with about seventeen million consumers far from being an important market, Chilean-Chinese trade grew from $6.9 billion in 2005 to $32.5 billion in 2012 (DIRECOM 2014). Chile's main export product is copper, accounting for more than 50 per cent of its total exports. China consumes more than 40 per cent of the world copper production, while producing less than one-sixth of its own copper needs. China has hence become Chile's main trading partner, and Chile as the main supplier of copper (around 25 per cent of all Chinese copper imports) is of special importance to China. Consequently, Chinese copper hunger has resulted in a constant trade surplus for Chile, reaching almost $5 billion in 2012. In order to secure copper, China invests strategically in the Chilean mining sector (Gonzalez-Vicente 2012). In 2005, a joint venture worth $2 billion guaranteed China access to Chilean copper for more than fifteen years at far below market prices (Dosch and Goodman 2012: 9). In 2010, China invested another $2.3 billion in a joint venture with the state-owned Chilean mining company CODELCO and additionally approximately $2 billion in iron ore mines. In 2013, China announced it would invest $1.1 billion in photovoltaics to reduce energy costs for copper production (The BRICS Post 2013). These are huge sums for the comparably small country of Chile. Particularly noteworthy is the sustained attempt to coordinate closely (or closer) with democratic Chile in view of the crash of commodity prices and oversupply due to still high commodity production levels over the last half a decade; a phenomenon which does apply to Chile's copper exports as well even if of lesser magnitude. Much reported was also the currency swap agreement that reached between Chile's Central Bank and the People's Bank of China in 2015. Thought to affirm and support the intense bilateral economic cooperation, it can also be seen as another Chinese effort to use its partnership with a non-autocratic country like Chile to further internationalize its currency. China has similar agreements with Argentina and Brazil, other lucrative, non-autocratic economic cooperation partners.

To highlight the strategic importance of Latin America in economic terms, China has named Brazil, Mexico and Peru as 'comprehensive strategic partners' and Venezuela, Chile and Argentina as 'strategic partners'. China has also established Free Trade Agreements with Chile (2006), Peru (2010) and Costa Rica (signed 2010, in effect since 2011) and has become one of the leading trade partners for Brazil and Chile (ECLAC 2011: 19). These actions make clear that in terms of intensity and assigned importance, patterns of economic exchange between China and Latin America are by no means tilted towards autocratic states. By far, the most important economic partner is Brazil, being perhaps a special case as part of the BRICS network.

Institutional and soft power diplomacy

Institutional and soft power diplomacy represent further dimensions that China has highlighted in the region in order to protect its interests since Hu's promotion of soft power in 2007 (Cardenal 2017). Overall, China has increased its diplomatic presence in multilateral institutions of the region. In 2004, it received permanent observer status at the OAS in 2004, marking a clear indication of China's growing interest in the region. It is also an observer of UNECLAC and maintained 130 policemen as part of the UN peacekeeping forces in Haiti (MINUSTAH). China became a member of the Inter-American Development Bank in 2008, having invested $350 million. It sits on the committee overseeing loans to highly impoverished countries, including countries like Haiti and Honduras which still recognize the Republic of China as the legitimate China (Ellis 2011a: 88). China has also been active in 'track two diplomacy'. It is an active participant in the Forum of East Asia-Latin America Cooperation and has also initiated China-Latin America Summits as well as established the first China-Latin America Think Tank Forum. In 2014, China initiated the China-CELAC-Forum, which held its first meeting in 2015 in Beijing (Cardenal 2017).

In all these instances, China has sought cooperation and improved its organizational presence without positively discriminating in favour of autocracies. If at all, it rather looks as if it discriminates against ALBA. Despite several official invitations by Venezuela, China has apparently abstained from showing any commitment towards ALBA, the alliance of Venezuela, Cuba, Bolivia, Ecuador and some small Caribbean island states created in 2004 (Ríos 2013). This organization, aimed at improving trade relations among member states with a decidedly anti-imperialist stance against the United States and offering Venezuelan oil for members at special rates, even appealed to Iran, Syria and Russia as observing members. In this sense it arguably approximates being a club of (mostly) autocracies. While China has avoided ALBA, it immediately acquired observer status at the newly founded Pacific Alliance, a regional organization of Mexico, Chile, Peru and Colombia, promoting free trade and investment (Alianza del Pacifico 2018). Hence, the organizational presence may not be due to any considerations of regime type but rather motivated by long-term interest in the region.

In terms of public diplomacy, a higher profile in the region helps China to win the recognition race with Taiwan as well as to support its increased economic activity in the region (see Heine and Beal 2018). In line with this strategy, Chinese leaders have expanded their ties with Latin America. Jiang Zemin, Hu Jintao and Xi Jinping have visited the region several times between 2001 and 2018 (see Table 10.4).

Analysing this travel diplomacy, we can see a slight bias in favour of Cuba. Cuba has been visited five times, a surprisingly high number of state visits considering the low importance in economic affairs, in contrast to four visits in Chile, four in Brazil and Mexico, and three in Venezuela. Interestingly, in the short time since its recognition of the PRC instead of Taiwan, Costa Rica has been visited two times. Diplomatic recognition remains a goal for China in Latin America, as seven out of the nineteen remaining countries that recognize Taiwan in 2018 are located in Latin America (see Table 10.5, also Dosch and Goodman 2012). Costa Rica switched sides from Taiwan to China in 2007, after receiving $83 million to build a football stadium, along with other financial aid; Panama switched in 2017, the Dominican Republic in 2018.

Table 10.4 China, Presidential Visits to Latin America

Date	President	Country
2001	Jiang Zemin	Chile, Argentina, Uruguay, Brazil, Venezuela, Cuba
2002	Jiang Zemin	Mexico (APEC Summit)
2004	Hu Jintao	Chile, Brazil, Argentina, Cuba
2005	Hu Jintao	Mexico
2008	Hu Jintao	Peru, Costa Rica, Cuba
2010	Hu Jintao	Brazil, Venezuela, Chile
2011	Xi Jinping (Vice-President)	Cuba, Uruguay, Chile
2013	Xi Jinping	Trinidad and Tobago, Costa Rica, Mexico
2014	Xi Jinping	Brazil, Argentina, Venezuela, Cuba
2015	Li Keqiang	Brazil, Colombia, Peru, Chile
2016	Xi Jinping	Peru (APEC Summit), Chile, Ecuador

Source: own compilation.

Table 10.5 Diplomatic Relations with China/Taiwan 2018

Country	Relations with Taiwan	Country	Relations with China (PR)
Paraguay	1957	*Cuba*	*1960*
Guatemala	1960	*Chile*	*1970*
El Salvador	1961	Peru	1971
Honduras	1965	Mexico	1972
Nicaragua	1990	Argentina	1972
		Venezuela	*1974*
		Brazil	1974
		Ecuador	1980
		Colombia	1980
		Bolivia	1985
		Uruguay	1988
		Costa Rica	*2007*
		Panama	2017
		Dominican Republic	2018
		Panama	2018

Source: own compilation.

Table 10.6 Confucius Institutes in Latin America 2018

Country	Number of Institutes
Mexico	5
Peru	4
Brazil	10
Colombia	3
Chile	2
Argentina	2
Cuba	1
Costa Rica	1
Ecuador	1
Bolivia	1
Venezuela	1

Source: Hanban 2018, own compilation.

In this respect, Cuba really is in China's good books. Cuba was the first country in Latin America to recognize the People's Republic of China in 1960, a diplomatic move China has not forgotten until today (Hearn 2012). Up until that point, Latin American countries had followed US policy in recognizing the ROC/Taiwan, further isolating the PRC at a time of the Sino-Soviet split. Although in terms of travel diplomacy, one can thus argue that there is a slight favouritism towards Cuba in particular, it is necessary to bear in mind that counter examples for any authoritarian nexus are also at hand.

Moreover, China is trying to build up its image through the establishment of language institutes, Spanish-speaking television, the sponsoring of student exchange programmes and its general image of a successful, rising developing country. By 2018, China had established over thirty Confucius institutes throughout the region to promote the study of Chinese language and culture. As seen in Table 10.6, it has established one Confucius Institute in Cuba, but one in Costa Rica as well, while there are two in Chile and one in Venezuela. The outstanding case here is Brazil with ten institutes, and Chile with the regional headquarter in Santiago de Chile in 2014. Hence, if we are to compare our cases (Cuba–Costa Rica, Venezuela–Chile), we certainly see that regime type does not explain the variance, while a mixture of economic and cultural/diaspora linkages, such as in the cases of Brazil and Mexico may be of more predictive value.

To sum up, the assumption of the creation of an authoritarian nexus through soft power instruments (i.e. producing cultural affinity as a means for stabilizing any special relationship) is not supported.

Conclusion: China in Latin America and the absence of an 'authoritarian nexus'

This chapter set out to trace the specifics of Chinese foreign policy activities in Latin America, guided by the question whether there is a discernible authoritarian streak to Chinese activities in the region. A structured, focused comparison of Chinese foreign policy towards Latin American authoritarian regimes (Cuba and Venezuela) and towards comparable democratic countries (Costa Rica and Chile) was conducted in order to detect if there was any 'authoritarian nexus'. This term was to designate patterns of favouritism towards autocratic states.

From a theoretical perspective, IR theories and foreign policy analysis, three hypotheses have been derived. In a realist perspective, China should not cooperate especially with other autocracies or promote autocracy, in a liberal perspective this may happen, in a constructivist perspective this should happen because of common norms.

Based on our analysis of structurally similar, comparable cases of autocracies (Cuba and Venezuela) and democracies (Costa Rica and Chile, respectively), we conclude that there is no pattern of outright favouritism for autocracies or a sustained will to nurture autocratic regimes in the Western hemisphere. Military cooperation, arms sales, patterns of economic exchange and public diplomacy efforts may be, to different degrees, important in Chinese relations with Cuba and Venezuela, but they are either comparable to or even dwarfed by the activities towards similarly structured democratic countries or the general level of activity within the whole region. High-level Chinese travel diplomacy confirmed the impression that the countries visited had been selected on grounds of economic attractiveness and opportunity, not supposed political affinity. Beyond that, in seeking allies for the promotion of China's vision of global governance (Hearn 2012; Leiteritz 2012; Pei 2018; Nolte 2018), Brazil, the regional democratic heavyweight, is, as a partner within the BRICS-group, far more important than Cuba or Venezuela (Christensen 2016; Stuenkel 2016). Hence, China has declared Brazil as well as Peru and Mexico (all being democratic countries) a 'comprehensive strategic partner', not Venezuela or Cuba. Even with the most likely case, Cuba, we see no special relations. Despite rhetoric of socialist brotherhood, the Chinese aim at economic benefits, as the Cubans clearly know. 'The Chinese are very clear about one thing: they're not going to be benefactors for Cuba like the Soviets were. I was once told in no uncertain terms by a Chinese diplomat: Our relations with Cuba have to be mutually beneficial or they will not work' (the former Cuban ambassador to China, Mauro García Triana, quoted in Hearn 2009: 5). This exact sentiment was expressed in a personal meeting in 2013 by an economist at the Ministry of Sugar.

In its 2016 Policy Paper, the Chinese government addresses the whole of Latin America and the Caribbean without ever referring to specific bilateral relationships. If one reads the document closely, it seems to be markedly devoid of any specific expectations as regards preferred cooperation partners in the region except for the fact that (a) there has to be mutual benefit (economic-wise) and (b) the 'One China'-principle is respected. As the key institutional venue for cooperation, the hemisphere-wide CELAC has been singled out, with the China-CELAC Forum mentioned several times. Hence, there is not even a suggestion of favouritism towards specific (autocratic leaning) partners which can be read off this policy guideline.

Judged from the results of our empirical analysis conducted through a structured focused comparison, we have to conclude that there is no special relationship of China with either Cuba or Venezuela. Neither were there closer institutional bonds corroborated by especially strong and constantly re-affirmed cultural-ideological affinity, as expected by constructivism, nor did patterns of economic interaction seem to follow a logic of preferential treatment, as expected by liberalism.

Hence, the idea of China promoting autocracy in Latin America is so far not supported. China's advancing engagement in Latin America is due, first, to Latin America's impressive abundance of resources and primary goods; secondly, to the Latin American market with a population of more than 600 million people; and thirdly, to the issue of diplomatic recognition (e.g. Leiteritz 2012; Nolte 2018). The empirical analysis supports the realistic hypotheses of China pursuing a pragmatic foreign policy, following national interest. Within this framework of interests, regime type does not play a pivotal role in finding cooperation partners. There is no evidence of China discriminating in favour of autocracies or deliberately working towards an offshore stabilization of autocracies in Latin America.

Latin America continues to be as a whole an important region for Chinese activities. However, several recent developments lead to rising questions concerning Chines-Latin American relations. First, observers note a remarkable difference between rhetoric and reality. Margaret Myers, director of the Asia & Latin America Program at the Inter-American Dialogue in Washington, D.C., speaks of 'China's cooling interest in Latin America' (Myers 2019). Many promises were made, but only few deliveries can be seen. Since 2002, about 150 infrastructure projects in Latin America have been discussed by Chinese companies and banks, as of 2018, only half a dozen has started construction phase. The cooling interest has several reasons, a slowdown of Latin American economic growth; turmoil in international trade and economy associated with the Trump administration, but especially growing resistance in Latin America about China's role in Latin America. Predatory loans, land grabbing, the acquisition of strategic minerals like lithium, problems with Huawei concerning 5G and the BRI raised concerns. New conservative governments in Argentina, Ecuador, El Salvador, but especially in Brazil criticized China. President Macri in Argentina as well as President Bolsonaro in Brazil refused so far to join the BRI. Bolsonaro and his Foreign Minister Araújo pursue a fierce anti-China rhetoric, criticizing the 'sale' of Brazil to China. In February 2018, as presidential candidate, Bolsonaro visited Taiwan, the first visit of an official candidate since Brazil's diplomatic recognition of the People's Republic of China in the early 1970s. After Bolsonaro's election in 2018, China's FDI in Brazil dropped from $11.3 billion in 2018 to $2.8 billion in 2018, because of the uncertainties related to Bolsonaro's future China policies. However, China remains an important economic partner for Brazil, and in office, Bolsonaro's tone softened. In 2019, Brazil's vice-president Murão visited China to convince Xi Jinping that Brazil is a reliable partner for China. As Richard Lapper wrote in *Americas Quarterly*: 'Bolsonaro took Aim at China. Then Reality Struck' (Lapper 2019).

It remains to be seen how the new conservative electoral tide in Latin America affects Chinese-Latin American relations. So far, China remains an important economic partner for the whole region, no matter which government, whether democratic or authoritarian, is in office.

Bibliography

Agustín, Óscar García, 'Venezuela and China: Independency and Dependency in the Context of Interdependent Hegemony', *Journal of China and International Relations*, Special Issue 104–127 (2016).

Alianza Del Pacifico (2018). Available at https://alianzapacifico.net (accessed 4 June 2018).

Arias, L., 'Costa Rica, China Sign Cooperation Agreements Worth Nearly $2 Billion', *The Tico Times*, 2 June (2013).

Bader, Julia, 'China, Autocratic Patron? An Empirical Investigation of China as a Factor in Autocratic Survival', *International Studies Quarterly*, 59 (1) (2014), pp. 23–33.

Bader, Julia, *China's Foreign Relations and the Survival of Autocracies* (London: Routledge, 2015).

Brand, Alexander, Susan McEwen-Fial and Wolfgang Muno, 'Der Drache im Revier des Adlers: China in Lateinamerika', in Günter Meyer, Wolfgang Muno and Alexander Brand (eds.), *China in der Dritten Welt* (Mainz: Interdiszipl. Arbeitskreis Dritte Welt Universität Mainz, Mainz, 2013), pp. 9–34.

Brand, Alexander, Susan McEwen-Fial and Wolfgang Muno, 'An "Authoritarian Nexus"? China's Alleged Special Relationship with Autocratic States in Latin America', *European Review of Latin American and Caribbean Studies* No. 99, October (2015a), pp. 7–28.

Brand, Alexander, Susan McEwen-Fial and Wolfgang Muno, 'Ein "autoritärer Nexus"? Chinas vermeintliche Sonderbeziehungen zu autokratischen Staaten in Lateinamerika', in Harnisch, Sebastian, Klaus Brummer and Kai Oppermann (eds.), *Sonderbeziehungen als Nexus zwischen Außenpolitik und internationalen Beziehungen* (Baden-Baden: Nomos, 2015b), pp. 133–58.

Brand, Alexander, Susan McEwan-Fial, Wolfgang Muno and Andrea Ribeiro Hoffmann, *BRICs and U.S. Hegemony: Theoretical Reflections on Shifting Power Patterns and Empirical Evidence from Latin America*. Mainz Papers on International and European Politics, 2012/04 (Mainz: Chair of International Relations, Johannes Gutenberg University, 2012).

Brand, Alexander, Susan McEwen-Fial, Wolfgang Muno and Andrea Ribeiro-Hoffmann, 'Hegemoniale Rivalität? Brasilien, China und die US-Hegemonie in Lateinamerika', in Nölke, Andreas, Christian May and Simone Claar (eds.), *Die großen Schwellenländer. Ursachen und Folgen ihres Aufstiegs in der Weltwirtschaft* (Wiesbaden: Springer VS, 2014), pp. 395–412.

Breslin, Shaun. 'China and the Global Order: Signaling Threat or Friendship?' *International Affairs*, 89 (2013), pp. 615–34.

Briceño Ruiz, José, 'From the South America Free Trade Area to the Union of South American Nations', *Latin America Policy*, 1 (2010), pp. 208–29.

BTI [Bertelsmann Transformation Index]. 'BTI Transformation Project', (2018). Available at http://www.bti-project.org/en/country-reports/ (accessed 19 June 2018).

Burnell, Peter, *Is There a New Autocracy Promotion?* FRIDE Working Paper 96 (2010a).

Burnell, Peter, 'Promoting Democracy and Promoting Autocracy: Towards a Comparative Evaluation', *Journal of Politics and Law*, 3 (2010b), pp. 3–14.

Cardenal, Juan Pablo, 'China in Latin America: Understanding the Inventory of Influence', *National Endowment of Democracy*, (2017). Available at https://www.ned.org/wp-content/uploads/2017/12/Chapter1-Sharp-Power-Rising-Authoritarian-Influence-China-Latin-America.pdf (accessed 19 June 2018).

Carvalho, Raquel, 'China in Latin America: Partner or Predator? *South China Morning Post*, 25 May (2019).

CEPAL, 'Exploring New Forms of Cooperation Between China and Latin America and the Caribbean, *United Nations*, (2018). Available at https://repositorio.cepal.org/bitstream/handle/11362/43214/1/S1701249_en.pdf (accessed 19 June 2018).

Christensen, Steen Fryba, 'How Prioritized Is the Strategic Partnership between Brazil and China', in Li, Xing and Steen Fryba Christensen (eds.), *Emerging Powers, Emerging Markets, Emerging Societies: Global Responses* (London: Palgrave, 2016), pp. 87–109.

Cota, Isabella, 'China Lends Costa Rica $400 Million on Xi Visit', *Reuters*, 3 June (2013).

Creutzfeld, Benjamin (ed.), *China an América Latina: Reflexiones sobre las relaciones transpacíficas* (Bogotá: Universidad Externado, 2012).

Diamond, Larry, Marc Plattner and Christopher Walker (eds.), *Authoritarianism Goes Global: The Challenge to Democracy* (Baltimore: Johns Hopkins UP, 2016).

DIRECOM [Ministerio de Relaciones Exteriores, Dirección General de Relaciones Económicas Internacionales, Chile], 'Evaluación de las Relaciones Comerciales entre Chile y China. A Siete Años de la Entrada en Vigencia del Tratado de Libre Comercio', (2014). Available at http://www.direcon.gob.cl/wp-content/uploads/2013/09/Evaluación-TLC_China_7_años-1.pdf. (accessed 19 June 2018).

Dosch, Joern and David Goodman, 'China and Latin America: Complementarity, Competition, and Globalisation', *Journal of Current Chinese Affairs*, 41 (2012), pp. 3–19.

Doyle, Michael, 'Kant, Liberal Legacies, and Foreign Affairs', *Philosophy and Public Affairs*, 12 (3) (1983), pp. 205–35.

ECLAC, *People's Republic of China and Latin America and the Caribbean. Ushering in a New Era in the Economic and Trade Relationship*, (2011). Available at http://www.eclac.cl/comercio/publicaciones/xml/4/43664/People_Republic_of_China_and_Latina_America_and_the_Caribbean_trade.pdf (accessed 19 June 2018).

Ellis, Evan, *Venezuela's Relationship with China: Implications for the Chávez Regime and the Region* (Miami: University of Miami, 2010).

Ellis, Evan, 'China-Latin America Military Engagement: Good Will, Good Business, and Strategic Position', (2011a). Available at http://www.strategicstudiesinstitute.army.mil/pubs/download.cfm?q=1077 (accessed 19 June 2018).

Ellis, Evan, 'Chinese Soft Power in Latin America: A Case Study', *Joint Forces Quarterly*, 60 (2011b), pp. 85–91.

Ellis, Evan, 'The Strategic Dimension of Chinese Engagement with Latin America', Perry Paper Series No. 1, (2013). Available at http://chds.dodlive.mil/files/2013/12/pub-PP-ellis.pdf (accessed 20 June 2018).

Ellis, Evan, Indian and Chinese Engagement in Latin America and the Caribbean: A Comparative Assessment, (2017). Available at http://strategicstudiesinstitute.army.mil/pubs/display.cfm?pubID=1346 (accessed 4 June 2018).

Elman, Colin, 'Horses for Courses: Why Not Neorealist Theories of Foreign Policy?' *Security Studies*, 6 (1) (1996), pp. 7–53.

Erdmann, Gero, André Bank, Bert Hoffmann and Thomas Richter, *International Cooperation of Authoritarian Regimes: Toward a Conceptual Framework*, GIGA Working Paper No. 229 (Hamburg: GIGA, 2013).

Evan Ellis, R., *China in Latin America: The Whats and Wherefores* (Boulder: Lynne Rienne, 2009).

Fierke, K. M., 'Constructivism', in: Tim Dunne, Milja Kurki and Steve Smith (eds.), *International Relations Theories: Discipline and Diversity*, 4th ed. (Oxford: Oxford UP, 2016), pp. 166–84.

FMPRC [Foreign Ministry, People's Republic of China], 'Assistant Foreign Minister Zhang Kunsheng Lectures at the 1st China-Latin America High Level Forum on Defence', 13 November (2012).

Freedom House, 'Freedom in the World', (2018). Available at https://freedomhouse.org/report/freedom-world/freedom-world-2018 (accessed 20 June 2018).

Gachúz, Juan Carlos, 'Chile's Economic and Political Relationship with China', *Journal of Current Chinese Affairs*, 41 (2012): 133–54.

Gallagher, Kevin and Roberto Porzecanski, *The Dragon in the Room: China and the Future of Latin American Industrialization* (Palo Alto: Stanford UP, 2010).

George, Alexander, 'Case Studies and Theory Development: The Method of Structured, Focused Comparison', in Gordon, Paul (ed.), *Diplomacy: New Approaches in History, Theory and Policy* (New York: Free Press, 1979).

George, Alexander and Andrew Bennett, *Case Studies and Theory Development in Social Sciences* (Cambridge: MIT Press, 2004).

Giacalone, Rita and José Briceño Ruiz, 'The Chinese-Venezuelan Oil Agreements: Material and Nonmaterial Goals', *Latin American Policy*, 4 (2013), pp. 76–92.

Gonzalez-Vicente, Ruben, 'Mapping Chinese Mining Investment in Latin America: Politics or Market?' *The China Quarterly*, 209 (2012), pp. 35–58.

Hanban, 'Confucius Institutes', (2018). Available at http://english.hanban.org/ (accessed 20 June 2018).

Hearn, Adrian, 'Cuba and China: Lessons and Opportunities for the United States, Commissioned Report for the Cuba Info Series', *The Cuban Research Institute, Florida International University*, (2009). Available at http://cri.fiu.edu/research/commissioned-reports/cuba-china-hearn.pdf (accessed 20 June 2018).

Hearn, Adrian, 'China, Global Governance and the Future of Cuba', *Journal of Current Chinese Affairs*, 41 (2012), pp. 155–79.

Heine, Jorge and Anders Beal, 'The Strategy Behind China's Diplomatic Offensive in Latin America', *Americas Quarterly*, 14 May (2018). Available at http://www.americasquarterly.org/content/strategy-behind-chinas-diplomatic-offensive-latin-america (accessed 20 June 2018).

Horta, Loro, 'In Uncle Sam's Backyard: China's Military Influence in Latin America', *Military Review*, (September/October) (2008): 47–55.

Ikenberry, John G., 'The Rise of China and the Future of the West', *Foreign Affairs*, 87 (2008), pp. 2–7.

Kagan, Robert, 'League of Dictators?', *Washington Post*, 30 April (2006).

Kleine-Ahlbrandt, Stephanie and Andrew Small, 'China's New Dictatorship Diplomacy', *Foreign Affairs*, 87 (2008), pp. 38–56.

Krauss, Clifford and Damien Cave, 'Cuba's Prospects for an Oil-Fueled Economic Jolt Falter with Departure of Rig', *New York Times*, 9 November (2012).

Kurlantzick, Joshua, *Democracy in Retreat* (New Haven: Yale UP, 2013).

Lapper, Richard, 'Bolsonaro Took Aim at China: Then Reality Struck', *Americas Quarterly*, 23 April (2019).

Layne, Christopher, 'This Time It's Real: The End of Unipolarity and the Pax Americana', *International Studies Quarterly*, 56 (2012), pp. 203–13.

Leiteritz, Ralf 'China y América Latina: ¿el matrimonio perfecto?', *Colombia Internacional*, 75 (2012), pp. 49–81.

Lindsay, James M., 'The Future of US Global Leadership', *International Affairs*, 87 (2011), pp. 765–80.

Marcella, Gabriel, 'China's Military Activity in Latin America', *Americas Quarterly*, Winter (2012), pp. 67–9.

Mattes, Michaela and Mariana Rodríguez, 'Autocracies and International Cooperation', *International Studies Quarterly*, 58 (3) (2014), pp. 527–38.

Mearsheimer, John, 'Structural Realism', in Tim Dunne, Milja Kurki and Steve Smith (eds.), *International Relations Theories: Discipline and Diversity*, 4th ed. (Oxford: Oxford UP, 2016), pp. 71–88.

MOFCOM [Ministry of Commerce, People's Republic of China], Costa Rica Trade Newsletter, April (2013).

Moravcsik, Andrew, 'Taking Preferences Seriously: A Liberal Theory of International Politics', *International Organization*, 51 (4) (1997), pp. 513–53.

Moravcsik, Andrew, 'Liberal International Relations Theory: A Scientific Assessment', in Elman, Colin and Miriam Fendius Elman (eds.), *Progress in International Relations Theory* (Cambridge: MIT Press, 2003), pp. 159–204.

Myers, Margaret, 'The Reasons for China's Cooling Interest in Latin America', *Americas Quarterly*, 23 April (2019).

Navejas, Haro, Francisco Javier, 'China in the Central American and Caribbean Zone', *Latin American Policy*, 4 (2013), pp. 144–56.

Nolte, Detlef, 'China Is Challenging but (Still) Not Displacing Europe in Latin America', *GIGA Focus Latin America*, 1 (2018). Available at https://www.giga-hamburg.de/en/publication/china-is-challenging-but-still-not-displacing-europe-in-latin-america (accessed 20 June 2018).

O'Donnell, Thomas, 'Russia Is Beating China to Venezuela's Oil Fields', *Americas Quarterly*. (2016). Available at http://www.americasquarterly.org/content/russia-be ating-china-venezuelas-oil-fields (accessed 20 June 2018).

Panke, Diana and Thomas Risse, 'Liberalism', in Tim Dunne, Milja Kurki and Steve Smith (eds.), *International Relations Theories: Discipline and Diversity*, 4th ed. (Oxford: Oxford UP, 2016), pp. 89–108.

Pei, Minxin, 'A Play for Global Leadership', *Journal of Democracy*, 29 (2) (2018), pp. 37–51.

Ríos, Xulio, 'China and Venezuela: Ambitions and Complexities of an Improving Relationship', *East Asia*, 30 (2013), pp. 53–65.

Roett, Riordan and Guadalupe Paz (eds.), *China's Expansion into the Western Hemisphere: Implications for Latin America and the United States* (Washington DC: Brookings Institution Press, 2008).

Roett, Riordan and Guadalupe Paz (eds.), *Latin America and the Asian Giants: Evolving Ties with China and India* (Washington DC: Brooking Institutions Press, 2016).

Stuenkel, Oliver, *Post-Western World: How Emerging Powers Are Remaking Global Order* (Cambridge: Polity Press, 2016).

Tarrow, Sidney, 'The Strategy of Paired Comparison: Toward a Theory of Practice', *Comparative Political Studies*, 43 (2010), pp. 230–59.

The BRICS Post, 'China Investing Heavily in Chile', *The BRICS Post*, 23 January (2013). Available at http://thebricspost.com/china-invests-heavily-in-chile/#.UxSEhaMwfqQ (accessed 20 June 2018).

Vanderhill, Rachel, *Promoting Authoritarianism Abroad* (Boulder: Lynne Rienner, 2013).

Venezuelanalysis, 'China Approves US$5Bn Loan for Venezuelan Oil Development', (2018). Available at https://venezuelanalysis.com/news/13918 (accessed 6 July 2018).

Walker, Christopher and Jessica Ludwig, 'From "Soft Power" to "Sharp Power": Rising Authoritarian Influence in the Democratic World', *National Endowment for Democracy* (2017). Available at https://www.ned.org/wp-content/uploads/2017/12/Introduction-Sharp-Power-Rising-Authoritarian-Influence.pdf (Accessed 19 June 2018).

Williams, Adam, 'Costa Rica Halts $1.3 Billion China-Funded Refinery Plan', *Bloomberg*, 21 June (2013).

WSJ [Wall Street Journal], 'Cuba Seeks Closer Ties with Beijing', *The Wall Street Journal*, 5 July (2012).

WTO [World Trade Organization], 'Cuba, Costa Rica', *WTO Trade Profiles* (2018). Available at http://stat.wto.org/CountryProfile/WSDBCountryPFView.aspx?Country=CU,CR. (accessed 19 June 2018).

Waltz, Kenneth, *Man, the State, and War* (New York: Columbia UP, 1959).

Waltz, Kenneth, *Theory of International Politics* (Reading: Addison-Wesley, 1979).

Wendt, Alexander, 'Anarchy Is What States Make of It: The Social Construction of Power Politics', *International Organization*, 88 (2) (1992), pp. 384–96.

Wendt, Alexander, *Social Theory of International Politics* (Cambridge: Cambridge UP, 1999).

11

China in sub-Saharan Africa

Implications for democracy promotion

Earl Conteh-Morgan

Introduction

As the Western powers make policy pronouncements to promote democracy in sub-Saharan Africa, many observers argue that China's growing influence in the continent and its very successful manifestation of free-market dictatorship could influence African leaders to revert to outright undemocratic politics. Pro-human rights groups have repeatedly criticized China for bolstering dictatorial and corrupt African regimes such as Angola, Sudan, Equatorial Guinea or Zimbabwe, among many others. In other words, China's critical raw materials (oil in particular) imperative has made it susceptible to criticisms of undermining democracy and human rights because of its seemingly neutral role in African countries experiencing civil strife (e.g. Democratic Republic of Congo), democracy struggles (e.g. Zimbabwe) or blatant elite corruption (e.g. Angola, Nigeria). The charges are as follows: (1) China's foreign policy is so commercially focused that it turns a blind eye to African conflicts and human rights violations; (2) it provides aid to authoritarian states that consistently ignore human rights abuses; and (3) it uses its veto power in the Security Council to protect authoritarian African states from the threat of sanctions. It is China's strategic/critical resource imperative that impelled it towards Africa underlined by the momentum of economic globalization and China's determination to enhance its power economic capabilities and sustain its phenomenal industrialization growth. China, accordingly, has recognized the potential of Africa as an economic power house of lucrative minerals, a source of other raw materials, and a market for finished Chinese products, an outlet for Chinese investments, as well as a source of political support in its competition with Taiwan, and in its objective of a 'One China' policy. First, this analysis is predicated on the argument that ongoing Sino-African relations are based on three broad factors that could impact the promotion of democracy and human rights observance in sub-Saharan Africa. The following are the three factors: (1) mutual geo-economic and geo-political importance and dependence; (2) similar political–historical experiences and (3) sociopolitical/cultural proximity. In other words, is China's extensive and close ties with Africa and preoccupation with access to critical raw materials in Africa undermining democracy promotion or the observance of human rights within African states? In addition, the analysis will also focus in some detail, on China's political behaviour vis-à-vis countries such as Sudan and Zimbabwe that are well known for their consistent violations of human rights and subversion of democratic ideals. The democracy and human rights records of some African countries that are currently interacting extensively with China have been troubling to the international system.

This analysis, however, assumes the following about the reality of democracy and human rights in Africa: (1) China is not the only great power that is benefitting from authoritarian tendencies in Africa; (2) Most African states have been negatively affected by colonial rule, and the ongoing influence of neocolonialism which foster and perpetuate non-democratic tendencies; (3) Perhaps some African states are inherently not susceptible to liberal democratic values because of their history of social cleavages and economic realities and (4) the West which has had a longer span of interactions and hegemonic influence over Africa has not actually seriously invested in the promotion of democracy and human rights in Africa. Its rhetoric about democracy promotion far surpasses its actual efforts to do so in the continent.

China to a large extent is operating within the authoritarian political culture within most of Africa bequeathed by the colonial era. In most African states post-independence era politics in the continent has oscillated between military regimes and one-party civilian authoritarian regimes with interludes of multiparty competition that border episodes of political strife. In political–historical terms the authoritarian political cultures and tendencies of Africa's post-colonial regimes are a residue of the colonial state which shaped African societies even though its rules had no indigenous roots in society, especially in the politically salient areas of authority, legitimacy and leadership. Stated differently, the African state up till now has not been able to invest itself with legitimacy because of the following reasons: (1) the inherited imbalance between state and society; (2) the half-hearted attempts by the West to aid Africa in its democratization efforts and (3) the dependent character of African states and the impact of external imperatives and impositions which undermine and dislocate state–society relations even more thereby making authoritarian tendencies even more attractive. Accordingly, China has become 'attractive' to many African states because of its policy of non-interference and minimal aid transfer conditionality in its relations with African states.

Conceptual clarifications

Mutual geo-economic and geopolitical importance of Africa is defined as the critical role played by Africa's strategic resources in China's industrialization process including Africa's diplomatic support for, and political importance, in China's 'One China' policy. Secondly, it also includes the political and economic importance of China to Africa defined as the role played by China as a counterweight to Western conditionalities (calls for good governance, transparency or fiscal probity). China's foreign policy in the last decade in particular has been focused on two broad politico-economic goals: (1) to ensure the success of its 'One China' policy and (2) to secure access to critical resources, sources of investments and markets for its manufactured goods. Accordingly, Africa has presented itself as a key avenue for the realization of these two objectives. China's geo-economic/political importance to Africa is reflected in the regular Forum on China–Africa Cooperation (FOCAC) summits that bring together African states and China. For instance, during the 2006 FOCAC Summit in Beijing, President Hu Jintao outlined the following economic benefits that China would extend to African states: (1) double its 2006 assistance to Africa by 2009; (2) provide $3 billion of preferential loans to African states; (3) set up a China–Africa Development Fund; (4) cancel the debts of very indebted Africa states; (5) open up more of China's market to African goods and (6) establish three to five trade and economic cooperation zones in Africa, among others.[1] All other FOCAC summits have been marked by greater economic commitments to African states. On the other hand, Africa's geo-economic importance to China is manifested in Africa's critical resources that are strategic to China's continuing industrialization. These are resources such as oil, bauxite, iron ore, tin and platinum, among many others, found in many African countries. The geo-economic importance of African states is reflected in the role of those critical resources in China's rapid industrialization. For example, PetroChina purchases tens of thousands of barrels of oil per day from Nigeria since 2005. China National Offshore Oil Corporation (CNOOC) is also very active in Nigeria. Gabon's declining oil industry got a boost from investments by China National Petro-Chemical Corporation (SINOPEC).[2] South Africa, Zimbabwe, Angola, Equatorial Guinea and Algeria all supply critical resources to China. In order of geo-economic importance, the following usually fall within the top five trading/investment partners of China: Angola, South Africa, Sudan, Nigeria and Egypt. According to the *China Daily* (October 2010), Sino-African trade outperformed that of China's major trade partners, including the United States and the EU. In other words, China is now Africa's largest trade partner. In just eight years, from 2000 to 2008, China–Africa trade reached annual growth rates of more than 33 per cent and a peak of $106.8 billion in 2008. Similarly, in terms of investments in 2009, Africa became the fourth largest overseas Foreign Direct Investment destination for China, and in terms of value it stood at $1.44 billion from a low of $210 million in 2000.[3]

Similar politico-historical experiences refer to the fact that both regions (China and Africa) in the recent past were victims of external subjugation and fought hard to gain freedom and sovereign statehood. They have interacted and cooperated in bodies such as the Non-Aligned Movement, UNCTAD and the UN itself to ensure their freedoms as developing nations. China's support for African liberation wars in particular and its assistance to nations like Zimbabwe and Angola are cases in point. In terms of recent historical and political interactions in the post-Second World War world, China's relations with Africa began in May 1956 when Egypt became the first African country to establish diplomatic relations with China. Less than ten years later, China had established diplomatic relations with countries such as Algeria, Guinea, Morocco and Sudan, among others. China's foray into Africa intensified with the beginning of the twenty-first century. But unlike the United States, or major European states like Britain or France, China's presidents and prime ministers have, since the early 1960s, visited several African countries. For example, between 1963 and 1965 Chinese premier Zhou Enlai made three visits to several African countries culminating in the establishment of diplomatic relations with many of them. Currently, almost all of the fifty-four African countries maintain diplomatic relations with China, and most since the end of the 1970s. China's presidents and prime ministers have continued the political tradition of paying high-level visits to several African countries on a periodic basis. For example, in May 1996, former Chinese president Jiang Zemin visited Kenya, Egypt, Ethiopia, Mali, Namibia and Zimbabwe. Similarly, in April 2006, Chinese president Hu Jintao visited Morocco, Nigeria and Kenya. The current Chinese president Xi Jinping paid visits to three African states (Tanzania, South Africa and the Republic of Congo) a week after being elected President in March 2013. There are many other examples of such visits. Since 2000 these political, diplomatic and historical ties have culminated in regular FOCAC meetings that bring together China and all African states that maintain diplomatic ties with China and support the 'One China' policy. In 2005, President Mugabe declared that

> it is very important for us in Zimbabwe to develop the Look East Policy because that is where people who think like us are, same history of colonialism as ourselves, people who have started developing their economies, are more advanced than Africa, and relations with them will be reciprocal and rewarding.[4]

In this statement, President Mugabe underscores the sociopolitical, historical, cultural and economic similarities between China and Africa. The former is a developing country, but on the path of rapid industrial development, and with a mind-set and experiential knowledge of what it means to have been a colonial subject, along with all the constraints that go with it.

Sociopolitical/cultural proximity is defined as similarity in values and norms related to communal societies or developing society political culture. It underscores the extended family orientation, strong loyalty to the clan, tribe or ethnic group and/or to the community rather than to the entire nation, compared to Western individualism and the competitiveness that goes with it. There are many expectations, obligations or responsibilities that are associated with being part of a communal oriented society, just as there are of the individual in a modern advanced industrial society characterized by individualism. At times, the values and obligations inherent in more communal/ group oriented societies produce more nepotism, 'graft' or 'bribery' which result from the pressures of cultural expectations to provide for one's kith and kin. For example, in African and Chinese economic interactions, the tendency of extending gratitude prior to consolidating an economic deal is very common and acceptable. In a Western value system if gift exchange precedes the sealing of a deal, it is considered bribery, corruption and therefore unethical. It is not uncommon for the Chinese to construct stadiums, hospitals, schools and 'donate' them to African governments while at the same time negotiating lucrative mineral mining deals with African governments. A Western nation would frown on such economic interactions because it would be considered unethical or bribery. When and if it takes place, it would be done in a subtler, secretive or indirect manner, often benefitting only the top political elite. There is more of a culture clash between African and Western value systems than between African and Chinese cultural norms and communal expectations. It is probably not very surprising that African elites tend to prefer the Chinese style of economic and political interaction over the Western one. The factors of sociocultural proximity and shared sociopolitical and historical experiences spawn willingness to cooperate around shared goals, generate common expectations on issues of cooperation between two or more nations on issues related to national interest shaped largely by mutual experiences, and mutual power dependence in the pursuit of their domestic and international objectives. In sum, Sino-African mores, values and customs are much more proximate to one another compared to the sociocultural distance that exists between Sino-Western mores, values and customs. Problems of authoritarianism, corruption and nepotism, in general, underlie economic and political relations in developing nations. In terms of level of political culture, China and Africa are to a large extent on the same level. Many African leaders would no doubt prefer to exercise a more authoritarian rule just as in China. They would prefer to be left alone to run their country as they see fit and not be bothered by Western impositions about good governance. The West, which is characterized by a more developed democratic capitalist culture, therefore tends to experience more culture clash with China than Africa. According to the West, African nations are supposed to be liberal democracies which hold regular free and fair elections, and respect freedom of speech, assembly and tolerate a free press, among other aspects of the rule of law. In other words, the close bilateral ties between Africa and China are being cemented not just because of geo-economic importance of the latter, but because of the sociocultural proximity, and politico-historical and cultural legacy of these nations strengthened by the legacy of the revolutionary era for nations like Zimbabwe, Tanzania, Egypt, Guinea, Mali and Algeria, among others. China played a significant role in the struggles of many African nations for independence from colonial rule.

China's relationship with Africa has gone through some significant transformations from the era of independence and liberation struggles in the 1960s and 1970s, to the 1980s when the focus on anti-imperialism and anti-colonialism gave way to issues of economic development. Around this time, China also introduced a new policy of reform and opening up that focused on economic transformation. In this era of globalization, China has embarked on a broad-based, and at times, intensive series of transactions with Africa. Consistent Chinese activities with Africa include investments, African personnel training, timely humanitarian assistance to some African countries and debt forgiveness for some of the heavily indebted African countries. Since the first ministerial conference of the Forum on China–Africa Cooperation (FOCAC) in 2000, China has cancelled debt totalling 10.9 billion Yuan ($1.4 billion) owed by the heavily indebted poor countries and the least developed countries in Africa that have diplomatic relations with China. China, in other words, acts outside of the Western debt regime in its dealings with African nations, and its unilateral debt forgiveness may encourage African nations to ignore Western conditionalities about debt forgiveness. For example, the Paris Club is integral to the Western debt regime. The objective of the Club with regards to debt is predicated on the norm that it is the moral, legal and material obligation of a debtor nation to repay all debt in a timely manner. Before debt forgiveness is adopted the Club first reschedules the debt of countries that are affected. Besides, debt rescheduling is only adopted if IMF and World Bank conditionalities are not being violated by the country in question.[5] China, on the other hand, cancels the debts of the least developed and heavily indebted countries without adhering to the rescheduling strategy of the Club, and regardless of whether the indebted country implements economic policies deemed sound by the International Financial Institutions (IFIs) and the West. In other words, China uses the FOCAC multilateral forums to engage in massive debt cancellations for the poorest of African nations. Accordingly, debt forgiveness was part of the first FOCAC in 2000. Again, in 2003 during the second FOCAC, China forgave another $750 million. China's interactions with Africa seem to be consistently free of conditionalities and reiterated at the Beijing Summit of FOCAC in 2006, when the two regions pledged to establish a 'new type of Sino-African strategic partnership' on the basis of political equality, mutual trust, economic cooperation, win-win and cultural exchanges. The essence of relations is summarized by China this way:

> Not like western countries that offer aid to Africa with rigorous political and economic terms. China's aid, without any political or economic terms, aims at promoting the development of African countries and consolidating Sino-African friendly cooperation. Moreover, China never poses as an almsgiver. It tries to avoid words like 'donor', 'aid receive', 'poverty' and 'backwardness' as far as Africa is concerned. Instead China emphasizes 'solidarity', 'mutual help', 'equality' and 'mutual benefit and common development' in the course of cooperation, which constitutes a remarkable difference from western countries.[6]

It seems as if China has so far kept to the blueprint of its African policy. In return China has gained the support of African countries for over fifty years now. They reciprocated by supporting China at the UN where issues of Taiwan or human rights are concerned. In 1971, seventy-one countries voted for China's resumption of its legal seat in the UN. Twenty-six of those seventy-one countries were African countries.

In particular, China has been very consistent in its policy orientation towards African nations. Often the same or similar principles formulated since 1949 and 1963 have guided Sino-African relations. Since 1949 when the People's Republic was founded, Chinese leaders have underscored the importance of forging closer relations with African nations. Between 1963 and 1964 Zhou Enlai further emphasized the importance of Africa to China through the five principles of Peaceful Coexistence that should guide Sino-African relations. The Africa Policy Paper of 2006 is almost an exact replication of those five principles of Peaceful Coexistence including the subsequent additional Eight Principles of Foreign Aid that, according to Zhou Enlai, should underlie Sino-African relations. Similar themes are found in all three pronouncements –the five principles of Peaceful Coexistence, the Eight Principles of Foreign Aid, and the Africa Policy Paper. These themes range from opposition to imperialism, safeguarding national independence, pursuing a policy of peace, neutrality, non-alignment, equality and mutual benefit, respect for sovereignty of recipient states in the aid-giving process, among others. The Chinese government tries to set itself apart from the West's economic behaviour towards developing countries. This strategy is especially captured in the last four of the Eight Principles of Foreign Aid formulated by Zhou Enlai as underlying China's foreign aid policy to developing countries. These principles claim to help recipient countries increase their income through Chinese projects that require less investment but yield quicker results. China also claims to provide the most effective but efficient equipment in carrying out its projects, while also making sure the recipient nation is satisfied with the completed project. In the area of technical assistance, the Chinese government promises to ensure that the recipient country acquires the knowledge, skills and techniques related to the assistance. The last of the Eight Principles of Foreign Aid states:

> The experts dispatched by China to help in construction in the recipient countries will have the same standard of living as the experts of the recipient country. The Chinese experts are not allowed to make any special demands or enjoy any special amenities.[7]

These principles stand in stark contrast to the attitude of the West or IFIs like the IMF and World Bank regarding aid or technical assistance to Africa. Although these principles were formulated in the 1960s, China still regards them as part of the guiding principles of Sino-African relations.

China and authoritarian African regimes: Growing mutual dependence?

China's economic activities in Africa are structured by the former's national interest, the geo-economic importance of some African states and the overall perception of China in the current global system and with regards to Africa in particular. The civil strife and/or authoritarianism in some African states tend to elicit criticisms of China's relationship with them. The conflict situations in Sudan, Zimbabwe and the Democratic Republic of Congo (DRC) in particular, or the pervasive corruption and human rights violations in Equatorial Guinea, and Angola are such examples. The existence of conflicts, human rights violations or blatant corruption and inequality leads to three outcomes: (1) an ever-present need by China to escape such national entanglements and present a clean image to the international system of its role in Africa; (2) serious challenges for China should national and /or regional tensions escalate into crisis situations and (3) the unintended establishment, or support for dictatorships by China that undermine the progress achieved so far in human rights and democracy promotion in African countries. In all three outcomes, China will find itself working against the prevailing international ethos of democracy promotion and respect for universal human rights in all African countries.

The corrupt practices of many African regimes do not deter China from forging strong bilateral relations with them. China, in particular, approaches Africa with no preconditions of political liberalization, respect for human rights or balanced budgets.

This policy posture is part of China's non-interference, or mutual cooperation or equality in its transactions with African states. China consistently maintains a non-political interference, and non-patronizing, and non-economic conditionality policy posture with African nations. For example, China signed economic deals worth over $7 billion just a few weeks after the Guinean military junta massacred over 150 people and openly raped women in the streets of Conakry, Guinea, on 28 September 2009. In particular, Chinese aid to Africa is free of all political, economic and social conditionalities often imposed by Western or OECD countries. The overall cultural affinity between China and Africa in the area of political culture, similarity in several areas of economic development, as well as in national and international aspirations, is stronger than with the West. This relatively strong cultural and developmental closeness has produced areas of convergence between the two regions in terms of frequent and closer multilateral and bilateral consultations, mutual support in multilateral organizations where human rights issues in particular are concerned, the shared objective of promoting a new just and rational international political and economic order informed by their historical experience as victims of colonialism, and imperial aggression. For example, with the support of twenty-six African states, China ousted Taiwan as one of the Big Five powers in the Security Council of the United Nations. On many issues, China enjoyed the diplomatic backing of African states, especially support against condemnation of China by the UN Human Rights Commission.

The current positive and strengthened ties between China and Africa are a result of political, economic and diplomatic interactions in the recent past (i.e. between the 1950s and 1980s). In addition to the strong diplomatic overtures during the Bandung Conference, in the 1960s and 1970s many African states and liberation movements sought and secured the political and military support of China during their wars of colonial liberation and/or struggles for control over the proper boundaries and policies of the state. From the perspective of China and based on China's foreign policy towards Africa during this era of ideological struggles, Africa was (1) viewed as a region which could boost China's international recognition and minimize its actual and perceived diplomatic isolation by the West and later by the USSR; (2) seen as an integral part of the 'third world front' against neocolonialism and imperialism; (3) a major theatre of its (China's) political and ideological struggles against the Soviet Union; and (4) as now is seen as a source of formidable support for its 'One China' policy against Taiwan. Besides, foreign aid had long played the role of cementing Sino-African relations. What is currently unfolding has had a precedent because Africa received the lion's share (over 40 per cent) of China's aid commitments to developing countries between 1961 and 1975.[8] The affinity and mutual understanding between China and Africa is such that with the help of the latter, China is assured the diplomatic support of African states. For example, in 2004, fifteen African countries out of twenty-eight voted against a resolution condemning China's human rights record at the 60th Session of the Human Rights Commission. China, in these instances, gets more support from African states (fifteen in 2004) than from Asian states (only eight in 2004). During the era of ideological struggles China was particularly supportive of the goals and objectives of states like Egypt, Guinea, Mali, Tanzania and Algeria. Currently China enjoys a strong and special relationship with these countries, among many others.

In terms of political culture and behavioural characteristics related to political and economic transactions, China has a great deal more with Africa than the West. Issues of graft, nepotism and incumbent regime control over political and economic liberalization are problems that are shared, lived or experienced by both regions. This advantage on the part of China is coupled by the fact that China makes a vigorous attempt to court Africa through its multilateral summits and frequent visits by its top leaders to African states. For example, China declared 2006 as 'the year of Africa'. During the Sino-African summits of 2000, 2003, 2006, 2009, 2012 and 2015 China underscored its 'equality' with Africa, its mutual cooperation, mutual respect, benefit and focus on a 'win-win' relationship. The overall theme during those summits can be summarized as one of mutual dependence and mutual respect. This Chinese strategy of wooing African states has a strong positive appeal to African government elite. Compared to the longstanding Western attitude towards Africa, China's attitude is very effective. The West's attitude towards Africa has often been one of condescension, punctuated by a superior–inferior rhetoric. In 2005, according to James Traub:

> The industrial nations conducted a sort of moral crusade, with advocacy organizations exposing Africa's dreadful sores and crying shame on the leaders of wealthy nations and those leaders then heroically pledging, at the G8 meeting in July, to raise their development assistance by billions and to open their markets to Africa. Once everyone has gone home, the aid increase turned out to belargely ephemeral and trade reform merely wishful.[9]

However, is it possible that China's rhetoric and actions towards Africa and its demonstration of a free-market dictatorship may be negatively impacting Africa's march towards democracy? The Chinese rhetoric is backed up by tangible and substantial aid, trade and investment activities that also appear more 'generous' than those of the West. In November 2006, Chinese president Hu Jintao announced that between 2007 and 2009 China would not only substantially increase aid to Africa, but would cancel the debts of many African states.

Since democracy and capitalism are intertwined, China's neglect or hands-off approach to political liberalization (democracy) practices may also be reflected in the stifling of economic liberalization or practices that would ensure fair and efficient economic practices. For example, both the private and public Chinese business firms in Africa are often accused of (1) flagrant violation of local African laws; (2) exploitation and maltreatment of African labourers by Chinese businessmen and contractors; (3) monopolizing African markets by predatory dumping of goods that undercut African firms and business enterprises; (4) meagre salaries paid to African workers; (5) a lack of backward and forward linkages with African economies and societies, among others. Some of these accusations may be more manifest in some African countries than in others. For example, in the area of textiles, South Africa is an example of how China may be subverting the growth of African capitalism and therefore the destruction of a bourgeois (middle) class. By 2007, China's exports of textiles and clothing to South Africa had increased tremendously. However, this significant growth of Chinese goods to South Africa resulted in a severe loss of jobs in the South African textile industry. Between 1996 and 2004, roughly 76,000 South Africans lost their jobs as the market share of China in textile and related products increased significantly. A similar situation regarding textiles and clothing is being repeated in many other African countries where inexpensive clothing, footwear, medicine and the like undercut the entrepreneurial efforts of local African producers. Besides, the African political elite are slow to condemn these practices because conditions within the African economies at the end of the Cold War, and the 'fatigue' of the West regarding African development problems, made China very attractive to Africans. Moreover, in terms of sociocultural proximity, Chinese business behaviour is very similar to that of Africa. The willingness by the Chinese to upgrade infrastructure and construct much-needed hospitals, schools and roads is very attractive to both the African elite and the masses. While such undertakings are often linked to mining concessions for oil, bauxite, copper and the like, they are nonetheless much appreciated by Africans plagued by pervasive dilapidation of infrastructure. In some African countries, negative attitudes about China's economic role in Africa are in contrast to positive ones. For example, Ethiopian officials commend the Chinese firms because of their ability to keep costs down. This ability means major contracts are usually awarded to Chinese firms. Ethiopian officials also admit that although wages paid to Africans by Chinese are low, nonetheless large numbers of local workers are employed. On the positive side for the Chinese, there is the consensus that African workers are learning new skills because of the increase in Chinese funded projects.

The African government elite and Chinese multinationals which are largely state owned seem to have developed a symbiotic relationship especially in the area of economic transactions. In particular, in the areas of trade and oil extraction, Chinese MNCs are protected by host African governments in countries such as Nigeria, Sudan, Angola and Equatorial Guinea, among others. In Nigeria and Sudan this tight relationship between the host government and Chinese extractive companies such as China National Petroleum Corporation (CNPC), China National Petrochemical Corporation or SINOPEC, and China National Offshore Oil Corporation (CNOOC) has at times spawned violence, kidnappings or intensified insurgencies against both government and Chinese MNCs. For instance, in January of 2006 Chinese workers in the Delta region of Nigeria were kidnapped by insurgents fighting for the Ogoni cause. In Sudan similar incidents of violence and kidnapping of Chinese workers occur. China's policy of non-interference in the political affairs of host countries is interpreted by marginalized and deprived citizens of host African countries as a case of Chinese collusion with corrupt and authoritarian regimes. In Nigeria for instance, China does not in any way try to put pressure on the Nigerian government to alleviate the deprivations suffered by the inhabitants of the Niger Delta who are frustrated by the collusion between oil MNCs, including Chinese ones, and the Nigerian government.

Key Chinese bilateral relationships: Sudan and Zimbabwe

China's policy of turning a blind eye to the authoritarian and corrupt practices of African states is especially manifested in its relationship with Sudan and Zimbabwe, among others. For instance, in 2004 China derailed US efforts to impose sanctions on

Sudan for its alleged support of genocide against the people of Darfur. Sudan is of geo-economic importance to China because it supplies roughly 10 per cent of its oil. While the world was protesting genocide in the Darfur region, China rationalized its policy of non-interference in the domestic affairs of host countries. On several occasions, China has frustrated attempts by the Security Council to impose sanctions on Sudan and on government elites involved in gross human rights violations. On no occasion has the Chinese government criticized or condemned the Sudanese government's role in the extra-judicial killings. In July 2004, China's ambassador to the United Nations blocked a more direct and forceful UN resolution that threatened the Khartoum government with sanctions if it did not prosecute the Janjaweed responsible for atrocities against the people of Darfur. China's decision to forego adopting a tough diplomatic posture vis-à-vis Sudan's gross human rights violations in Darfur goes far beyond a policy of non-interference in the domestic affairs of host countries to one of geo-economic importance of Sudan. This geo-economic importance is manifested in the following way: China and Sudan have had a longstanding investment relationship that has lasted over forty years now. Accordingly, China has invested several billion dollars in Sudan. The import of up to 10 per cent of oil makes China Sudan's largest trading partner. On the political cultural dimension, China finds it impossible to criticize Sudan on issues of human rights and democratic rule because it does not respect human rights either. China's oil investments in Sudan are the largest Chinese overseas investments in terms of production. Apart from owning oil fields in Sudan, China, according to Human Rights Watch, has contributed to the militarization of Sudanese society through its financing of weapons factories.[10] Chinese weapons such as antitank mines, ammunition, tanks, helicopters and jet fighters have played a big role in Sudan's civil war since the 1990s. These weapons contribute to the gross violations of human rights in both Sudan's civil war and the Darfur crisis. According to the International Crisis Group (ICG) report of 2002, China deliberately foments civil strife in Sudan in order to enhance its business opportunities.[11] There is no doubt that many of these weapons were used by the North in its atrocities against the people of Darfur. Furthermore, China openly advertises its close military relationship with the Sudanese government. While Chinese weapons were being used by the Khartoum regime to commit atrocities in Darfur, China frustrated efforts to deploy a joint UN-African Union peacekeeping force in the region. The Chinese leadership rationalizes its behaviour vis-à-vis authoritarian states like Sudan and Zimbabwe as one based on a diplomacy that is subtler and more respectful of sovereign states. Instead of making public statements, the Chinese leadership would rather discuss sensitive internal matters behind closed doors thereby obviating the necessity to use threatening or strong-arm tactic diplomacy.

Apart from over one billion dollars invested in the oil industry and refinery infrastructure, China maintains a lucrative trade relationship in aircraft parts and munitions equipment often amounting to tens of millions of dollars. In 2005, the figure was over $80 million. Specifically, China sold the Khartoum regime $24 million worth of arms and munitions, $57 million worth of aircraft parts and equipment, and $2 million worth of parts for helicopters and airplanes.[12] The advanced fighter jets that China provides the Khartoum government can prove very lethal in attacks against the south and Darfur regions. It is not surprising that China has consistently voted against or abstained in UN-sponsored resolutions to take effective action against Sudan. Another explanation for China's philosophy of non-interference in Sudan's internal affairs could simply be a difference in political culture and philosophy with the West. The following statement can be found on its foreign ministry website:

> China had suffered imperialist aggression and oppression for over 100 years before the founding of the Peoples Republic in 1949. Therefore, China regards the hard-earned rights of independence as the basic principle of foreign policy.[13]

The opposition to international sanctions as an instrument to influence foreign governments, or any form of intervention in the domestic affairs of foreign nations, has been a consistent and long-term policy of China even before its current economic boom and its seeming energy imperative. In a similar fashion, where oil revenues in Sudan are concerned, China has long adopted a very rigid and non-transparent policy. The inequality involved in distribution of oil revenues between the North and South Sudan was one of the thorny points in the North–South divide. China, which buys the vast majority of Sudanese oil, does not take any steps to ensure that oil revenues are benefitting the South. China, to a large extent, did not make any efforts at peace-building between North and South, or ensure that there is an equitable share of oil revenues between the regions. Between January and March of 2007, South Sudan's share of oil revenues had declined by 50 per cent from $80 million to $40 million per month.[14]

However, as far as the Darfur crisis is concerned, and with Western diplomatic pressure on China, and condemnation of its policy of non-interference, its subtle diplomacy seemed to work. After President Hu Jintao discussed the issue of UN/African Union peacekeeping with Sudan's president, it resulted in the latter's concession to a deployment of 3,500 UN peacekeepers in Darfur in 2007. At the same time, despite China's policy of non-interference and effective behind the scenes diplomacy, its inclination to encourage, befriend and maintain close economic, political military relations with overtly authoritarian regimes could negatively impact the attitudes of other African regimes towards efforts to promote democracy and human rights on the continent. They could continue to view China as an effective alternative to the West, an alternative that is easier to handle or deal with where resource transfers, investments, trade and political expectations are concerned.

Apart from Sudan, Zimbabwe is another authoritarian regime with close political, economic and diplomatic ties to China. This is in stark contrast to the West's response to Zimbabwe's downward spiral into authoritarian rule under President Robert Mugabe. China–Zimbabwe relations are based on economic, political and military transactions. The Zimbabwean regime, in the last five years in particular, has engaged in many gross violations of civil rights and political liberties of its citizens. In January 2010, in a speech commemorating thirty years of China–Zimbabwe diplomatic relations, the Chinese ambassador to Zimbabwe emphasized the frequency of high-level contacts, increasingly strong mutual trust and ever deepening cooperation in economic, educational, cultural and military affairs. In particular, since 2008 Sino-Zimbabwean ties have been cemented through the provision of the following by China: (1) $470 million concessional loan and $200 million buyer's credits to Zimbabwe; (2) China trains 300 Zimbabwean officials annually in China amounting to $5 million; (3) a $10 million China–Zimbabwe Friendship Hospital; (4) the $1.5 million construction of two rural schools; and (5) establishment of an agricultural demonstration centre of 108 hectares; among many other projects and donations. In total roughly $4300 million of aid was extended by China to Zimbabwe.[15] In other words, China's economic, political and military ties with Zimbabwe are just as deep and extensive as those with Sudan. Its involvement includes the cell phone industry, the media (radio and television) and power generation. Besides, China is Zimbabwe's largest tobacco buyer. In terms of significant transportation projects, a Chinese company was involved in the construction of a terminal at Beira on Mozambique's coast that will help transport oil to Zimbabwe by pipeline.[16] In particular China is helping to enhance tourism between the two countries. While Zimbabwe received international condemnation for its land reform programme, China strongly supports it.[17] The relationship between China and Zimbabwe is so strong that in addition to FOCAC, they maintain other high-level diplomatic exchanges as a manifestation of the special relationship between them. For example, in July 2010, Zimbabwe and China held the 8th session of their Joint Permanent Commission. In addition to further pledges to strengthen ties and mutual cooperation, President Mugabe reaffirmed his commitment to the 'Look East Policy' first announced in 2003. Because of the Western backlash against President Mugabe's land distribution, Zimbabwe adopted the Look East Policy as a way to counter the West's reaction as well as its policy of conditional aid and imposition of sanctions. The Look East Policy will, in other words, continue to maintain, and even increase, China's trade and investment with Zimbabwe. In July 2010 during the Joint Permanent Commission summit between the two countries, President Hu Jintao promised Zimbabwe a loan of $950 million to aid in the country's economic recovery. The strong and special relationship between China and Zimbabwe is largely structured by the latter's strategic minerals – coal, chromium ore, asbestos, gold, nickel, copper, iron ore, vanadium, lithium, tin, platinum group metals, diamonds and uranium – many of which are essential to China's industrialization process. Accordingly, China–Zimbabwe relations are still strong and mutually supportive under President Xi Jinping.

China is supporting a country that has consistently refused to uphold democracy in both its presidential and parliamentary elections. Both the 2002 and 2005 parliamentary elections were characterized by the intimidation of voters and the opposition, as well as the disqualifying of opposition candidates. During the 2008 elections in particular, Mugabe's ZANU-PF party executed a campaign of repression and terror on the opposition MDC party activists and voters. In its audit of Zimbabwean elections, the Research and Advocacy Unit (RAU) came up with some shocking findings that underscore the blatant violation of election rules in Zimbabwe. As far as the voters' roll is concerned, the RAU Report entitled '2013 Vision – Seeing Double and the Dead' found among other things, that those aged between 90 and 100 numbered 82,456 people. The only problem with these figures is that in Zimbabwe the average life expectancy is thirty-four for females, and thirty-seven for males. Besides, according to the WHO only 14.7 per cent of people have a life span of over sixty years.[18] Civil society in general is constrained by government oppression and intimidation. The harassment, beatings and arbitrary arrests by security forces are frequent occurrences. All of these negative incidents constitute severe constraints on efforts by civil society to create democratic space. Most sectors of the Zimbabwean political system are far removed from transparency, freedom of speech or a positive democratic culture. The judiciary is far from independent and corruption is rampant among the ruling political elite. With the help of China which sold radio jamming technology to the regime, the government jammed broadcasts of the opposition and even seized radios belonging to rural populations. Overall, where liberty is concerned, the government consistently stifles the freedom of assembly, speech and press. To a large extent, the Mugabe regime, can afford to blatantly violate democratic rules and individual human rights because of the economic and political support it gets from China. China is increasingly becoming an alternative to the West where Zimbabwe is concerned, thus the 'Look East' policy of President Robert Mugabe. China is breaking the West's monopoly of being the major provider of economic support to Zimbabwe.

There is no doubt that China is credited among many African states for supporting the continent's struggle against colonialism and oppression. However, in its current policy posture towards Africa, it rigidly and blindly supports any incumbent regime within the continent without regard to its human rights record. China manifests a strong and unflinching support for the ruling elite in African countries at the expense of post-independence and twenty-first-century struggles by ordinary Africans for democracy and human rights. In 2009 China vetoed UN sanctions targeted at the political elite within President Mugabe's regime. The blatant violations of democratic and election rules did not dissuade China from abandoning its laissez-faire policy in the ordinary peoples struggle for justice, transparency and respect for human rights, as well as the overall need to promote a more democratic rule. China is imposing its domestic market dictatorship in Africa because its priority goal is more economic than political. Its economic interests are considered far more important than the civil liberties and political rights of ordinary people. China continues to forge close ties with the Zimbabwean regime and is not bothered by its pariah status. Chinese firms are busy in Zimbabwe in the mining, aviation, agriculture, defence and other sectors of the economy. In particular, China International Water and Electric, National Aero-Technology Import and Export Corporation (CATIC) and North Industries Corporation (NORINCO) have signed lucrative deals in the key sectors of the Zimbabwean economy.[19] The strong ties between China and Zimbabwe may in fact be influencing President Mugabe to subvert the multiparty system in Zimbabwe by rigging elections, brutalizing the opposition and violating human rights. The Chinese presence in Africa not only subverts the promotion of human rights and democracy in Africa, but also stifles the promotion of Africa's own indigenous forms of human rights and individual freedom which predated the current universal human rights regime. To a large extent, critics of China's foreign policy are baffled by the insensitivity of China's foreign policy towards Africa especially in countries like Sudan and Zimbabwe where gross human rights violations are concerned. According to the UN and Amnesty International, more than 200,000 people were killed, 2.5 million displaced and numerous women raped during the Darfur crisis. For a very long time, China not only did fail to stop the carnage, in the midst of international protests against the bloodletting, but also traded in weapons with the Khartoum regime.

China and Zimbabwe solidify their relationship in four areas. First, they do so through elite level contacts, cordial intergovernmental exchanges or at the level of political parties and parliaments. Secondly, they promote and expand economic cooperation based on mutual beneficial transactions and proper implementation of joint bilateral decisions. Thirdly, China is ever willing to develop Zimbabwe's human resources through personnel training. This goal covers cooperation in cultural, educational and health issues, among many others, that contribute to Zimbabwe's national development. Fourthly, China-Zimbabwean relations are cemented through mutual support in the UN and other multilateral bodies.[20] In May 2010, the Communist Party of China (CPC) and Zimbabwe's ZANU-PF launched a deliberate effort to strengthen their inter-party relations as a basis of promoting bilateral economic cooperation. This was all part of the 30th anniversary of Zimbabwe's independence as well as thirty years of China-Zimbabwean diplomatic relations. During the ceremony, visiting senior Chinese party official Wang Gang, a member of the CCP Central Committee Political Bureau proposed four areas of inter-party cooperation: (1) strengthen high-level exchange; (2) improve exchange in ruling experiences; (3) promote bilateral cooperation; and (4) promote folk or informal exchanges between the two countries.[21] The goal is to achieve comprehensive Sino-Zimbabwean relations. As a pariah nation to the West, Zimbabwean president Robert Mugabe is solidly supportive of China's approach to the African continent. His approval of China's foreign policy to Zimbabwe, in particular, and Africa in general, is captured in these words:

> China's relations with Africa are based on sincere friendship and equal treatment and China is moreand more welcome in the continent. All African countries are ready to deepen traditional friendship, develop cooperation in all areas and strengthen coordination in international affairs with China.[22]

The decision by China to continue a cooperative partnership with states experiencing civil strife could be interpreted in three ways: (1) to continue to promote investments within the host country so that the economic and political ties already forged are not lost within that country; (2) to ensure Chinese access to (Sudanese and Zimbabwean) resources, or political support from the country affected; and (3) to continue to maintain support for China within the host country and at the UN, thereby keeping Taiwan out. This means that China's economic activities in Africa are structured by China's national interest, the geo-economic importance of some African states and the overall role perception of China in the current global system, with regards to Africa in particular. The effect that China's economic and political relationship with African states has is to embolden African states to reject Western conditionalities circumventing rules and regulations on transparency, fiscal probity and political liberalization by some African states that have extensive ties with China. For example, in 2005, Angola was very reluctant to adhere to Western demands for improved transparency in its oil sector, as well as calls for other reforms as preconditions for a donor's conference. The reluctance on the part of Angola was interpreted as the result of a Chinese loan that Angola had received. Angolan officials even stated that they did not see the need for transparency as a condition for the donor's conference. To some extent, China is serving as an alternative to the much resented Western policy posture of economic and political conditionalities for the donor–recipient aid relationship. China, on the other hand, rigidly adheres to the pre-globalization ethos of the sacrosanct nature of sovereignty and therefore its belief that the sovereignty of nations should be above any other concerns. Accordingly, China's aid and debt forgiveness is free of any conditionalities such as good governance or transparency. These economic and political conditions with their attendant austerity measures have been the weapons utilized by Western nations and IFIs, in particular the IMF and the World Bank.

In the Chinese approach to Africa, it is possible to discern strong overtones of Chinese sociocultural values and political culture. In authoritarian states like Zimbabwe, Sudan and Equatorial Guinea, China's 'hands off' approach could also be interpreted as a lingering effect of Confucian values which emphasize obedience, authority and hierarchy. This Chinese tendency to defer to African rulers and the Western tendency to promote universal human rights constitutes a culture clash between China and the West in Africa. If the persistence of Confucian values is to be taken into account, it means China's African policy assumes that the African masses are supposed to be obedient and subservient to the political elite.

The promotion of democracy and human rights in African countries is not a priority in Chinese foreign policy, neither is it one of the preoccupations of the Chinese political elite regarding China's domestic policies. What is currently at the top of the Chinese agenda is to establish strong diplomatic ties with as many countries as possible that would support the One-China Policy, and/or be a source of critical resources that China needs in its ongoing industrialization. Moreover, what makes China uncompromising about its policy of non-interference and refusal to condemn human rights abuses in African countries is the fact that Western condemnations of authoritarian or dictatorial regimes are selective. For instance, while the West condemns Zimbabwe, Sudan and other countries, it continues to support Egypt, Equatorial Guinea, Tunisia and Saudi Arabia that do fall into the category of gross human rights violators. Thus, from a foreign policy/national security perspective, China is also focused on cementing relations with external allies that will prove useful in the pursuit of economic, political, military and cultural objectives. The problem with authoritarian African regimes is that the pro-democracy stance of the West makes them gravitate towards China. These governments recognize that China can take the place of the West and provide the means to ensure their political survival. Accordingly, the trend in Africa is that collusion takes place between China and the African regime to protect the former's economic activities. It is not surprising that China supplies arms that are used by the host government to protect Chinese investments. For example, China sells some of the most advanced weapons to valued African clients including F6 class fighter planes, Z-6 type helicopters, self-propelled artillery units and F-7 jets.[23]

The fact that China's historical interactions with Africa are free of colonial and imperial oppression makes African perceptions of the Chinese relatively more positive than perceptions of most European countries. The African political elite are particularly more open to Chinese economic and political behaviour on the continent. Apart from its past positive role in Africa through support of liberation wars and decolonization in particular, the Chinese are further enhancing their image on the continent by engaging in extensive investments in varied sectors related to infrastructure (roads, transportation) health, personnel training and agriculture. However, among the African masses, perceptions and attitudes towards Africa are both positive and negative for several reasons. The Chinese in some regions of Africa are perceived as solely focused on oil exploration and extraction. China has still not abandoned its 1972 policy posture of 'right to pollute' argument in response to the West's demand for environmental (pollution in particular) concerns in the process of industrialization. Accordingly, its behaviour in Africa is seen to correlate with this policy posture and is reflected in little to no regard for environmental standards. Such an attitude is likely to encourage the African elite to stifle civic organizations, or domestic African non-state actors who might want to encourage environmental concerns as part of the democratic process in Africa. Similarly, China's neglect of labour standards and harsh working conditions is not conducive to the growth of labour unions and occupational and safety standards for workers that are an integral part of a democratic process. In other words, China may be directly or indirectly influencing the African political and economic elite to discourage the growth of interest groups or a civil society in the areas of the environment, labour and working conditions that enrich and strength democracy in Western societies.

In some countries, China has been a source of conflict between the incumbent regime and the opposition parties. Apart from Sudan, violence against Chinese investment is well documented. Its policy of non-interference has led the opposition in many countries to level criticisms of backing corrupt and dictatorial regimes. Its policy of non-interference has also resulted in its investments either directly or indirectly falling prey to violence. According to the Brussels Institute of contemporary China Studies:

> Chinese business activities often fall prey to endemic instability and violence in economic partner states. Between 2007 and 2009, at least thirty Chinese citizens were killed in violent incidents and more than seventy were abducted. In five countries Chinese energy operations were attacked. In six countries rebel groups threatened to sabotage Chinese companies.[24]

This manifestation of Sinophobia in several parts of Africa could be the result of China's adherence to a rigid non-interference policy, which also translates into a lack of interest to aid in conflict resolution efforts between the incumbent regime and opposition or rebel groups.

In terms of recent historical interactions between China and Africa, China's current African policy is no different in terms of substance from the 'five principles of Peaceful Co-existence' outlined by Premier Zhou Enlai in 1953 at a meeting with an Indian delegation. The five principles of Peaceful Coexistence were a source of unity or rallying point for countries that had experienced the burden of colonial or Western imperial intervention. The five principles of Peaceful Coexistence – mutual respect for territorial integrity and sovereignty, non-aggression, non-interference in internal affairs, equality and mutual benefit, and peaceful co-existence – are again very similar to the China–Africa policy Paper enunciated in 2006. China's current policy of non-interference, aid with no strings attached, and investment in neglected sectors of Africa's economies, is an example of China continued adherence to the Maoist African policy of adopting the moral high ground and distancing itself from any suggestion of external impositions that many African elites resent. Accordingly, China condemns, in particular, US hegemonism (domineering attitude) vis-à-vis developing countries, while it underscores its friendship and cooperation with African and other developing countries. A cornerstone of Chinese foreign policy in Africa is to promote itself as a positive contrast to what it knows the Africans will resent – Western domination, impositions and 'dictatorial' tendencies manifested in economic and political conditionalities, threats of sanctions and the like. Gerald Schmitt of the Donor Committee for Enterprise Development contrasts the African attitude to Chinese involvement compared to the West's in this manner:

> In most African countries, the new Chinese engagement is highly appreciated, especially at political level. It counters the 'post- colonial hegemony' of the West and gives additional room for manoeuvre in negotiations with donors. Large infrastructure projects, constructed by Chinese companies in very short time and financed by Chinese loans at cheap conditions, are highly welcome, especially in post-conflict countries. China's support is known to be realized fast – it does not involve tedious negotiations with a high number of conditionalities attached. China's philosophy of support with 'no strings attached' except the 'One China principle' and its tied aid is preferred to support from the West involving the whole governance agenda.[25]

This dual Chinese strategy of political non-interference and focus on African development through large infrastructure development is bound to make many African governments look increasingly to China as a model of political and economic development.

The question is often discussed in the democratization literature of whether democracy can thrive in a non-bourgeois society? The answer for most has been a resounding 'no'. China's predatory dumping of poor quality Chinese goods in Africa is undercutting and dampening the efforts of African producers because local Africans opt for cheaper Chinese goods. This has resulted in thousands of workers in the textile industries of South Africa, Lesotho and Kenya to lose their jobs. The unfair Chinese economic competition in textiles, pharmaceuticals and other sectors undermine African economies thereby either directly and/or indirectly undermining the growth of a middle class (a bourgeois class) which is usually the engine for growth in democratic values. Closely related to this problem of Chinese goods undercutting African goods is the problem of a Sino-African trade imbalance manifested in growing trade deficits. If China contributes to increasing subversion of trade and industrialization in Africa, African states could adopt protectionism thereby interfering with global calls for trade liberalization.

Summary and conclusions

Sino-African relations are very comprehensive, diversified and encompass four broad areas of bilateral cooperation as follows: (1) the political dimension which comprises of high-level visits, exchanges between legislative bodies and political parties, mutual support in international affairs, and even exchanges between local governments; (2) the economic sector comprised of trade, investment and agricultural cooperation, as well as issues of debt reduction and tourism; (3) education, health, cultural cooperation and the like; and (4) peacekeeping and military cooperation, and related activities. Although the extent and depth of China's monetary involvement in Africa is not yet as significant as that of the West, nonetheless it is gradually becoming an alternative to the West's bilateral and multilateral relationship with the continent. China has certain advantages over the West in Africa: (1) the reality and perception that it is also a Third world nation that is complementary to African needs and resources; (2) its sociocultural and politico-cultural proximity to Africa in areas of governance, economic goals and cultural norms; (3) its industrial success as a market dictatorship which could further appeal to many African states still gripped in authoritarian rule; and (4) its policy orientation towards Africa based on non-conditionality of aid, non-interference in domestic politics and what seems to be a more direct involvement in African development issues compared to the West. Pariah states like Zimbabwe, under pressure from the West, are forced to look to China and are even willing see China as an alternative to Western models of development.

As the new great actor in Africa, China is igniting both positive and negative concerns about its political and economic involvement on the continent. Many observers note that China is enhancing economic development in Africa by investing in sectors such as roads, transportation, health and education that have long been neglected by the West. Such observers also underscore the differences in style between China's relationship with Africa and that of the West. The West emphasizes on austerity measures or conditionalities that have caused a great deal of misery and deprivation on the continent. At the same time critics of China in Africa point to China's willingness to use bribery as a way of cementing economic and political deals with African states. Secondly, they charge that China's extension of aid with no strings attached encourages authoritarian regimes to subvert any efforts at democratization. Thirdly, it is also argued that its non-conditional aid policy undermines the West's efforts, including IFIs, at macroeconomic reforms. Considering the tight connection between capitalism and democracy, it would mean that the Chinese model would not only stifle African markets, but would also derail the growth of civil society which is an integral part of a democratic society.

Finally, the problem for good governance is that African states that view China as an alternate model of development could be (1) reluctant to adhere to principles of good governance or respect for human rights since China does not itself encourage or observe democratic values and (2) the China–Africa economic relationship which is mostly asymmetrical in favour of China could end up stifling the growth of a bourgeois (middle) class which is essential for the growth of democracy and capitalism in any country.

However, it is important to point out that China is simply working within the context of authoritarian tendencies that have long been present within the continent as a result of colonial and neocolonial influences. At the same time, it could be argued that China is also complicit in encouraging or fostering non-democratic tendencies because of its policy of non-interference in matters of liberal democracy and human rights observance. The objective of the West and China is to ensure that their interests are protected within a stable Africa, whether democratic or not. This often translates into helping to protect and preserve dictatorial, authoritarian and illegitimate regimes.

Notes

1 See, full text of Chinese president Hu Jintao's speech at FOCAC 2006, Beijing, 4 November 2006. http://www.fmprc.gov.cn/zflt/eng/tptb/t404200.htm (accessed 6 May 2012).
2 For more details, see Brooks and Shinn (2006).
3 See Qingfen (2010).
4 The Herald (Harare) (2005).
5 For details on the debt regime, see Rieffel (1985).
6 FOCAC Beijing Summit Adopts Declaration (2006).
7 *People's Daily* Online, http://english.peopledaily.com.cn/200605/16/eng 20060516_266153.
8 For details, see Li Anshan, 'Transformations of China's Policy towards Africa', Paper submitted to the Workshop 'China-Africa Relations: Engaging the International Discourse', organized by China's Transnational Relations Center at Hong Kong University of Science and Technology, 11–12 November 2006; and Guillaume Mounmouni, 'Domestic Transformations and Change in Sino-Africa Relations', paper presented at the Workshop 'China-Africa Relations: Engaging the International Discourse', Hong Kong University of Science and Technology Center on China's Transnational Relations. 11–12 November 2006.
9 Traub (2006).
10 Human Rights Watch (2003).
11 International Crisis Group (ICG) (2002).
12 For more details see Pan (2006), Chung-lian (2004).
13 See, Ministry of Foreign Affairs of the People's Republic of China, www.fmprc.gov.cn/mfa_eng/wjb_663304/.
14 See, Harman (2007).
15 See, for example, briefing by H.E. Xin Shunkang at the Launch of the 30th anniversary celebrations of establishment of China–Zimbabwe Diplomatic Relations, Harare, 21 January (2010), in http://zw.china-embassy.org/eng/xwdt/t653147.html (accessed 15 March 2011).
16 The Herald (2004).
17 Agence-France Presse (AFP) (2004).
18 For more details, see, Hickman (2009), and : Derek Matyszak, ' 2013 Vision – Seeing Double and the Dead: A Preliminary Audit of Zimbabwe's Voter Roll, Research and Advocacy Unit (RAU) Harare, Zimbabwe, 13 October (2013).
19 See Moyo, http://www.newzimbabwe.com/pages/opinion 335.18494.html.

20 Official Chinese News Agency Xinhua – New China News Agency (2005).
21 Communist Party of China (CPC) and ZANU-PF (2010).
22 See, 'Zimbabwean President and Prime Minister meet respectively with Chinese Foreign Minister Yang Jiechi', (2011).
23 Pan (2006), and Jiang (2004).
24 See Kaplinsky and Morris (2010).
25 Schmitt (2007: 8).

Bibliography

Agence-France Presse (AFP), 'Chinese Envoy Supports Zimbabwe Land Reforms', 2 November (2004).

Anshan, Li, 'Transformation of China's POLICY TOWARDS AFRICA,' paper submitted to the workshop, 'China-Africa Relations: Engaging the International Discourse,' organized by China's transnational relations center at Hong Kong University of Science and Technology, 11 November (2006).

Brooks, Peter and Ji Hye Shin, *China's Influence in Africa: Implications for the United States* (Washington, DC; Report Asia: The Heritage Foundation, 22 February 2006).

Communist Party of China (CPC) and ZANU-PF, Xinhua- *People's Daily* Online, 31 May (2010).

Easterly, William, *The Whiteman's Burden: Why the West Effors to Aid the Rest Have Done So Much Ill and So Little Good* (New York: The Penguin Press, 2006).

'FOCAC Beijing Summit Adopts Declaration', 5 November (2006a). Available at www.focac.org/eng/dwjbzjjhys/t952503.htm (accessed 15 April 2011).

'FOCAC Beijing Summit Adopts Declaration', 5 November (2006b). Available at http://englishfocaccri.cn/2946/2006/11/05/53@159216.htm (accessed 15 January 2012).

Harman, Danna, 'How China's Support of Sudan Shields a Regime Called "Genocidal"', *The Christian Science Monitor*, 26 June (2007). Available at http://www.csmonitor.com/2007/0626/p01s08-woaf.html (accessed 11 April 2012).

Herald (Harare), 'President to Retire in 2008', 22 April (2005), https://zimbabwesituation.com/old/april2005_arch

Hickman, John, 'Does Electoral Competition Cause Post-Election Intimidation and Violence? Evidence from the March 29, 2008 Zimbabwean General Election', *Paper presented at the 27th Annual Meeting of the Association of Third World Studies*, Cape Coast, Ghana, 21–24 November (2009).

Human Rights Watch, 'Sudan, Oil, and Human Rights', New York, 24 November (2003). Available at http://www.hrw.org/en/reports/2003/11/24/sudan-oil-and-human-rights (accessed 27 May 2011).

International Crisis Group, *God, Oil and Country: Changing the Logic of War in Sudan*. ICG Africa Report, No. 39. Brussels, Belgium, October (2003).

International Crisis Group (ICG), *God, Oil and Country: Changing the Logic of War in Sudan*, Africa Report, No. 39, 10 January (2002).

Jiang, Chung-lian, 'Oil: A New Dimension in Sino-African Relations', *African Geopolitics*, 14 (Spring) (2004)

Jintao, Hu, 'Speech at FOCAC 2006', Beijing, 4 November (2006). Available at www.gov.cn/misc/2006-11/04/conent_432652.htm (accessed 28 June 2012).

Kaplinsky, Raphael and Mike Morris, 'The Policy Challenge for Sub-Saharan Africa of Large-Scale Chinese FDI (ARI)', *Reall Instituto Elcano*, 169 (2010). Available at http://www.realinstitute.oelcano.org/wps.portal/rielcano eng/Print?WCM (accessed 20 March 2012).

Matyszak, Derek, *2013 Vision-Seeing Double and the Dead: A Preliminary Audit of Zimbabwe's Voter's Roll*, Research and Advocacy Unit (RAU). Harare, Zimbabwe, 13 October (2013).

Ministry of Foreign Affairs of the People's Republic of China. Available at www.fmprc.gov.cn/mfa_eng/wjb_663304/ (accessed 19 August 2011).

Mounmouni, Gillaume, 'Domestic Transformation and Change in Sino-Africa relations,' *Paper Presented at the Workshop 'China-Africa Relations: Engaging the International Discourse,' Hong Kong University and Technology Center on China's Transnational Relations*, 11–12 November (2006).

Moyo, Last, 'From Sudan to Zimbabwe, China Is Part of the problem', newzimbabwe.com. Available at http://www.newzimbabwe.com/pages/opinion 335.18494.html (accessed 17 March 2011).

Official Chinese News Agency Xinhua—New China News Agency, 'Chinese Zimbabwean Presidents Sign Economic Cooperation Deal', 28 July (2005).

Pan, Esther, *China, Africa, and Oil* (Washington, DC: Council on Foreign Relations Backgrounder, 12 January 2006).

People's Daily Online, 'Fairly Looking upon Sino-African Relations', 16 May (2006). Available at http://english.peopledaily.com.cn/200605/16/eng 20060516_266153 (accessed 18 June 2012).

Qingfen, Ding, 'Trade with Africa Set to Achieve Record High', *China Daily*, 15 October (2010).

Rieffel, Alexis, *The Role of the Paris Club in Managing Debt Problems*. Essays in International Finance, No. 161 (New Jersey: Princeton University, December 1985).

Schmitt, Gerald, 'Is Africa Turning East? China's New Engagement in Africa and Its Implications on the Macro-Economic Situation, the Business Environment and the Private Sector in Africa', *Donor Committee for Enterprise Development African Regional Consultative Conference*, October (2007).

The Herald (Harare), 'Joint Venture to Ease Country's Fuel Woes', 17 December (2004), https://allafrica.com/stories/200412170323.html

The Herald, 'Zimbabwe: President to Retire in 2008', 22 April (2005).

Traub, James, 'China's African Adventure', *The New York Times*, 19 November (2006).

Wenping, He, *New Actors in International Development: The Case of China in Africa* (Washington, DC: Brookings, 13 May 2013).

Xinhua-New China News Agency, 'Chinese Zimbabwean Presidents Sign Economic Cooperation Deal', 28 July (2005).

'Zimbabwean President and Prime Minister Meet Respectively with Chinese Foreign Minister Yang Jiechi', 11 February (2011). Available at om.chineseembasy.org/eng/xwdt_2_1_1/t794415.htm (accessed 20 November 2011).

12

China's autocracy, global democracy and their limits in an age of uncertainty

Miao-ling Lin Hasenkamp

To what extent has China's authoritarian regime influenced, by example or by action, other states to develop authoritarian features? How can China's growing influence be evaluated? Is there a causal link between China's rise, persistent and competitive authoritarianism, the democratic recession, and the rise of authoritarian populism in old and young democracies? These are questions which require comparative empirical and longitudinal research for getting satisfactory answers. The findings of this volume and the existing literature have provided some first hints while addressing these questions.

As this volume has demonstrated, China is not on a road towards democracy. Its internal development counters two important findings gained from empirical research on democracy: first, the CCP's authoritarian rule has resisted the contemporary wave of democratization, in spite of Western engagement efforts towards China and a continuous rise in the number of democratic states.[1] Secondly, though comparative studies on democratization observe a strong correlation between economic growth and democratization, China's emerging middle class stands loyally behind the CCP's rule. This signals a limit of the economic theory of democracy. It also urges us to rethink institutional, sociocultural and economic prerequisites of democracy (e.g. the existence of a democratic culture with civil society's participation and engagement, see Hadenius and Teorell 2005; Congleton 2003: 44).

The following paragraphs present two synthesized accounts in highlighting the relationship between China's autocracy, its influence abroad, persistent authoritarian regimes and the democratic recession in old and young democracies. First, in spite of its rising authoritarian influence, China falls short of establishing a solid authoritarian nexus due to the lack of transparency, credibility and consistency of its global engagements. Secondly, democracy is less challenged by the rise and persistence of authoritarian regimes than by its own structural weaknesses and varied crises it faces at home.

China's autocracy and its political influence: Is the deepening of authoritarianism inevitable?

China's growing influence on the global stage marks a success for competitive authoritarianism and becomes a factor in contributing to authoritarian survival and diffusion (Levitsky and Way 2010; Bader 2015a). Its political weight can be felt in diverse fora of international cooperation. Prior to the 13th summit of G20 in December 2018, China and other powerful authoritarian regimes (Russia, Turkey, Saudi Arabia, etc.) had constituted 60 per cent of the world's economic performance – a facilitating environment for China to promote authoritarianism.[2] Studies on diffusion have shown different mechanisms that support the spread of ideas – democratic or authoritarian alike – and the pursuit of interests of powerful states (e.g. through learning, emulation, competition, coercion, control, conditionality and persuasion (Barry 2012; Burnell 2010; Bader 2015a; Levitsky and Way 2006, 2010). While they view geographical proximity and regional peer pressure as crucial for such diffusion process (Miller 2013), evidence also demonstrates how regime change takes place depending on the degree of leverage, linkage and organizational capacity powerful states have beyond the region (Levitsky and Way 2010; Tolstrup 2013). For Levitsky and Way (2010: 26–32ff), 'Leverage refers not to the exercise of external pressure, *per se*, but instead to a country's vulnerability to such pressure.' If a target state lacks bargaining power and is heavily affected by punitive action of powerful states, leverage is high. In conceptualizing 'linkage to the West', Levitsky and Way (2010: 26–32ff) define linkage 'as the density of ties (economic, political, diplomatic, social, and organizational) and cross-border flows (of capital, goods and services, people, and information)' between target states, powerful states and multilateral institutions dominated by leading Western democracies and non-Western autocracies. In particular, the existence of historical links, gatekeeper elites as well as state capacity in resisting external influence or organizing the scope of diffusion are important factors in shaping regime outcomes.

By including the aspect of legitimacy in the study of authoritarian diffusion, Ambrosio (2010) suggests a framework in terms of ideology and interests, in which the appropriateness and effectiveness of autocracy can be assessed. Namely, the stronger an authoritarian regime is legitimized, the more assertive is its leadership in exercising its influence at home and abroad. Also, the more effective a regime exercises its political and economic influence abroad, the more many states will follow its model. The Belt and Road Initiative (BRI) introduced by President Xi Jinping in 2013, for instance, has become a Chinese version of the Marshall Plan. Not only has it found broad domestic support. It also reveals China's ambition 'to write new rules, establish multilateral institutions' through connecting Africa, Asia and Europe and expanding infrastructure projects on an unparalleled scale that reflect Chinese interests and 'reshape "soft" infrastructure'.[3] The impacts of China's offensive engagements in Africa are paramount: through the BRI, student and journalist exchange programmes, China has been able to present itself perceived as 'a civilized, democratic, open, and energetic country'. Following a newspaper source *Business Daily* based in Kenya, in March 2018, China constitutes 72 per cent of Kenya's bilateral debt with foreign states, eight times more than France – a traditional donor in Kenya. As noted by the John Hopkins University, between 2000 and 2015, a credit sum of $94 billion have flown from China to Africa.[4] More initiatives are on the way: China plans to set up international courts in Shenzhen and Xi'an, which are the former hub of the original Silk Road. The aim is to resolve commercial disputes related to the BRI area. A further example is the Asian Infrastructure Investment Bank (AIIB) initiated by China. As China has successfully gained support from Germany and other important Western states as members, in summer 2017, the AIIB has obtained a high credibility score by the international rating agencies, who have given the World Bank and other multinational banks the same rank.[5]

The elaboration of novel concepts has further helped enhance our knowledge of authoritarian diffusion and its effects (Kneuer et al. 2018; Tansey 2015; Melnykovska et al. 2012; Ambrosio 2012). Tansey (2015: 141) suggests to strictly define 'autocracy promotion' as the existence of 'a clear intent on the part of an external actor to bolster autocracy as a form of a political regime as well as an underlying motivation that rests in significant part on an ideological commitment to autocracy itself'. Furthermore, the use of the concept 'authoritarian gravity centres' (AGC) detects how authoritarian regimes use regional organizations (ROs) or create new ROs for the pursuit of their interests, thereby contributing to the building of AGC across different regions. As observed by Kneuer et al. (2018), AGC such as the Gulf Cooperation Council (GCC) and the Bolivian Alliance for the Peoples of Our America (ALBA-TCP) have served as 'a transmission belt and a learning room for disseminating autocratic elements'. Tansey et al. (2017) present the concept 'autocratic linkage' to detect how the strengthening links between autocrats have facilitated authoritarian survival and diffusion.

Indeed, powerful authoritarian regimes such as China often use (inter)-regional fora and launch new initiatives to counter Western influence and pursue their interests (Ambrosio 2012, 2008). Guided by 'Shanghai Spirit', both Russia and China have considered the Shanghai Cooperation Organisation (SCO) as an important channel to exercise their power and to pursue their geostrategic and economic/energy interests in Central Asia. The SCO's adoption of the principles of 'diversity' and 'non-intervention' and a common authoritarian rhetoric of a 'fight against terrorism and separatism' has proved to be effective in legitimizing authoritarian rule and justifying repressive measures against political opposition groups, minorities and dissenters (e.g. China's 're-education camps' in Xinjiang,[6] see also Ambrosio 2008). Also, China's decade-long dialogue relations and cooperation with the Association of Southeast Asian Nations (ASEAN) in different issue areas have posed a challenge against traditional US dominance in the region.[7]

For its regional counterparts, the so-called 'Beijing consensus', 'China option' (*Chong guo fan an*) or 'China model' has become a source of inspiration. In October 2018, Vietnam has followed China's mode of one-man leadership and elected Nguyen Phu Trong as its new president, who is also the leader of the ruling Communist party. Despite the territorial conflicts with China and deep-rooted anti-Chinese resentments in the local population, Trong has pledged to strengthen its relations with China. As such, his presidency will differ from his predecessors' pro-Western foreign policy.[8] Similarly, some elected governments have looked to their regional counterparts and resorted to neo-nationalist rightist discourses while incorporating authoritarian elements into their rule.[9]

In view of rising authoritarian influence reflected in China's comprehensive global engagements and the persistence of hybrid regime, scholars of democratization and comparative politics have begun to reconsider the validity of the 'transition paradigm' (Carothers 2002; Diamond et al. 2014). Evidence reveals that a stable democracy is not necessarily a natural outcome following the installation of democratic institutions and regular elections. Several longitudinal empirical studies unambiguously unravel the limited effects of Western linkage and leverage policies through foreign aid, economic sanction or military intervention while promoting democracy abroad (Knack 2004; Escribà-Folch and Wright 2015). The lack of effectiveness might be resulted from the narrow focus of Western aid policy on the requirement of introducing democratic institutions as a core leverage and linkage attribute without paying appropriate attention to the power structure and resource allocation in target states. Instead, China's growing influence has not only confirmed the results of early studies of the resilience of a one-party regime in countering Western influence. It also has helped entrench the persistence of hybrid regimes through ongoing autocratic linkages at bilateral, regional and multilateral level, thereby bringing the third wave of democratization in the post-Cold War era into a state of stagnation or even recession. In this sense, we observe a mutually reinforcing relationship between the rise of China, its expanding influence and the persistence of hybrid regimes.

Notwithstanding, the results of several empirical studies of autocracy promotion offer a highly ambivalent picture of the effects of leading authoritarian regimes' engagements abroad. Melnykovska, Plamper and Schweickert (2012: 75) use three dimensions – leadership or participation of regional organizations, economic cooperation, direct interference and threat – to examine autocracy promotion. Their qualitative study shows the impacts of different strategies Russia and China have implemented in Central Asia. Unlike Russia's dominance mode of operation in its exercise of influence, 'China's doing-business approach towards its neighbours in Central Asia may have – although unintentionally – even positive effects in terms of improving governance and undermining autocratic structures'. Bader's study (2015b) illuminates a strong causal link between China's economic support and authoritarian survival involving also a one-party system similar to that of the CCP. However, one observes a strong degree of variation of the effects of China's economic cooperation upon other types of regime (electoral military regime or dictatorship) due to different circumstances in target states and the difference of scope and content of interactions.

The authors in this volume have also pointed out ambivalent effects of China's rise on democracy promotion and authoritarian diffusion. On the one hand, China's engagements in Africa have detrimental effects on Western democracy promotion efforts. Not only has China's party-state regime encouraged autocrats to follow its model by strengthening their political control and suppressing dissident voices at home. It also has provided authoritarian leaders (e.g. in Zimbabwe and Sudan) with alternative choices to resist Western democracy promotion programmes (i.e. with the requirements of good governance, the rule of law and respect of human rights). On the other hand, echoing the results of several empirical studies, this volume finds *little* evidence of China's influence in building an authoritarian nexus in Latin America.

Herein arises the question of the reasons of the limited influence of leading authoritarian regimes like China in building a solid nexus of autocracy, intra- or cross-regionally. Four reasons may account for such limitations.

First, as found in several comparative empirical studies of diffusion of authoritarianism (Chou et al. 2017: 175; Ziegler 2016; Way 2016, 2015; Muno et al. in this volume), the limited direct influence of authoritarian external actors (e.g. Russia in Central Asia and China in Latin America) is due to the lack of consistency of autocracy's foreign support. The case of Russia shows that Moscow supports 'opposition and greater pluralism in countries where anti-Russian governments are in power, and incumbent autocrats in cases where pro-Russian politicians dominate' (Way 2015).

Secondly, despite the adoption of a common authoritarian rhetoric, powerful authoritarian regimes lack a clear-defined consistent political ideology and a credible agenda to promote autocracy. For instance, since the 1990s, China has presented several political ideas that were to demonstrate China's unique role as a great power and possible contribution to world peace and prosperity. The idea of 'building a harmonious society' pervaded at all levels was considered as the CCP's attempt to restore Chinese traditional values and to address social conflicts resulting from former president Jiang Zemin's success in driving the country towards 'moderate prosperity'. As such, China's political elites and scholars were also eager to explore the applicability of this concept that could be adopted as a guideline for international cooperation (e.g. the suggestion of a Chinese School of the Theory of International Relations (IR)). At the same time, under the shibboleth 'harmony', it can reach out to different peoples with different meanings. It covers a variety of different ideological colours (with inspiration in socialist, republican and liberal principles articulated in Chinese ancient texts (i.e. Confucian, Taoist, legalist, and Buddhist ones)) with which the CCP may risk to lose control in dictating its scope and content.[10] Later, the 'harmony' discourse was replaced by Hu Jintao's concept of 'the scientific outlook of development' and Xi's discourse of global engagement through the BRI. By connecting with the glorious past after the rupture of revolution, CCP's ongoing discursive deliberation efforts prove to be selective by picking up hierarchical and paternalistic aspects of its heritage. They have been mainly driven by the CCP's calculations to legitimize its top-down monopoly of decision-making power, to combat excess capacity at home and to effectively pursue its interests through expanding China's presence at the global level. The propaganda of different political discourses has thus raised concerns about its content, appropriateness, consistency and credibility. Critics point out that President Xi's Silk-Road'-project can be of dual use: usable not only for an expanded commercial presence, but also for political and military purposes. Particularly in some key Belt and Road countries, Beijing have been successfully using its projects to give China both favour and leverage among its clients, tying them to its military ambitions. Following a confidential plan reviewed by the *New York Times* in December 2018, Pakistan and China for instance have agreed to expand their projects planned in the so-called China–Pakistan Economic Corridor that include new military and space cooperation. While Pakistan might have found alternative sponsor to help address its domestic economic desperate situations in facing the recent decision of United States to suspend billions of dollars of security aid, some Pakistani officials have expressed their concerns of losing sovereignty to its deep-pocketed Asian ally which may leave Pakistan little choice but to go along with China.[11] As such, the new Sino-Pakistani military cooperation has confirmed 'the concerns of a host of nations who suspect the infrastructure initiative is really about helping China project armed might'.[12] Furthermore, evidence shows how China's intensive engagements in Africa have been able to gain cross-issue support in international fora such as in the UN Human Rights Council during its regular universal periodical review procedure.[13]

Thirdly, the lack of transparency and increasing discrepancy between the rhetoric and motivation found in China's growing involvement in global development cooperation (e.g. lending and debt release measures) have further evoked critiques of the consequences of its investment activity for world trade and economy. Analysts find that in extreme cases, China has used 'debt-trap diplomacy' to 'extract strategic concessions – such as in the territorial disputes in the South China Sea or silence on human rights violations'.[14] In other words, China lends into very high risk environments with a hidden motivation to create leverage used for purposes *unrelated* to the original loan. For instance, in 2011, Tajikistan got an undisclosed debt release from China in exchange for 1,158 square kilometres (447 square miles) of disputed territory.[15] This evidence immediately echoes what some commentators warn against rising authoritarian influence named as '"sharp power" that pierces, penetrates, or perforates the political and information environments in the targeted countries' (Cardenal et al. 2017: 6). In view of the high risks Belt and Road countries may encounter, commentators urge Western countries to be vigilant towards China's lending activities, particularly in the forum of multinational banks (e.g. the AIIB), in which the Chinese leadership may easily facilitate the creation of a world order that would make human rights and democratic values obsolete.[16] Similarly, in view of Beijing's cultural and informational influence in open democratic societies (e.g. in the United States and Australia), observers suggest to promote 'constructive vigilance' between China and democratic states that should serve as the basis for protecting the integrity of democratic institutions, core values, norms and laws (Hoover Institution 2018: ix). Moreover, in its 2018 annual meeting, the twenty-two members of the Paris Club have urged China to respect international rules and to apply for a membership of the Paris Club.[17] The 2019/20 coronavirus outbreak in China has unambiguously revealed the anarchic face of a huge country and an uncertain social-political environment under Xi's absolutist rule (i.e. the anxiety and obedience of local authorities towards Beijing reflected not only in the censors erasing anything that veers from the official narrative but also in a surge of reported cases and a jump in the number of deaths following Xi's instruction to vigorously respond to this outbreak before the Lunar New Year holiday in January 2020). The lack of transparency, reliable sources as well as clarity of the CCP's willingness to comply with international rules while tackling such a public health crisis has become a test case for China's proclaimed ambition and leadership, domestically and internationally. In this respect, China's authoritarian influence remains limited as long as its behaviour is constantly under suspicion and its status as a reliable lender and global leader has not yet established.

Finally, China's growing influence might constitute a disquieting reality, coupled with the increasing assertiveness of other authoritarian regimes and the shortcomings and crises leading democracies face. Namely, with their growing influence abroad, autocrats' arbitrary rule may be justified while pursuing their political interests abroad, thereby running the risk of violating international norms and impeding the functioning of institutions that defend human rights and democracy. Some recent cases illustrate such a risk of cross-border despotism. One is the 'political murder' of the Saudi dissident journalist Jamal Khashoggi in the Saudi Arabia's general consulate in Turkey. Another is the disappearance of Interpol's chief Meng Hongwei during his visit to China. These cases reveal not only how unscrupulous authoritarian rulers pursue their political interests through cross-border arbitrary arrest and killing, kidnapping and manipulation of information. They also make visible the vacuum of a reliable global authority that can effectively scrutinize state behaviour on behalf of international norms.[18] Meanwhile, the 2019 turmoil in Hong Kong shows how autocracy's imperious style and concentration of power through breaking the promise of 'One State, Two Systems' and eroding people's civil liberties and political rights can backfire. Ultimately, the drawbacks of such authoritarian rule (i.e. the lack of a democratic check-and-balance system) have contributed to the Chinese government's mishandling of the crisis and misreading of the scope of discontent in Hong Kong.[19]

Considering the limits autocracy faces, the inevitability of the deepening of authoritarianism remains open. This view suggests that autocracy may pose fewer challenges for democracy than many have assumed at the beginning (Way 2016). Instead, we need to understand why some authoritarian regimes remain persistent, why among some young democracies, elected governments have moved towards an authoritarian rule and what are the driving forces that have caused the democratic recession in some old democracies.

The looming of an authoritarian and populist age? Reviving democracy as a survival strategy

In spite of the rising number of democratic states, the quality of democracy which looks beyond electoral process and ensures pluralism and civil liberties decreases. According to its 2017 Democracy Index, the Economist Intelligence Unit (EIU) saw democratic erosion in eighty-nine states. It found the 'democratic recession' in some of the oldest democracies in the world (notable in Western Europe) reflected in declining popular participation in elections and politics, declining trust in democratic institutions, a growing influence of unelected and unaccountable institutions, and a widening gap between political elites and electorates.[20] It seems that democracy is *less* challenged by the rise of autocracy on the global stage than by a variety of crises and structural weaknesses it faces at home.

Anti-democratic voices have been viewed as heretical and illusionary in the post-Cold War era with the triumphal claim 'The End of History'. But contemporary voices appear to echo old critiques from philosophical, theological and technocratic perspectives which can be traced back to the ancient, enlightenment and inter-war periods. The warnings found in the work of Plato, Thomas Aquinas and Thomas Hobbes as well as French observers during the inter-war period regarded democracy as bringing a disastrous 'every man's struggle against all' (Hobbes, Leviathan, i. xv.: 79), running the risk of being ruled by the mob, therefore being constantly in a state of conflict and incompetent to tackle problems.[21] Critics point to democracy failure trapped in a variety of mutations and contradictions engendered by neoliberal globalization, technological change and the rise of social media, the construction of a technocratic state, and fear of multi-ethnic democracy (Runciman 2018; Mounk 2018; Doyle 2018: 185; Zuboff 2018). Both young and old democracies as well as the authoritarian world witness the end of 'an absolute victory of the democratic principle'[22] and see their societies are torn between the erosion of civility and their realization of the necessity to reinvent democracy 'in a form that will match the new abstract mode of social cohesion' (Doyle 2018: 188). Not only do old democracies (i.e. the United States and France and Germany) experience an unprecedented crisis of their representative politics, which, cut from the symbolic, is increasingly mired in insignificance (Gauchet 2017a, IV: 721, here cited in Doyle 2018: 189). As such, they attest the rise of authoritarian populism as a reaction to counter the feeling of the loss of common purpose in a globalized and digitalized world. Some young democracies in Europe, African and Latin America also become frustrated about the unsatisfied translation of democratic dividends into tangible outcomes in the people's daily life and have therein injected authoritarian elements into their democratic institutions (Brazil, Poland and Hungary as the most prominent examples). Democracy malaise appears to provide autocracy in Asia and Central Asia its best justification to boost their reign at home.

Though the causes of the authoritarian turn in some elected governments, the persistence of autocracy and democracy malaise differ greatly, depending on the specific historical, sociocultural, economic and political context involved, commentators highlight some direct and indirect links between them and reveal how the banalization of liberal democracy as an ensemble of relatively general principles (popular sovereignty, individual rights, etc.) takes place with serious repercussions (e.g. by leaving room for the rise of radical and authoritarian discourses). First and foremost, the identification of different root causes helps explain why some elected governments have become illiberal democracy and authoritarian regimes remain resilient. They include weak democratic prerequisites (e.g. the existence of illiberal civil societies which regard democracy as an alien and incompetent governance system and the lack of resources), parallel regional diffusion effects (Miller 2013), and broad public silence and ignorance towards the past dictatorship (Way 2015; Ziegler 2016). Due to the lack of judicial and non-judicial issues implemented to redress legacies of its past military repressive regime, Brazil, for instance, has voted to be subject to an authoritarian populist control. Also, in Eastern Europe, the weak consolidation of democracy has paved way for authoritarian populist parties' coming to power whose policies have violated democratic principles.[23] Diamond (2008) further dissects the causes of the 'democratic recession' in critical states which include the crime-infested oligarchy in Russia and the strong-armed populism of Venezuela. In this sense, the spread of authoritarian populist politics is both a product of democratic processes and a cause of the democratic recession.

In particular, in his efforts to bring out what is historically specific in modern democracy, Marcel Gauchet writes of a 'banalization' of liberal democracy, whose complex composite between democratic and liberal traits with the mode of representation often has been taken for granted without properly considering its dynamics of evolution and inherent tensions.[24] In dissecting democracy's ailments, Wendy Brown's theory of de-politicization (2006) and Gauchet's theory of de-symbolization (2017) well elucidate how the construction of a technocratic state driven by neoliberal capitalism has leered out the meaning of 'the political', thereby making the state increasingly detached from the society, whose meta-power of institution is deemed to sustain the state's legitimacy while exercising its power. For Brown, de-politicization of democracy involves 'a process of which personalizes political phenomena (such as social conflict, inequality and margionalization), and culturalizes or even naturalizes them' (cited in Doyle 2018: 190). Seen from this prism, the discourse of securitization has been used to divert attention from the structural failures of Western societies (e.g. unemployment and cultural fragmentation).

Coupled with the de-politicization of democracy, de-symbolization of the political that sees the convergence of market fundamentalism and the extension of individual rights has caused another symbolic mutation found in the crisis of representative politics (Doyle 2018: 191–2). As discussed by Doyle (2018: 190–1),

> We have seen how Gauchet's work deepened the distinction (between the ground power of society and the explicit power of the state), introducing the question of society's meta-power of institution through his discussion of the symbolic logic of processual autonomy which makes all human socieites create their durable worlds of meaning. Gauchet's discussion of contemporary neo-liberal capitalism … provides a much more deeply theorised account of the coherence of the new culture that underpines it and operates at a deeper level than that of (Foucault's) governmentality, that is, a deeper level than that of institutions. It addresses the existence of an underlying level of the political, on which the totally de-symbolised mode of neo-governmentality associated with neo-liberal culture ultimately relies despite the false appearances. This approach opens up a totally different understanding of the economic rationalisation of the state denounced by Brown or of the discourse of security which has accompanied the depoliticisation of democracy.

In other word, as neoliberalism has become 'thinkable and believable' in the contemporary form of social life (Gauchet 2017: 605), the convergence of two seemingly contradictory forces – the right-wing market fundamentalism and the left-wing extension of individual rights – has paradoxically contributed to the loss of explicit common political purpose. The older vision of societal inclusion has been displaced and replaced by a proliferation of 'micro-political projects of individual emancipation which pushed for the recognition of the specific needs of various segments of society subject to discrimination' (Doyle 2018:192). Hence, as rights movements go forwards, democracy faces a paradox, in which democratic politics have been driven by greater individual aspirations and running the risk of becoming degraded in its original republican meaning of collective self-determination (Gauchet 2015: 178, here cited in Doyle 2018: 192).

Ultimately, the combined forces of de-politicization and de-symbolization have contributed to all the pathological manifestations of democracy which are the results of the loss of control in striking a proper balance among various tensions and contradictions. They can be detected in four forms: (1) the crisis of representative politics that sees the alienation of traditional class-based constituencies now embracing populist parties and the increasing social fragmentation and unresolvable ideological conflicts; (2) the construction of a technocratic state which has lost its social meaning in serving explicit common collective purpose; (3) the resurgence of neo-nationalism and radicalization as a response to protest democracy's failure to invent a new symbolic mode of collective existence against the backdrop of a digitalizing and globalizing world; (4) the decay of the US leadership in the democratic world, whose neo-nationalist isolationist politics under the President Trump have eroded the principle of multilateralism in international cooperation and triggered aggravating effects upon democracy,[25] thereby feeding the growth of the political influence of powerful authoritarian regimes such as China on the global stage.

Even though democracy has seen its best days, commentators have not lost their optimism regarding its future. As noted by Gauchet in his recent work 'Le nouveau monde' (2017), the current crisis democracy faces is not ultimately the truth of democracy's history. Instead, it also paves the way for a renewal. Hence, the future of democracy will depend on the extent to which it can effectively tackle those challenges and reinvent itself through creative design of norms, institutions and procedures. Any failure to revive democracy through the restoration of society's meta-power of institutions while redefining a new mode of symbolic representation may offer opportunity for autocracy to attract more democratic states to install authoritarian and neo-nationalist elements in the name of guaranteeing collective interests and people's sovereignty.

A variety of ideas have emerged to revive democracy: some have suggested to support good governance – the rule of law, security, protection of individual rights and shared economic prosperity – and free civic organizations. Others have proposed to reimagine the principle of 'popular sovereignty' and introduce a new constitution with innovative institutional designs that will enhance participation and democracy's credibility (Diamond 2008; Peonidis 2013). In the midst of the search of renewal strategies, as Doyle reminds us (2018: 232), it is of ultimate importance to interrogate the question: 'How can we regain sovereignty over our historical existence?' If democracy cannot provide proper answers to this question, the challenges posed by China will become direct and pressing.

Notes

1 The number of democratic states increases gradually and witnesses some breakthroughs: 26 states in 1956, 63 states in 1991, 87 states in 2009, and 103 in 2015, a year which saw transition to democracy in Tunisia solidified, and positive breakthroughs in Myanmar, Burkina Faso, Nigeria and Sri Lanka. It is worth

mentioning that in 2015, more than the half of the world population lived in a democracy (56 per cent). In contrast, almost 40 per cent of the world population lived in an autocracy (open and closed autocracy), most of them in China (four out of five people in the world that live in an autocracy live in China). The rest world population lived in country in transition or no data. See Roser (2018). See also Miller (2018).

2   At the first summit of G20 bringing together the leading and emerging economies together in 1999, the democratic world had a dominant position with 85 per cent of the world's economic performance. See Hulverscheidt (2018: 17).

3   For Jonathan Hillmann, director of the Reconnecting Asia Project at the Center for Strategic and International Studies based in Washington, BRI is 'about more than roads, railways and other hard infrastructure'. BRI, originally known as 'One Belt, One Road (OBOR)'-Initiative came into existence in 2013 with the aim to connect Asia, Africa and Europe. It covers almost all aspects of Chinese engagement abroad. According to one analysis, in the past five years, China has spent more than 210 billion for this project, the majority in Asia. Here cited in Kuo and Kommenda (2018).

4   Sources cited in Strittmatter (2018: 9).

5   See Horta (2018).

6   China has fiercely defended its crackdown and re-education camps in the far western province of Xinjiang as necessary for security. Shohrat Zakir, a high-ranking Xinjiang government official, has justified the mass internment of the mostly Muslim Uyghur minority group deemed to fight against '"terrorism and extremism" in its own way, and in accordance with the United Nations resolutions'. See Westcott and Fang (2018).

7   See, for instance, the ASEAN-China Joint Statement on Comprehensively Strengthening Effective Anti-Corruption Cooperation, signed in 13 November 2017 in Manila, Philippines at the 20th ASEAN-China Summit. ASEAN-China Dialogue Relations commenced when China was invited to attend the opening session of the 24th ASEAN Ministerial Meeting (AMM) in July 1991 in Kuala Lumpur, Malaysia. Later China was accorded full Dialogue Partner status at the 29th AMM in July 1996 in Jakarta, Indonesia. See ASEAN Secretariat Information Paper, Overview of ASEAN-China Dialogue Relations, August (2018).

8   For coverages concerning the spread of autocracy and neo-nationalism in Vietnam, the EU (Poland, Hungary) and Latin America, see Perras (2018: 8), Petzold (2018), Sabatini and Galindo (2017).

9   In October 2018, Brazil has followed Cuba, Bolivia and Venezuela and voted for an authoritarian populist president who is ready to recur to repressive measures and violence against dissenters and in fighting crime. See the Economist (2018). Even within the EU, the neo-nationalist populist governments in Poland, Hungary and Italy have violated democratic norms and the EU's laws through the adoption of laws restricting freedom of expression, violating the principle of academic autonomy and the EU's criterion for household stability. Hungary's high education policy (e.g. the abolition of gender studies as a master study programme) directly collides with the academic autonomy, whose new regulations have brought some renowned universities such as Central European University (CEU) into a state of complete uncertainty. See Münch (2018: 23).

10 For angry farmers who are upset about poverty and corruption and anxious middle classes who worry about their property, the promise of 'building a harmonious society' becomes an olive branch either to criticize or to defend CCP's authoritarianism. For the CCP's hardliners it means repression even in the name of 'harmony'. Delury observes a boom of articles featuring 'harmony' in their titles from around 30 in 2003 to 6,600 in 2005. At least, under the banner of 'harmony' as

an ideological framework, the ideal becomes an interesting test case 'to see how the resurgence in native Chinese values and statecraft thought might affect the future of the Chinese polity'. See Delury (2008).

11 Pakistan has been the flagship site of the BRI since 2013, with some $62 billion in projects planned, some of them had clear strategic implications. For instance, a Chinese-built seaport and special economic zone in the Pakistani town Gwadar has given China a quicker route to get goods to the Arabian Sea. See Abi-Habib (2018).

12 Ibid.

13 Cited in Kuo and Kommenda, EN3. Being able to profit from China's investment policy in Africa, Sambia for instance, has praised China's newly introduced point system in regulating citizens' social behaviour. See SZ (2018: 7).

14 Cited in Kuo and Kommenda, EN3.

15 Ibid.

16 See Horta, EN5.

17 See Gammelin (2018: 22). Information about the Paris Club, see Committee of the Abolition of Third World Debt (CADTM) (2016).

18 See Kornelius (2018b: 4), Deuber (2018: 4).

19 Protests and clashes with the police in Hong Kong incited by a bill that would have allowed the extradition of criminal suspects to the mainland see Myers, Buckley and Bradsher (2019); Deubner, Giesen, and Strittmatter (2019: 11–13).

20 Based on sixty indicators, the EIU since 2006 has ranked the quality of democracy in 167 countries on a scale of 0 to 10 since 2006. Therein states' political development and performance are assessed in four categories: (1) authoritarian regime (0–4); (2) hybrid regime (4–6); (3) flawed democracy; (4) full democracy. In 2017, old democracies such as France and the United States have seen the democratic recession at home marking a score of 7.80 and 7.98, respectively. Eastern European transformation countries such as Hungary (6.64) and Poland (6.67) are on the brink of becoming a hybrid regime. See the Economist Intelligence Unit (2017).

21 For an overview of the limits of democracy found in the anti-democratic critiques in the nineteenth and twentieth centuries, see Sara Gebh, Aus Angst vor Konflikt. Zur Kontinuität vormoderner und moderner Demokratiekritik; Michel Dormal, '"Vertrauensblick zu einer anderen Instanz von Bessermachenden". Der Formwandel der Demokratie- Kritik nach dem Ersten Weltkrieg'. Both papers have been presented during the 27th scientific convention of the German Political Science Association (DVPW), Frankfurt am Main, 27 September (2018).

22 See Tocqueville21 (2018).

23 In the midst of a failing economy, Brazil has elected Jair Messias Bolsonaro as its next president, see EN9. According to Eliane Brum, the reason why the majority of Brazilian population have decided to vote for an authoritarian populist leader is due to the ignorance and silence of the Brazilian society towards the legacies of its repressive military regime between 1964 and 1985. For some observers, Bolsonaro turns out to be Latin America's latest menace. Brazil's decision to be subject to a radical rightist leader who has even admired dictatorship (i.e. Carlos Alberto Brilhante Ustra) marks a heart attack for the young democracy. See Brum (2018: 2), Herrmann (2018: 4); Herrmann and Schoepp (2018: 9).

24 See EN18.

25 See Kornelius (2018a: 4).

Bibliography

Abi-Habib, Maria, 'China's "Belt and Road" Plan in Pakistan Takes a Military Turn', *The New York Times*, 19 December (2018)

Ambrosio, Thomas, 'Catching the "Shanghai Spirit": how the Shanghai Cooperation Organisation Promotes Authoritarian Norms in Central Asia', *Europe-Asia-Studies*, 60 (8) (2008), pp. 1321–44.

Ambrosio, Thomas, 'Constructing a Framework of Authoritarian Diffusion: Concepts, Dynamics, and Future Research', *International Studies Perspectives*, 11 (2010), pp. 375–92.

Ambrosio, Thomas, 'The Rise of "China Model" and "Beijing Consensus": Evidence of Authoritarian Diffusion?' *Contemporary Politics*, 18 (4) (2012), pp. 381–99.

Bader, Julia, 'China, Autocratic Patron? An Empirical Investigation of China as Factor in Autocratic Survival', *International Studies Quarterly*, 59 (2015a), pp. 23–33.

Bader, Julia, 'Propping Up Dictators? Economic Cooperation from China and its Impact on Authoritarian Persistence in Party and Non-Party Regimes', *European Journal of Political Research*, 54 (4) (2015b), pp. 655–72.

Brown, Wendy, *Regulating Aversion: Tolerance in the Age of Identity and Empire* (Princeton, NJ: Princeton UP, 2006).

Brum, Eliane, 'Land des Schreckens', *Süddeutsche Zeitung (SZ)*, 25 October (2018), p. 2.

Burnell, Peter, 'Promoting Democracy, Promoting Autocracy: Towards a Comparative Evaluation', *Journal of Politics and Law*, 3 (2) (2010), pp. 3–14.

Cardenal, Juan P., Jacek Kucharczyk, Grigorij Meseznikov, Gabriela Pleschová, *Sharp Power: Rising Authoritarian Influence*. National Endowment for Democracy (NED), International Forum for Democratic Studies, December (2017).

Carothers, Thomas, 'The End of the Transition Paradigm', *Journal of Democracy*, 13 (1) (2002), pp. 5–21.

Chou, Mark, Chengxin Pan and Avery Poole, 'The Threat of Autocracy Diffusion in Consolidated Democracies? The Case of China, Singapore and Australia', *Contemporary Politics*, 23 (2) (2017), pp. 175–94.

Claus Hulverscheidt, 'Geisel der Machtpolitik', *Süddeutsche Zeitung (SZ)*, 27 November (2018).

Committee of the Abolition of Third World Debt (CADTM), What Is Paris Club? 4 March (2016). Available at http://www.clubdeparis.fr/?What-is-the-Paris-Club (accessed 10 October 2018).

Congleton, Roger D., 'Economic and Cultural Prerequisites for Democracy', in A. Breton, G. Galeotti, P. Salmon and R. Wintrobe (eds.), *Rational Foundations of Democratic Politics* (New York: Cambridge UP, 2003), pp. 44–67.

Delury, John, 'Harmonious in China', *Policy Review*, 31 March (2008). Available at https://www.hoover.org/research/harmonious-china (accessed 15 September 2018).

Deuber, Lea, 'Meng Hongwei: The Chairperson of the Interpol Who Disappears in China', *SZ*, 8 October (2018).

Deubner, Lea, Christoph Giesen and Kai Strittmatter, 'Stadt, Land, Frust', *SZ*, 7/8 September (2019).

Diamond, Larry, *The Spirit of Democracy: The Struggle to Build Free Societies Throughout the World* (London: Macmillan, 2008).

Diamond, Larry, 'Facing Up to the Democratic Recession', *Journal of Democracy*, 26 (1) (2015), pp. 141–55.

Diamond, Larry, Francis Fukuyama, Donald L. Horowitz and Marc F. Plattner, 'Discussion. Reconsidering the Transition Paradigm', *Journal of Democracy*, 25 (1) (2014), pp. 86–100.

Doyle, Natalie J., *Marcel Gauchet and the Loss of Common Purpose: Imaginary Islam and the Crisis of European Democracy* (Lanham/Boulder/New York/London: Lexington Books, 2018).

Escribà-Folch, Abel and Joseph Wright, *Foreign Pressure and the Politics of Authoritarian Survival* (Oxford: Oxford UP, 2015).

Gammelin, Cerstin, 'Show Your Credits: The Western Industrial Nations Urge China to Lay Open Its Investitions', *SZ*, 22 October (2018), p. 22.

Gauchet, Marcel, *Le nouveau monde. Vol. IV. L'avènement de la démocratie* (Paris: Gallimard, 2017).

Hadenius, Axel and Jan Teorell, 'Cultural and Economic Prerequisites of Democracy: Reassessing Recent Evidence', *Studies in Comparative International Development*, 39 (4) (2005), pp. 87–106.

Harcourt, Alison J. and Claudio M. Radaelli, 'Limits to EU Technocratic Regulations?' *European Journal of Political Research*, 35 (1999), pp. 107–22.

Herrmann, Boris, 'Der Anti-Demokrat', *SZ*, 30 October (2018), p. 4.

Herrmann, Boris and Sebastian Schoepp, 'Nur beten Hilft', *SZ*, 30 October (2018), p. 9.

Horta, Korinnna, 'Die Bank an Chinas Seite', *SZ*, 28 September (2018). Available at https://www.sueddeutsche.de/politik/aussenansicht-die-bank-an-chinas-seite-1.4145718 (accessed 19 October 2018).

Hoover Institution, *Chinese Influence & American Interests: Promoting Constructive Vigilance*. Report of the Working Group on Chinese Influence Activities in the United States, co-chairs Larry Diamond and Orville Schell, Stanford, California (2018).

Knack, Stephen, 'Does Foreign Aid Promote Democracy?' *International Studies Quarterly*, 48 (1) (2004), pp. 251–66.

Kneuer, Marianne, Thomas Demmelhuber, Raphael Peresson and Tobias Zumbrägel, 'Playing the Regional Card: Why and How Authoritarian Gravity Centres Exploit Regional Organisations', *Third World Journal*, Published online: 4 June (2018). Available at https://www.tandfonline.com/doi/abs/10.1080/01436597.2018.1474713 ?journalCode=ctwq20 (accessed on 29 October 2018).

Kornelius, Stefan, 'Trumps Weg' (Trump's Way), *SZ*, 10–11 November (2018a), p. 4.

Kornelius, Stefan, 'Wie es mir gefällt' (Just as It Pleases Me), *SZ*, 10 October (2018b), p. 4.

Kuo, Lily and Niko Kommenda, 'What Is China's Belt and Road Initiative?' *The Guardian*, 30 July (2018). Available at https://www.theguardian.com/cities/ng-interactive/2018/jul/30/what-china-belt-road-initiative-silk-road-explainer (accessed 19 October 2018).

Levitsky, Steven and Lucan A. Way, 'Linkage versus Leverage: Rethinking the International Dimension of Regime Change', *Comparative Politics*, 38 (4) (2006), pp. 379–400.

Levitsky, Steven and Lucan A. Way, *The Rise of Competitive Authoritarianism: Hybrid Regime after the Cold War* (Cambridge, UK: Cambridge UP, 2010).

Melnykovska, Inna, Hedwig Plamper and Rainer Schweickert, 'Do Russia and China promote autocracy in Central Asia', *Asia Europe Journal*, 10 (2012), pp. 75–89.

Miller, Michael, *The Origins of Electoral Authoritarianism and Democracy*. APSA 2013 Annual Meeting Paper; American Political Science Association 2013 Annual Meeting (2013). Available at SSRN: https://ssrn.com/abstract=2299196 (accessed 25 September 2018).

Miller, Nick, 'The Question of Democracy: Is It Winning or Losing the Global Contest?' *The Sydney Herald*, 23 February (2018).

Münch, Peter, 'Der lange Arm des Viktor Orban', *SZ*, 29 October (2018), p. 23.

Myers, Steven L., Chris Buckley and Keith Bradsher, 'Is Xi Mishandling Hong Kong Crisis? Hints of Unease in China's Leadership', *The New York Times* 7 September (2019).

Peonidis, Filimon, *Democracy as Popular Sovereignty* (Lanham, MD: Lexington Books, 2013).

Perras, Arne, 'Das Kollektiv und der Starke Mann', *SZ*, 25 October (2018).

Petzold, Andreas 'Das Memo: Riechen Sie es? In Europa kriecht der Gestank diktatorischer Regime durch die Ritzen', *Stern*, 27 September (2018).

Roser, Max, 'Democracy'. Published online at OurWorldInData.org (2018). Available at https://ourworldindata.org/democracy (accessed 23 October 2018).

Sabatini, Christopher and Jimena Galindo, 'It's Not Just Venezuela: Elected Governments Don't Necessarily Defend Democracy or Protect Human Rights', *The Washington Post*, 11 August (2017).

Strittmatter, Kai, 'Chinas Glück im Süden' (China's Luck in the South), *SZ*, 25 July (2018).

SZ, 'Massive Kritik an China im Menschenrechtsrat' (China under Massive Pressure in the UN Human Rights Council), 7 November (2018).

Tansey, Oisín, 'The Problem with Autocracy Promotion', *Democratization*, 23 (1) (2015), pp. 141–63.

Tansey, Oisín, Kevin Koehler and Alexander Schmotz, 'Ties to the Rest: Autocratic Linkages and Regime Survival', *Comparative Political Studies*, 50 (9) (2017), pp. 1221–54.

The Economist, 'Jair Bolsonaro, Latin America's Latest Menace: He Would Make a Disastrous President', 20 September (2018). Available at https://www.economist.com/leaders/2018/09/20/jair-bolsonaro-latin-americas-latest-menace (accessed 21 October 2018).

The Economist Intelligence Unit, Democracy Index (2017). Available at https://infogra phics.economist.com/2018/DemocracyIndex/ (accessed 11 November 2018).

Tocqueville21, 'Marcel Gauchet: "There Has Been an Absolute Victory of the Democratic Principle"', interview conducted by Jacob Hamburger, 29 January (2018). Available at https://tocqueville21.com/interviews/marcel-gauchet-absolute-victory-of-the-demo cratic-principle/ (accessed 25 October 2018).

Tolstrup, Jakob, 'When Can External Actors Influence Democratisation? Leverage, Linkages, and Gatekeeper Elites', *Democratization*, 20 (4) (2013), pp. 716–42.

Way, Lucan A. 'The Limits of Autocracy Promotion: The Case of Russia in the "Near Abroad"', *European Journal of Political Research*, (2015). Available at https://doi.org/10.1111/1475-6765.12092.

Way, Lucan A., 'Weaknesses of Autocracy Promotion', *Journal of Democracy*, 27 (1) (2016), pp. 64–75.

Westcott, Ben and Nanlin Fang, 'China Admits to Locking Up Uyghurs, But Defends Xinjiang Crackdown', *CNN*, 17 October (2018). Available at https://edition.cnn.com/2 018/10/16/asia/xinjiang-uyghur-china-camps-intl/index.html (accessed 11 November 2018).

Ziegler, Charles E., 'Great Powers, Civil Society and Authoritarian Diffusion in Central Asia', *Central Asian Survey*, 35 (4) (2016), pp. 549–69.

Zuboff, Shoshana, *Das Zeitalter des Überwachungskapitalismus (The Age of Surveillance Capitalism)* (München: ABOD Publisher, 2018).

Index